D0049379

Leaving the Saints

Leaving the Saints

How I Lost the Mormons

and Found My Faith

Martha Beck

CROWN PUBLISHERS NEW YORK

Published by Crown Publishers, New York, New York.
Member of the Crown Publishing Group, a division of
Random House, Inc.
www.crownpublishing.com

CROWN is a trademark and the Crown colophon is a registered trademark
of Random House, Inc.

Printed in the United States of America

Library of Congress Cataloging-in-Publication Data
Beck, Martha Nibley, 1962–
Leaving the Saints : how I lost the Mormons and found my faith /
Martha Beck.—— 1st ed.
p.   cm.
1. Beck, Martha Nibley, 1962–. 2. Ex–church members—Church of Jesus Christ of
Latter-day Saints—Biography. 3. Mormons—United States—Biography. I. Title.
BX8678.B43A3 2005
289.3'092—dc22   2004011333
ISBN : 0-609-60991-2
10 9 8 7 6 5 4 3 2 1
FIRST EDITION

They say that religion is for people who are afraid of going to hell, and spirituality is for people who've been there. If you're in the second category, this book is dedicated to you.

Acknowledgments

To write any sort of book, I need the support of many forgiving and generous people. To write this sort of book, I needed the kind of maintenance an emergency medical team might give the survivor of a plane crash—for years on end. My gratitude to the people listed below far exceeds anything words can convey, but since words are the tools I'm using, they'll have to do for now. One caveat: I suspect that some of the individuals mentioned in these acknowledgments may feel less than thrilled to be associated with the book. Accordingly, I will refer to them by pseudonyms I have invented myself. Others I won't specify even cryptically, but y'all know who you are.

First, I would like to thank my clients and readers, the reason I bother to keep typing at all. The fact that you are willing to read my stories, and sometimes tell me yours, lets me know that I am not living in the hell my childhood teachers called outer darkness. Even if we've never met, your support buoys me up every moment.

Huge thanks to the people at Crown Books who agreed to this project and urged me to be as honest and straightforward as possible, especially Chip Gibson, Steve Ross, Jenny Frost, Phillip Patrick, and Kristin Kiser.

Betsy Rapoport is both the most brilliant editor I've ever met, as well as a loyal, dauntless friend. She is a light to me and to the world, one of the main reasons I believe that Something is taking care of us all.

My agent, Beth Vesel, has been willing to jump into white water with my on many occasions, in many ways. Her openness, generosity, and incisive feedback have made me a better writer and a better person.

My magazine editors, including Jeanie Pyun at *Mademoiselle,* Marcia Menter at *Redbook,* and Carol Kramer at *Real Simple,* helped me develop as a writer until I worked up the courage to tell this story. Many thanks to all of them.

More recently, and in particular, the wonderful people at *O, the Oprah Magazine* have given me the opportunity and encouragement to speak in my real voice, to both discover and convey what I believe to be most true. I'm inspired by the leadership of the great O herself and editor-at-large Gayle King. I'm honored and incredibly fortunate to receive feedback from my editor Mamie Healey, and especially from the peerless Amy Gross. None of these people will ever know how much I owe them as an author and as a human being.

Along with the folks who helped me write this book, I want to thank those who helped me live it. I cannot express my gratitude to the Utah friends who helped me negotiate the events described in this book. Some I met at church, some at BYU, some in my amazing therapy group. I won't blow your cover here, but I'll never forget the priceless gift of your compassion.

Speaking of Utah, the good people at the R & R Ski Lodge have given me sanctuary for body and soul more times than I can count. Their intelligent and enthusiastic support are part of the foundation on which my right life is built.

My beautiful, hilarious, and ever-shapely cousins, "Diane" and "Miranda" Nom-de-Plume, make me proud to wear the tartan of our clan. They saved my soul and my hide when no one else could have done it.

Steve and Mary Ann Benson, my first friends in Arizona, are also the two best models of courage and integrity anyone is ever likely to meet. I am so grateful to know them.

My work with Stacey Shively, Kim Barber, and Al Preble has given me major infusions of strength, courage, and audacity. I owe them the singular gratitude a prisoner feels to those who have helped out in a jailbreak.

The pseudonymous Reilly Max, great writer and even greater friend, combines the traits of a war buddy, a poet, a therapist, and a stand-up comic. Again, words cannot express my thanks.

The Princess of Pink (not her real name) has donated generous infusions of her trademark genius, humor, and defiance, giving me the strength to tell my truth. Friends like her make me glad I survived the things I sometimes didn't want to survive.

To all those whose lives intersected with mine during the particular time I recount in these pages, please know that I have tried my best to make it as fully accurate and honest as possible. This was the most difficult truth I've ever had to tell.

John Beck was my staunch ally and companion through all the events recorded in this book. I hope that anyone who reads it will recognize what an extraordinary gift that was, and how deeply grateful I am for it. After the events I discuss in this book, John and I decided to live our lives separately but continue to raise our children together.

My children, Katie, Adam, and Elizabeth, were my motivation and inspiration for both living and writing this story. I am in constant awe that such beings could have spent their childhoods helping me learn how to be happy. The goal of my life is to return that favor.

Finally, Karen Gerdes is the gentle force that put me back together after the events of my life tore me apart, and the one that has kept me whole. Whenever I slip back into the world of shadows, she is the one who leads me back into the light.

To all these people, and to many more I haven't mentioned, I offer all the love and thanks my soul contains. They deserve none of the blame for this book, but all of the credit for anything worthwhile that may have strayed onto its pages. Having been blessed to cross paths with them, I can never doubt that we all have guardian angels.

Leaving the Saints

CHAPTER I

Room at the Inn

So there he stands, not five feet away from me. He looks almost un-changed since the last time I saw him, ten years ago—fabulous, for a man now in his nineties. His features are still sharply cut, his sardonic smile and turquoise eyes as bright as ever. The only difference I notice is that both his hair and his wiry body have thinned a bit. His trousers (probably the same ones he was wearing a decade ago) are now so baggy he's switched from a belt to suspenders.

A Shakespearean phrase pops into my mind: ". . . a world too wide / For his shrunk shank." From *As You Like It,* I think. That's something I seem to have inherited from this little old man in his shabby pants: a tendency to produce random literary quotations, from memory, to fit almost any situation. I don't do this on purpose; it just happens to me. The same way it happens to him. Despite the fact that we've rarely had a significant conversation, I know that my father understands the way I think, probably better than anyone on earth.

"Well, well, well," he says heartily, opening his arms. Hmm. This is new. Back when I knew him, my father wasn't the open-arms type. But, then, neither was I. I go forward and hug him. It does feel odd, but I've been practicing hugging the people I love for years now, and I get through it.

"Hello," I say, and stop there, at a loss for words. I can't bring myself to say "Hello, Daddy," but I don't know what else to call him. "Daddy" is the only title by which I and my seven siblings ever addressed him. "Dad" would sound disrespectfully casual, "Father" too formal, his given name completely bizarre. I settle for repeating "Hello," then gesture toward the easy chair by the door. "Please, sit down."

He sits, and I'm startled by another eerie jolt of familiarity: This man

1

moves just like I do. Nervous as I am, scared to death as I am, there is something unspeakably poignant about the fact that my posture and carriage are echoes of his. It's been a long time since I encountered so many of my own chromosomes in anyone besides my own children.

"I thought this day would never arrive," my father says, still wearing his most cheerful smile. "I thought you'd never come to your senses."

He assumes I've come to recant. He's wrong. I'm here for two reasons: to sew up the loose threads I left hanging when I fled my past and to make sure, as far as I can, that my father isn't afraid to die. If his model of the universe is correct, there must be serious retribution awaiting him in the afterlife, and in case this belief worries him I want to tell him I don't share it. The God to whom I pray is all parts unconditional love, no part vengeance or retribution. I once read that forgiveness is giving up all hope of having had a different past, and I reached that point a long time ago. But forgiving is not the same as obliterating memory. As Santayana wrote, "Those who do not remember the past are condemned to repeat it." This is something I do not want to happen. Not to my father, and certainly not to me.

"Oh, I stand by everything I've said," I tell my father as I sit down on the sofa a few feet away from him. "That hasn't changed at all."

His expression turns from cheer to scorn in a heartbeat. "Ridiculous," he says. "Utterly ridiculous."

Those sky blue eyes flash toward the door and I feel my throat tense with the fear that he's noticed it's slightly ajar, that someone is listening. He's used to people observing everything he says and does—so perhaps his spider senses are tingling. The hotel room where we're meeting is decorated in tasteful, neutral earth tones, ridiculously bland for a battlefield. But that's what it is, and we both know it. We also know it isn't level; my father practically owns the turf and has the advantages of age, gender bias, family expectation, psychological dominance, and religious legitimacy. Which is why I'm making sure there are witnesses to every word we say. Everything. Add secrecy to his other advantages, and my father will win walking away.

"I know you say it's ridiculous," I tell him gently. "We've established that. But there's a lot of evidence that squares with what I remember. Something happened."

"Nothing happened to you," he says firmly. "Nothing like that. Never."

"Well, then, nothing left an awful lot of scars." He already knows this. I told him about the scars a decade ago, when I met with him and my mother in my therapist's office. "It's not the kind of scar tissue a kid gets playing on the jungle gym. Someone put it there."

"Oh," says my father with a shrug, "that was the Evil One."

I can feel myself blink, the way you do when the eye doctor sends that little puff of air into your eyes to check for glaucoma. The Evil One? I've heard a rumor that my family of origin thinks I was consorting with the devil at the age of five, but I never believed they'd actually say such a thing. Even my family can't be that crazy, right?

I sit and stare for a moment as my mind frantically tries on several different interpretations of my father's statement. Does he actually think I spent my childhood hanging out with Lucifer? Is the Evil One the name he has for an aspect of himself? If he's suffering from a split personality or psychotic fugue states, is he aware of this intellectually or only at some dark subconscious level? Is my father a calculated liar, or is he certifiably insane, or could he actually be empirically correct? I have no idea. My mind feels like a tar pit. We've been talking for less than a minute, and already I feel the same blend of bewilderment, fear, and self-doubt that flavored my early years. Wow. You really can go home again.

"The Evil One," I repeat, squinting at my father, as if that will make things clearer. "Well, I'm not questioning that."

He taps the arm of his chair with his fingers. His hands are strong and squarish, with prominent tendons. Like my hands. Like my children's hands. I feel a rush of tenderness and suddenly realize that he probably thinks I'm recording our conversation in order to turn him over to the authorities—either legal or (worse) religious. I want to reassure him I have no such intentions. I have witnesses in place only because that's what I was trained to do in controversial situations, where every perception is clouded by conflicting interests. Later, when my father claims this conversation didn't happen the way I will remember it, I'll be able to check several sources.

My desperate thirst for data in any area related to my father is a tribute to his job skills. He's ostensibly a retired college professor, but his real life's work, the area in which he's built his reputation, is as an apologist for the Church of Jesus Christ of Latter-day Saints, otherwise known as Mormonism. The Mormon Church, whose headquarters is in Salt Lake City, Utah, is one of the few major world religions that traces its roots to recorded history, leaving the claims of its leaders open to factual testing—and the Latter-day Saint leaders, especially the religion's founder, Joseph Smith, have always been fond of making claims.

For instance, Smith taught that the American Indians are the descendants of a small group of emigrants from Jerusalem, who arrived on the continent in approximately 600 BC, and wrote their history onto a book of golden plates. Smith said he was led to these plates, which were buried in New York State, by an angel named Moroni (rhymes with "the PHONE eye") in 1823. Using a magical pair of spectacles buried along with the plates, Smith said, he translated the plates, and later published them as the Book of Mormon (Mormon was one of the original owners and authors of the golden plates). The problem, from a Latter-day Saint perspective, is that when scholars set out to test Smith's version of reality, they tend to bump into a lot of contradictory evidence (such as the fact that DNA analysis traces Native American ancestry to Asia rather than to the Middle East). This is the time for apologists to rush in, like white blood cells attacking a virus, to defend Joseph Smith and the subsequent Mormon leaders. Nobody does this better than my father.

In 2002, the year the Winter Olympics were held in Utah, the *New Yorker* published an article on the state's most prominent religion. The reporter who penned the story, a writer named Lawrence Wright, referred to my father as "the most venerable scholar in Mormonism, though he is little known outside of it." Wright interviewed the venerable scholar about some problematic aspects of Mormon scripture. Why is it, he asked, that after decades of archaeological work bent on verifying the Book of Mormon, "not a single person or place named in it has been shown to exist"?

My father's official published response, quoted in the *New Yorker,* was: "People underestimate the capacity of things to disappear." Wright also recorded what my father told him during their interview—comments tinged, according to Wright, "with some asperity." I know exactly the tone Wright meant: a stern, disdainful note my father adopts whenever his assertions are under attack.

"Well, if it was all pure fiction, who on earth had ever done anything like that?" my father said. "This is the history of a civilization, with all its ramifications having to do with plagues and wars. The military passages are flawless. Could you please tell me any other book like that?"

When I read the *New Yorker* article, several responses leapt to mind (for one thing, the "flawless" military passages in the Book of Mormon record battles waged between enormous populations who herded sheep and goats, operated mines, smelted metals, and rode wheeled chariots drawn by horses, none of which existed in North America prior to their introduction from Europe several centuries after the people described in the Book of Mormon allegedly arrived). But of course I knew that my father wasn't actually requesting input from Lawrence Wright. His response was rhetorical, a question that really meant the guy should stop asking so damn many questions.

This is the kind of thinking with which I grew up, the style of debate I took with me when I ventured out of Utah, the conservative-value capital of America, and off to a non-Mormon university in Cambridge, Massachusetts, where liberal attitudes are practically manufactured for export to other population centers. I still remember the immense relief I felt the first time one of my Harvard professors ripped into a paper I'd written, pointing out that my logic was circular, my language duplicitous, and my evidence shadowy. Part of me felt that my skin was being flayed off by sheer embarrassment, but a much larger part of me was practically screaming with relief that someone was dealing with reality more or less the way I naturally did, instead of reinforcing the way I'd been taught to think. "Thank God!" I remember thinking, though at the time I was an atheist. "Thank God, thank God, thank God!"

Thus began my love affair with evidence, which has ultimately brought me here, to a hotel room I have carefully arranged as a kind of psychological laboratory. Even after ensuring that I'll have multiple eyewitness accounts of our conversation, talking with my father still makes me feel as though my brain is twirling slowly in my head. I'm very grateful that my cousin Diane is parked next door, and Miranda is curled up in the closet across the room. I needed this kind of backup to gather enough courage to meet with my father at all, and though I feel weak and childish, there is huge comfort in knowing that people who would never hurt either of us are hearing this strange debate.

"Well, see, Dad," I say carefully, "I find your reaction to the scar thing kind of strange." I notice his eyes widening a little, perhaps because I'm openly disagreeing with him, perhaps because I called him Dad. This suddenly feels right. It feels like rebellion. It's the harshest, most disrespectful word I've ever deliberately said to him.

"If one of *my* daughters turned up with a lot of weird scars," I go on, enjoying the giddy, reckless feeling of saying what I actually think, "I wouldn't just blame the Evil One and drop the subject. I would want to find out what had happened to her."

"Nothing happened." My father's voice carries the ring of absolute assurance, absolute finality, that has made him a safe haven for so many Mormons whose faith is getting a little wobbly. The debate is resolved, the balcony is closed, the fat lady has sung, the last dog is hung, that's all she wrote.

This dead-certain tone is characteristic of many deeply religious folk, but Mormons are trained to use it about as thoroughly as any group of people I've ever known. As soon as they can talk, Mormon toddlers are held up to microphones in church meetings, lisping to hundreds of onlookers the words their parents whisper in their ears: "I know the Church is true. I know that Joseph Smith was a true prophet. I know our president is God's prophet on the earth. I know these things beyond a shadow of a doubt."

Mormons tend to know a whopping lot of stuff beyond a shadow of a doubt. I envy them. My whole life is shadowed by doubt. The only conviction I embrace absolutely is this: whatever I believe, I may be wrong.

For a moment, looking at the stern pioneer conviction on my father's handsome face, I'm so disoriented that I feel my brain twirling even faster—not in agreement but in familiar hopelessness, in the sickening conviction that no one will ever take my word over his. Everything seems to slither right off the hard drive in my head. He's right: People underestimate the capacity of things to disappear. At the moment, I can't even remember the chain of events that took me out of Mormonism, that have made me "a hiss and a byword" not only to my father, not only to my family, but to an entire religion.

Then I remember Miranda and Diane, just a few feet away, and my vision seems to clear. The whole thing comes back to me, the journey that has taken me out of religion and into faith. I recall its horror and beauty, the enormity of the things I have lost and the incalculable preciousness of the things I've gained. I wouldn't give up the journey, not a moment of it. On the other hand, I have no desire to live it again. If Santayana is right, this means I must be willing to remember the whole story. I close my eyes, take a deep breath, and force myself to go back to the beginning.

CHAPTER 2

Men Are from Mars,
Women Are from Venus,
I Am from Utah

The year was 1988, the month was June, and I was on the run.
My husband, John, and I had gone AWOL from Harvard, where
we had been enrolled, first as undergraduates and then as PhD
candidates, ever since we finished high school. Our getaway car was a
rented Buick LeSabre, which was presently headed southward from the
Salt Lake City airport to Provo, Utah, the city where both John and I
grew up. Our two-year-old daughter, Katie, was strapped into her car
seat behind John. Next to Katie, in his own small safety throne, sat the
main reason we were here: our three-week-old son, Adam.

Despite his tender age, Adam had already caused no end of consterna-
tion. He was diagnosed with Down syndrome when I was six months
pregnant, and I had bucked the advice of many doctors and advisers by
electing to continue my pregnancy rather than having a therapeutic abortion. This was why I'd fled Harvard for Utah, though I still had a dissertation to write. The Beehive State was one place where I knew no one
would question my choice or revile my son. As far as the Mormon residents were concerned—and Provo is more than 90 percent Mormon—
Adam's extra chromosome was a get-out-of-jail-free card: he was going
straight to heaven. I'm sure that growing up Mormon had influenced my
decision to keep Adam in the first place, but not as much as you might
think. It wasn't religion that nudged me into keeping my baby. It was my
baby who nudged me into keeping religion.

This is difficult to explain without writing another entire book (which, as a matter of fact, I've already done—it's called *Expecting Adam,* and you're more than welcome to read it). Suffice it to say that from the moment Adam was conceived, inexplicable things had been happening to me. I knew at some cell-deep level, well before his diagnosis, that there was something different about this baby. Though it took me months to articulate it, I felt as though this incipient child existed in an aspect of reality that did not register with my usual five senses. In short, I came to believe in spirits—my spirit, the spirit of my child, the spirit of everything and anything. And along with this belief came a yearning I could barely contain.

"As moderns," writes essayist Patricia Hampl, "we are born into a tradition of disbelief . . . The life of the spirit is not an assumption. It is a struggle. And the proof of its existence for a modern is not faith, but longing." From the time Adam was born, I was utterly possessed by this longing. The difficult aspects of my pregnancy had been sweetened by occasional surges of some inexplicable, ethereal joy, and these moments were so astonishingly comforting that by comparison, almost everything else in my life simply ceased to matter. Twenty-four hours a day, I yearned to feel again what I had felt in those dumbfounding moments of grace, and to that end, I was willing to try anything—even returning to my religious heritage.

To say this was humbling is a massive understatement. I'd been raised as a Mormon by two exceptionally devout parents, as had my husband, John. However, since adolescence, I'd been skeptical of religious belief, tolerating it by adopting a sort of wishy-washy relativistic agnosticism (there is no absolute truth; therefore, any one version of reality is worth as much as any other). As a practical matter, I followed the Baconian model of believing nothing until it was proven true. When Adam came along, with his grab bag of curious and magical properties, I performed a philosophical 180-degree turn. I made a conscious decision to believe anything—*anything*—until it was proven false. I no longer allowed myself to close my mind and roll my eyes at stories of reincarnation, miraculous healing, communication with the dead. Perhaps religion really was the opiate of the masses, as Marx had famously claimed; I didn't care. I'd taken a few hits by accident, and now I was a willing addict.

Naturally, the hefty caboodle of beliefs and traditions I'd inherited from my Mormon culture loomed prominently among the things I now refused to let myself dismiss. In many ways, it was a great relief to set aside my internal resistance to the religion that had dominated my family and community of origin. It gave me a sense of belonging I'd never felt before. For the first time in my life, I was not only willing but eager to blend in with the people who call themselves the Latter-day Saints. I felt like a salmon swimming home to the stream where I was spawned, guided by some built-in homing device, genetically bent on reproducing in a familiar environment.

.   .   .

John and I enjoyed a companionable silence, drinking in the scenery as our children took a rare synchronized nap. The sights, sounds, and scents brought tears of recognition and relief to my citified eyes. In any season, the place where I grew up is beautiful. In June, with everything fresh and growing and warm, it's breathtaking. Spacious skies, amber waves of grain, purple mountains majesty—you name it, Utah's got it. I could feel the stress of our life in Cambridge seeping away into the salty ground, into the sage-tinged air.

As John steered the Buick around the rocky promontory that separates Salt Lake Valley from Utah Valley, we saw the whole fair city of Provo sprawled across the sparkling landscape. All my muscles, still trying to recover from childbirth, relaxed. My heart was chief among them. Provo was where John and I were delivered by the same obstetrician in the same hospital, where we'd both learned to sit quietly in Sunday school, where we'd learned our alphabets and table manners and the Mormon Articles of Faith. Looking at Provo's tidy streets, its suburbs and strip malls, I knew that more than nine out of ten of its residents—the 90-plus percent who were Mormon—would automatically accept and protect my decision not to abort Adam, my newfound religiosity, my aching, Harvard-battered soul. They would look at the short fingers and slanted eyes of my tiny son and see what I saw: not a freak, but an angel. I rested my head against the passenger window and almost wept with relief.

And yet . . .

Looking back now, I clearly recall the twinge of doubt that pinched the corners of my consciousness as we neared Provo. I remember telling myself that I was experiencing culture shock, a normal New Englander's reaction to a sudden wave of niceness. It's an incredibly nice place, Provo. The weather is nice, the housing is nice, the natives are so nice they make the Trapp Family Singers look like Hell's Angels. You can slice Utah's pervasive niceness into decorative cookie-cutter shapes, slather it with decoupage, and hang it on the wall next to the photos of multitudinous blond families that grace every living room in Provo. This is a bit disorienting if you've been living in the Boston area, where the only strangers who wave at each other are prominently extending their middle fingers. As we rolled southward down the Wasatch Front, I kept telling myself that Beantown callousness was the only reason for the sick chill that tickled along my spine.

Then the Provo temple came into view, and I remembered my wedding day, and I had to admit, that had been a little weird.

There are layers and layers of Latter-day Saint culture, and niceness is only the top layer, the icing on a perfect home-baked cake (a flyer printed up for Mormon homemakers when I was a girl specified that making cakes from scratch was more likely to result in salvation than whipping up boxed alternatives, which I suppose were by definition devil's food). No one talks about the layers that lie beneath the surface, so most outsiders never know they exist—although many non-Mormons seem to sense it, smiling artificially and choosing their words carefully when interacting with the Saints. Even someone like me, an official Daughter of the Utah Pioneers, can remain blissfully oblivious to the complex subterranean foundations on which Mormon culture is based. That's why, as a refugee fleeing homeward, I looked back on my wedding day and its implications with some uneasiness. I won't tell you *all* about it here, but I'll hit the high points, the things I recalled most prominently on the day I returned to Utah. I think it will help you understand the seed of doubt that was already taking root in me that day, doubt that, to my eventual joy and sorrow, I chose to ignore.

To begin with, I knew next to nothing about what would happen at my wedding until the very moment it took place. This is because Mormons marry inside temples, which are not ordinary meetinghouses but sacred spaces (one might say *top*-sacred spaces) off limits to all but the most devout church members. The buildings where Latter-day Saints meet for Sunday services are similar in most ways to most Protestant chapels. Any old person off the street can wander into those and be warmly welcomed. The temples, by contrast, are much rarer, much more elaborate, and much harder to get into.

You can hear all about the structure of Mormon temples if you go to the grounds of the preeminent temple in Salt Lake City and locate one of the female missionaries who prowl the premises, guiding tours and looking for "investigators"—in other words, people interested in joining the one true Church. I have it on good authority that only the most attractive female missionaries are assigned to the temple grounds. (One of my Mormon friends likes to pose as a tourist, telling the "Temple Babes," as he calls them, that he's an atheist looking for religion. "I've never gotten so much attention from beautiful women," he told me one day. "Next week I'm going to ask them for a massage.")

The Temple Babes are carefully trained to discuss the temple without actually describing what goes on inside it (the temple rituals are considered necessary for salvation in the afterlife, but no one talks about them—*ever*—for reasons I will soon discuss). Typically, Mormon men go through the temple rituals at age nineteen, before they embark on their two years of missionary work. Unmarried females over the age of twenty-one, who were considered official "old maids" when I was young enough to consider this old, can also go through temple rituals before they wed. But most women, myself included, first enter the temple on the day they're married.

So, as my wedding day dawned, I followed Latter-day Saint bridal tradition by embarking on a whole series of bafflingly unfamiliar experiences. First, all my relatives and I packed little suitcases, me with my wedding dress, the others with a wardrobe of secret "temple clothes." We headed for the nearest Mormon temple, part of which had been reserved in advance for my nuptial ceremony. In one hand I clutched my "recommend," the scrap of paper certifying that I had been thoroughly interviewed by two Mormon leaders to ascertain that my past contained no flirtation with serious sins, such as committing murder or drinking coffee. Without a recommend, I'd have been barred from the temple and perhaps ended up getting married in a civil ceremony, which would have been an occasion of dark shame for me, John, and our families, since Mormon couples who wed outside the temple are generally assumed to have fallen prey to devilish lust, probably due to bad parenting. I exhaled in relief when the guardian at the temple door examined my recommend and smilingly ushered me in.

The interior of the temple felt otherworldly, the floor so thickly carpeted that it muffled all sound except for the soft footsteps and occasional whispers of various elderly Mormons padding around in white polyester slippers. Everyone wore pure white, top to bottom—long white dresses for the women, white jumpsuits for the men. Those who weren't bald had white hair, as well. These were official "temple workers," whose job it was to see neophytes like me through the rituals. They were clearly meant to do so with a minimum of words. One of them beckoned to me, so I followed her as my relatives bustled off with their suitcases to do I Knew Not What.

My chaperone led me to a counter, where women in street clothes were being given bundles of cloth. A few of these were other brides and their relatives, but as I was later informed, most were older women there to perform the temple rituals by proxy for the dead. Each was given a slip with the name of a deceased person on it and would go through the usual rites "for and in behalf of" that ghostly presence. Since Mormons believe that everyone, without exception, must go through these rituals to attain salvation, performing them by proxy for those who lived before Mormonism or who for some reason chose not to practice Mormonism during their lifetime seems only fair. (Several years ago the Jewish community responded rather obstreperously when it was discovered that Mormons were baptizing all the Holocaust victims into the Mormon church by proxy—a reaction that confused many a well-meaning Saint.)

I waited in line and got my bundle, which contained a confusing selection of archaic-looking clothing, all of it white except for a green satin apron embroidered with fig leaves. Carrying it, I followed my guide down a short hallway to a locker room. She whispered that I should undress completely, tie my hair back with a white ribbon, and cover myself with a shift I would find in my bundle. The shift turned out to be like a sheet with a large hole in the middle for my head. I draped it over my naked body and gripped it tightly as we walked to the chamber where I would undergo the Mormon "initiatory" ritual.

I won't describe this ritual in detail, because I think maybe I agreed to have my entrails carved out if I ever did such a thing, and there's nothing like a blood oath to put the old kibosh on one's natural chattiness. I will say that the ceremony involved a closed booth, a bull's horn filled with sacred oil, and a lot of memorized, muttered incantations. These were repeated by more elderly, white-clad women, who dipped their fingers in oil and then touched them to various parts of my body under my shift as they spoke. Later I would hear of people freaking out altogether during this unexpected procedure, but aside from clutching my shift rather too tightly, I went along with it in relative calm. I'd read enough anthropology to know that a lot of cultures have initiatory ceremonies, and I was quite fascinated to learn the customs of my own people. Still, it was . . . different. When I'd dreamed of my wedding day, my girlish fantasies never included having old ladies daub my naked body with oil. If they had, I seriously doubt that I would have been granted a temple recommend.

As we neared the conclusion of the initiatory ritual, the temple workers dressed me in my first set of sacred underwear, known to Mormons as the "regulation temple garment," or by their simpler nickname, garments. When I was a child, all the adults around me wore a single-piece garment with a flap at the crotch, like a baby's singlet, but in the wild 'n' crazy 1980s, the holy underthings had experienced a fashion update. I received a two-piece set, in white cotton mesh: a pair of leggings not unlike Bermuda shorts and a sort of T-shirt with a low, scooped neckline. Still, they were not exactly titillating—therein seems to lie much of their appeal (I know of only one store in the Provo area that supplies garments, but its sales record beats the local Victoria's Secret to smithereens).

Every Mormon who goes through the initiatory ritual gets a pair of garments, and once you put them on you take them off at your peril. All temple-going Saints submit to semiyearly interviews with religious leaders to ascertain that they, to quote the official interrogatory, "wear the regulation temple garment night and day." I have heard arguments both for wearing a brassiere *over* the garments, and wearing the bra *underneath,* thereby risking unprotected nipples. Not wearing the underwear at all is simply disastrous, first, because it's against the rules, and, second, because once an initiated Saint has passed through the temple, he or she becomes an absolutely irresistible target for Satan's minions. Garments, it is said, repel these demonic spirits.

The sacred underwear is also widely reputed to avert physical danger. Growing up, I heard many stories about Saints being saved from knives, bullets, and malfunctioning tractors by their garments. One faith-promoting rumor concerned a navy officer whose ship was bombed and burned by Japanese during World War II. After the battle, the devout Mormon officer was found with his arms, legs, and head burned off, but *not a single thread of his garment was even scorched by fire.* The skin under the holy long johns was as pink and clean as that of a newborn babe. I remember hearing this from a Sunday school teacher who was visibly moved by the miracle. We eight-year-olds sat solemnly, eyes wide, contemplating the power of garments and steadfastly refusing to say aloud what we were all thinking, namely, "His *head* burned off?"

Anyway, I managed to insert my oily self into my first set of garments without incident. I followed my guide out of the initiatory chamber and nodded dazedly as she instructed me that I should never let them touch the floor and that when a set of garments wore out, I should cut out the special symbols sewn into the fabric, burning them secretly before disposing of the remainder. She also told me that like many Mormons of her generation, she bathed with one arm outside her bathtub, garments dangling from her wrist, so she could put on a fresh set without ever removing the old ones. I didn't necessarily have to do that, she said, but you never know. Better safe than sorry.

I didn't have much time to ponder these developments, because now my chaperone whisked me back to the locker room and into my wedding dress (I'd chosen my own design, though it had to cover the garment— no sleeveless gowns allowed). Disaster loomed briefly when it was discovered that I'd worn an ivory-colored bra. This would never do—only pure white clothing is allowed in the temple, whether or not anyone can see it. After a few panicky moments, someone at the bundle desk managed to find an alternative bra, which fit me like a tarp (color, not cut, was the operative variable) but satisfied the dress code. Once dressed, I was led outside the locker room to meet up with my female kin. They hustled along with me to my second rite of passage.

This was a drawn-out affair known as the Endowment. I was delighted to discover that it consists largely of watching a movie. This was shown in a small theater rather like a shopping-mall cinema, though much more nicely appointed, with lush carpets, velvet drapes, and an altar at the front between the seats and the screen. We women filed into this room and sat down on the left side of the center aisle. The right side was already full of men: my father, father-in-law, assorted brothers and brothers-in-law, and, to my enormous relief, John. He was wearing a white jumpsuit. We waved to each other surreptitiously from our respective sides of the room as the house lights went down.

I thought the movie was fascinating, especially at the beginning, which dramatized the creation of the world, the Garden of Eden, and the story of Adam and Eve. The plot development was kind of confusing, though—extra people, like preachers and apostles, kept wandering in and having disconnected chats I found mostly incomprehensible. After an hour or so, just when Adam and Eve got run out of Eden, things definitely took a turn for the strange. Suddenly, the movie stopped, the house lights went up, and a booming recorded voice started giving the audience instructions about the clothing bundles in our laps. There followed a great deal of accessorizing, as everyone added new items of clothing—mainly robes and aprons—to the basic white outfits we were already wearing. The accessories were unfamiliar to me, and they were to be arranged in a very specific way, with knots in all the right places. This was not easy to learn without any kind of warning, let alone preparation.

Donning a veil, for example, is a highly counterintuitive operation—not something you want to attempt for the first time in front of an audience, smack-dab between being oiled by strangers and taking your wedding vows. All the older female Saints around me slapped on their veils deftly, then stood watching me. I kept trying on my own veil in any number of unsuccessful ways, until I was sweating with nerves and exertion and my hair had become so hypercharged with static electricity that it began to stand up in strange tentacles around my head. The whole ceremony ground to a deadly halt. Finally, one of the temple workers lunged at me, hissing like a puff adder (she was apparently forbidden to speak), and jammed the veil onto my head. Everyone in the room sighed in gratitude. I scraped the tentacles of hair from my eyes, looked over at John for support, and was startled to see him wearing a jaunty little hat that was—and I say this lovingly—not his optimal fashion selection. In combination with his jumpsuit and apron, it made him look like the Pills-bury Dough Boy.

But I was soon distracted from making worst-dressed comparisons, because now we'd reached the part of the ceremony where we promised that if we ever told certain temple secrets, we'd let ourselves be killed. This is why I have refrained from describing much of the actual content of the temple rituals, because the death vows were relayed very vividly, not just with words but with actions. Led by an ancient, feeble male tem-ple worker in much the same way aerobics classes are led by their in-structors, everyone in the room simultaneously pantomimed the various modes of death that would be inflicted on us if we broke the vows of secrecy.

I understand that this part of the temple ceremony used to be even gorier (one promised method of death was to have one's "tongue torn out by the root"). Nowadays, the whole murder/suicide pact segment of the ceremony has been eliminated. I think that's a damn shame. I can't imagine anything that could clean out your spiritual sinuses as fast as get-ting together with a bunch of clean-cut, normal-as-pie Mormons and performing a synchronized group mime of your own violent death. I found it so surreal it was truly marvelous, like watching an episode of *Leave It to Beaver* in which June and Ward take just a moment out of their busy day to agree that if they ever leak the family secrets, they'll hack off each other's limbs.

(ATTENTION: I would like to remind my readers, both Mormon and non-Mormon, that I have *not* told any of the specifically forbidden secrets here. If you're wondering about them, I've been told that they're very similar to certain Masonic ceremonies—Joseph Smith was a high-ranking Freemason—but I can't confirm this because I know *next to noth-ing* about the Freemasons, so please, all of you, just leave my entrails as they are. Thank you.)

And so, only three or four short hours after arriving at the temple, I was a fully "endowed" Latter-day Saint, aware that my fellow Mormons were poised and ready to end my life, and therefore—hurray!—ready for my actual marriage! Everyone in the wedding party bustled to yet another special chamber, this one known as a sealing room. Latter-day Saint couples (along with subsequent wives who are technically expected to come into the picture, either in this life or the next) don't just marry until death do them part. They're "sealed" to each other "for time and all eternity." (A "temple divorce" is a possible but rare event, mainly sought by women who wish to remarry. Men are allowed to marry without "temple-divorcing" their previous wives, because their eternal unions are expected to be polygamous.) The room where John and I would be sealed was small, with an altar in the center and mirrors on all four walls. The one thing I'd been told about the wedding before it happened was that I should look into the mirrors as John and I knelt together at the altar. Because they reflected each other, all the walls bore infinite repetitions of the two of us, which was meant to represent the generations of posterity we would produce as we, in classic Mormon fashion, were fruitful and multiplied and replenished the earth.

The actual wedding took about five minutes. After our relatives sat down in chairs that had been placed around the periphery of the room, a gracious old gentleman, dressed in full temple regalia with an especially fetching apron, gave John and me a little lecture, then asked us if we wanted to be married. As instructed, we nodded our heads and said, "Yes." Then we were allowed to exchange rings and a kiss, although this was not part of the official ritual. In the nick of time, I remembered to check out the walls. Sure enough, I saw endless versions of us (John! Martha! John! Martha! John!). Our joined image receded into the infinite distance, symbolizing the generations of children who would spring from our union and grow up to wear comical headgear.

•   •   •

John and I left Utah for Japan the very next morning so John could continue his doctoral and consulting work, and the bewildering events of my wedding day faded into the background of my memory. Five years later, as we rode our rental car past the temple, it all came back to me in a rush. I had to exert considerable effort to honor my new worldview by leaving my mind open to the Mormon rituals, but I managed it. I was a very different person from the bride who'd bumbled her way through those rituals five years earlier: older, sadder, more world-weary. Above all, I had a driving obsession to regain the sweetness I'd tasted in the fleeting moments during my pregnancy with Adam when I'd felt touched by another sense of spirit. I would do anything to get that feeling back, no matter what doubts I had to silence, no matter what oddities I had to accept.

Still, my thoughts did not wholly echo what Brigham Young had told the Mormon pioneers in 1847, when, having traveled thousands of miles over every sort of forbidding terrain hauling their possessions in handcarts, they finally crested the Wasatch Mountains and looked down upon the valleys of Utah. The prophet Brigham, who had succeeded the prophet Joseph after Smith was assassinated, was afflicted with fever, and he trekked the final miles lying in the back of a covered wagon. He is said to have raised himself from his sickbed, regarded the grassy expanse and vast, dead sea of Salt Lake Valley, and proclaimed, "This is the place. Drive on." That's what I meant to think when I returned in 1988. But instead, some troublemaking part of my psychology piped up with the same comment it had made years earlier, when I left the Provo temple with my newlywed husband at my side.

Whoa! I thought, looking around at a population made up almost exclusively of faithful Mormons. All these people are wearing *exactly* the same underwear!

That should have been the moment I realized there was trouble coming.

CHAPTER 3

Inner Darkness

I hear a rustling sound from the coat closet, and for a moment I stop breathing. My mind produces a quick succession of catastrophic images: Miranda wrestling boredom, claustrophobia, and cramped muscles until she can no longer stand it, then bursting out of her hiding place, gasping for air and space. My father startled into a fatal heart attack. An all-Mormon jury convicting me of murder by conversation—and don't think they wouldn't. As far as the Latter-day Saints are concerned, I've already committed the only sin worse than murder: I left the Church. Cold-blooded killers stand a chance of being forgiven by God, provided they undergo some form of execution that involves spilling blood (this is why at this writing, in 2003, Utah still practices death by firing squad). But we apostates are beyond help. After our deaths, no matter how bloody they may be, we get a one-way trip to outer darkness. This is the Mormon equivalent of hell, but a chilling one: no fire and brimstone here, just an endless emptiness, a cold, hopeless void that, come to think of it, sounds kind of like my childhood.

This thought relaxes me a little, because I suddenly remember that Miranda and I are from the same extended family, which means she is combat-ready to deal with my father and our confrontation. Miranda dealt with growing up in our clan by sitting for days in a fetal position, her long hair combed over her face, pretending to be invisible and darn near succeeding. When it comes to hiding, Miranda is a true virtuoso. Anyway, my father doesn't appear to have heard the rustling sound. He's still tapping the arm of the hotel easy chair, examining the lampshade just to the left of my head with a terse, wary expression. We have reached an impasse, an irresistible she-said force meeting an immovable he-said object.

I sigh, not in distress but in resignation. This is pretty much what I expected. Even if everything happened exactly the way I think it did, it's possible my father really doesn't remember. After all, I've watched him suffer at least one episode of amnesia as dramatic as any soap-opera plotline. For a couple of weeks, when I was ten, his famously photographic memory failed almost completely.

The episode began just before he was supposed to deliver an address on certain issues related to Mormonism and Egyptology, which, as you will see, figure prominently in my own personal history. Perhaps suffering from a little dry mouth as he prepared to speak, my father went to get a drink of water, then failed to find his way back to the lecture hall. He was discovered wandering around the building with no idea where he was or what he might be doing. For the next several days, he could barely recall the names of family members and seemed to know zilch about the rest of his life. I've talked to the neurosurgeon who examined my father during this spate of forgetfulness. He told me there was no stroke, no brain lesion, no physiological explanation at all. The doctor concluded that the amnesia was psychogenic, a mental mist that rose from some psychological or emotional conflict too intense for my father to bear. But whatever its source, there's no doubt it was real.

So, even before I grew up and saw for myself, I realized that memory—even the flypaper memory my father and I seem to share—is not the mechanical recording device people often think it is. Memory is anything but constant, anything but indubitable. It shifts and fades, blooms and dies, steps out for a cigarette and blows tendrils of information and emotion back under the door. It fills this room where I sit with my father, who seems as certain of his version of my life story as I am of mine. I don't know whether to accuse him of lying or accept that he really doesn't remember. But he offers no alternative explanation for the scars I carry in my flesh, and I have only one set of memories that accounts for them. Of one thing I am absolutely certain: I haven't invented a single thing.

Since developing a loosely defined but bone-deep belief in some sort of God, I take comfort in believing that there is some consciousness that does record events as they actually happen, that does not edit or forget the past, and that knows the empirical truth of my life story. For ten

years, I've wanted to talk about this with my father. Now, in this
memory-clouded room at the inn, I have my chance. I try to make my
voice as kind as it can be.

"Sometimes," I tell him, "I imagine what we'd say to each other if we
were standing in the presence of God."

My father twists his head slightly, like the Victrola puppy, but his
eyes stay fixed on the lampshade. "Oh, yes," he says, his voice curiously
cheerful again, his expression still suspicious, watchful. "Yes, indeed."
He has a habit of voicing agreement when he isn't tracking a conversation, the way I do when I'm trying to muddle through a discussion in a
language I haven't mastered or am at a cocktail party where I'm deaf-
ened by the music and inebriated by the fumes on the breath of other
conversationalists.

"For what it's worth," I say, "I don't think you have anything to fear.
I mean, I don't think there will be any fire and brimstone or anything. I
think we're here to learn from whatever happens to us, so maybe the bigger the mistake, the more we learn. Maybe it's a good thing."

I enjoy believing this, though of course I could be wrong. Another of
my beliefs, which I don't mention to my father, is that the process of
learning from our mistakes would necessarily involve each of us experiencing the full impact of the pain we've caused, as well as all we've
suffered. People who have had near-death experience sometimes say they
not only relived all their mortal interactions with others but also felt
every impact they had on those around them, as if they themselves were
both object and subject of their behavior. If that's how things work, it's
more than enough to satisfy my longing for justice and my anger at those
who do violence.

"Well, of course," my father says blankly. "Yes, of course." He shifts
his gaze to the wall above my head. I don't think he hears me at all, but
the reason I'm meeting with him is to clear out my own psychological
carburetor. Though I can't deny holding on to some hope, I've read,
thought, tried, and studied enough not to expect any particular reaction
from him.

"The thing is, I believe we're already in the presence of God, whatever God is. Right now. Always."

My father says nothing. He looks completely zoned out.

"Can't you feel it?" I ask him. "All that love? It's wonderful, isn't it?"

I've been looking forward to this part of our conversation, strained though I knew it would be, because I think my father is one of the few people I know who must be as preoccupied with the search for God as I have become. My spiritual quest is like being in love; it's so passionate and adventurous that I'm always looking for someone to help me celebrate it. I'm sure my father is one person who will understand. After all, whatever his mental illness, whatever his repressed or forgotten past, the man thinks religion twenty-four/seven. He is all about Mormonism, and there are more than a few areas in which Mormonism is all about him. To sustain that level of involvement, he must surely feel some of the grace unfolding, of God's presence. The Force must be strong with him.

But now that I've begun talking about my spiritual life, my father seems to have slipped away. He keeps tapping that chair arm, and now he's muttering to himself under his breath. Suddenly I remember that this is what happened whenever I tried to engage him in any serious conversation, something I did often during the period after I discovered spirituality, but before I left religion. I've seen him sit like this, muttering and tapping, for hours at a time. He did it the whole time I was growing up. It is such typical behavior for him that until this very minute, I never thought it was strange.

"I'm not trying to upset you," I tell my father. "I really just want to talk."

His empty eyes move up the frame of the cheap hotel print on the wall near my head as he thumps his private rhythm into his chair arm. He seems utterly indifferent, so maybe I'm just imagining that I can feel loneliness radiating from him like the vast, empty waves of outer darkness itself. Maybe I'm just projecting onto him the memory of how I felt for so many endless days and months and years before I began to sense the first hints of a loving presence in the universe. Tears come to my eyes, but I don't know whether they are for my father or for myself.

For both of us, I think.

It seems important that I continue to remember.

CHAPTER 4

The Milky Way

Just after Adam's conception, when I'd first had the odd, flickering impression of some indescribable, immense compassion around me, I simply dismissed the feeling as meaningless. When it arrived more frequently, and stayed longer, I thought it might be hormones, which were making me more emotional in general. As I began noticing that countless little (and some not-so-little) miracles were happening to me, I became perplexed, then resistant. It wasn't until after Adam's diagnosis of Down syndrome, when I was so sick and sad I could barely move, that I'd capitulated to the hope that there may in fact be some truth to the universal myth of a spirit world. Dazed with blood loss, I'd been infused with warmth and strength that seemed to come from outside my body. Crazed with grief, I'd been comforted by words that coalesced in my brain, clear as dewdrops, without ever taking the form of sound.

Nothing I do to describe these experiences can possibly convey the emotions that went with them. If there were a drug that could reproduce the same effect, I would be on that drug right now, and damn the side effects. Imagine a blend of all your favorite things: ice cream, sex, white sandy beaches, Beethoven's symphonies, all those happy times with your Garden-Weasel, the whole nine yards. Picture these experiences combined, boiled down into their most concentrated elements of pure joy, then multiplied by trillions and injected into every one of your cells. That might begin to help you imagine what I felt when the sense of Something Bigger emerged in the hurricane's eye of my life, surrounded by events that were otherwise completely devastating. The peace and joy were so dazzling, so potent, that I thought they would never fade.

But fade they had, much too quickly.

At the moment Adam was born, my love-drunk sense of the spiritual seemed to leave my body with him. It was a shock, one I'd never known could be part of the birthing process. Still, it made a kind of sense. If Adam was some sort of radio operator and I was just the broadcasting tower, no wonder the frequencies had all gone silent when he checked out and pulled the plug. It didn't occur to me, not yet, that there was another radio operator in there—let's call it my true self—who might do an adequate job on her own. All I knew was that I had lived for months halfway into heaven, and that mere earth, by comparison, felt almost unbearable.

During the days and weeks after Adam's birth, I grieved for his disability, but much more, selfishly, for my loss of connection to the divine. An aching sadness settled over me like broken earth over a grave. I told myself to get used to it. For all I knew, the normal human condition was one of perpetual spiritual hunger, never satisfaction. I tried to stop yearning for what I couldn't have, and go back to enjoying normal life— except that technically I couldn't, because now I knew that I'd never really enjoyed my normal life all that much. Before Adam, I'd been driven, even enthusiastic, but I had the emotional range of a department-store mannequin. Life at Harvard failed to produce anything like the radiant ecstasy I now knew I was capable of feeling. Working toward things like another academic degree, a faculty position, a tenured chair, blah, blah, blah, only pushed me further into a world where my son and my soul would be lifelong outcasts.

I thought it would help to return to my people, people whose spiritual focus shone through in practically every action, every conversation. Mormonism is what sociologists call a "life world" religion, not a back-of-mind relic that rises into conscious attention only during Sunday services but a way of living that flavors everything from watching television to choosing perfume to mowing the lawn. I told my friends at Harvard that moving to Utah was meant to make life easier while I raised my children and wrote my PhD dissertation. But really, I was looking for God.

. . .

John and I moved into a rented house on the eastern outskirts of Provo. We spent our first evening unpacking our luggage and setting up beds—

queen sized for me and John, a twin for Katie, and a crib for Adam, the baby bear. John and Katie actually got some use out of their beds that night. Adam and I had more important things to do. Our final check-in with a Boston neonatologist had revealed that my tiny guy was getting even tinier: he'd lost an ounce during his first two weeks of life. This was bad news, a sign that the muscles around his mouth weren't strong enough to create and sustain the suction he needed to nurse. Nevertheless, the doctor encouraged me to keep feeding him in Nature's Way, rather than switching to a bottle, because nursing was exactly what Adam most needed to build up the coordination that would later allow him to speak. I simply had to work with him harder, feed him more often.

There was certainly no supply-side problem in the nursing question. My body's always-exaggerated reaction to reproductive hormones had turned me into the Dairy Queen. I don't think that anyone who hasn't borne a child can really understand how bizarre it is to have one's own body suddenly begin manufacturing weirdly cantaloupe-flavored *milk*. You go around half expecting Oreos to pop out of your navel as serving suggestions. Anyway, my body had apparently expected to provide for a large dinner party, say the Romanian Army, rather than one suction-impaired seven-pound baby. It hurt. You know that plaintive bawling sound cows make when someone forgets to milk them? That is precisely the noise I would've made during my postpartum weeks if I weren't by nature a law-abiding woman.

So, as John and Katie slept, Adam and I retreated to our brand-new rocking chair—the only furniture in the living room—and redoubled our efforts to transfer calories from my body to his. I made sure that we were positioned for proper nursing and processed my usual moment of shock at the new-and-improved size of my mammary equipment (Will you look at that, I thought dolefully as Adam's tiny cranium entered nursing range. They're bigger than a human head). He started nursing with determined optimism and 100 percent effort, but after consuming very little he seemed exhausted. He fell asleep, resting up for his next attempt, before he could drink enough to reduce the painful milk-cow pressure in my chest.

At that point I probably should have put us both to bed, if only for a few minutes, to catch up on badly needed sleep. But I didn't. I just sat there . . . and sat there, and sat there. After a while I let myself notice that I wasn't following instructions from the La Leche League. I wasn't just awake and alert. I was waiting. At some level I expected that here, now, in this religious haven, surrounded by its cathedral of peaks, I could find God again. Especially in a moment of silence and darkness—not the sterile silence of the hospitals where I'd spent so much time over the past months, and not the oppressive darkness that had hidden behind the electric lights of Cambridge, but the pure, soft, rustling calm of a summer night in the mountains. Back in my homeland, I hoped that I'd be able to see beyond the boundaries of my physical condition.

But I couldn't.

I waited, barely moving, for at least an hour, every molecule saturated with that inexpressible yearning. I closed my eyes and strained my ears, hoping to pick up some trace of the soundless voice that had spoken to my soul a few times. Then I gave up listening and stared into the night sky beyond the open window. There was nothing to see: no God, no angels, no visions. The only light came from the vast, indifferent sprawl of the Milky Way, billions of miles beyond the living-room window.

I wondered idly if the name Milky Way reflected the ancient Chinese belief that the vast creator goddess Nu-ah formed the constellation by accident, when she was nursing the first human and her uncovered breast sprayed white droplets across the sky. At the time I heard that myth, I thought that the whole concept of a woman spraying milk was as weird and fictional as a "vast creator goddess." Now I could do it my own self, anytime I wanted to, often when I didn't. I wondered what other supposed impossibilities were only figments of my limited imagination.

Just thinking about nursing tripped some kind of physiological trigger in my chest, and I felt the strange stinging sensation of my milk letting down. I was once again, as Lady Macbeth put it, "too full o' the milk of human kindness" or, rather, the kindness of human milk. I bounced Adam gently to wake him up. He was clearly still hungry; he stirred, blinked, and began turning his head from side to side, seeking nourishment. We wrestled for a few minutes as his diminutive mouth clamped onto my upper arm, then my collarbone. By the time he finally got it right, my body was doing its best Nu-ah impression, spraying its own high-pressure Milky Way across our living room. It was too much for Adam; he choked, inhaled liquid, and began a tiny-baby coughing fit interspersed with angry wails. Combined with sleep deprivation and the grim prospect of a life without angels, the struggle overwhelmed me. I broke down and cried along with my son.

That was when, for the first time since his birth, it happened again. I felt a familiar tingle rush over and through my body, a slight electrical buzz that made the hair stand up on my nape and arms. I didn't hear or see anything, but suddenly my mind was filled with a thought that seemed to have come from somewhere both far beyond me and deep within me. I knew—I *knew*—that there was some infinite power whose relationship with me was being echoed by my relationship with Adam. It seemed to be telling me, without words but with perfect clarity, that my natural state was not hunger but fulfillment. More than that: this power yearned, longed, ached to nourish me, as intensely as I needed to feed my child. The only obstacle, for both Adam and me, was an impaired ability to receive.

In the half second that all these things seemed clear, the electrical sensation had already begun to flicker out, and with it went the indescribable comfort that had gone straight into me like a healing dagger.

I began to cry harder than ever, but now I was shedding tears of relief, not sorrow. I didn't have to be pregnant to feel connected to the Other Side. It was like seeing the warm, living smile of a loved one I'd given up for dead. I hugged Adam's soft little body, holding him on my shoulder and patting him until his cries mellowed into small, disgruntled squawks. Then I settled back in the rocking chair and stroked his velvet cheek, the way the neonatologist had told me to do, until he began to nurse. "There you go, boyo," I whispered as his tummy began to fill and his arms and legs went happily limp. "You've got it. It just takes a little practice."

I figured that was what I needed, too. Practice. Wasn't that what Asian mystics called their search for enlightenment? I would find out. In fact, I would research any spiritual practice I could. I would master them all. I would pray, fast, meditate, serve my fellow man, go to church, read the Bible—whatever it took to plug me into the source of that amazing joy. I was certainly in the right community to launch a spiritual quest. I'd grown up virtually ignoring all these good Utah people who spent so much of their time practicing their religion. Now I was going to listen to them as humbly as I could. I would hear and do and obey and believe and follow anything, anything at all, until I figured out how to let God feed my soul.

CHAPTER 5

The Kingdom of God

The next day, energized by renewed hope and faith, I got to work becoming a good Latter-day Saint. It was wonderful. It was restorative. It was *easy.*

Cambridge, Massachusetts, has many charms: cobblestones, historic sights, museums, libraries, good restaurants. But few of these attractions make life easier for a couple juggling two small children. By contrast, Provo is Baby Central. More infants are born in Utah Valley Medical Center, where both John and I first saw daylight, than in any other medical facility in the country. The infrastructure of the city is deeply influenced by this constant influx of infants. Public restrooms have special lounges for nursing. Dentists' offices feature play areas where youngsters can frolic while Mommy has a root canal dug into her jaw. Many grocery stores are outfitted with carts that seat at least two toddlers and also have bolted-on cradles for newborns. Ambulatory preschoolers push small plastic carts, also provided by the stores, alongside the mothers who cruise the aisles seeking industrial-sized crates of generic-brand diapers, children's Tylenol, macaroni and cheese.

Every time I turned around, another smiling, fair-haired person was trying to make my life easier. Tidily dressed teenagers opened doors for me and patted Katie's head as we shopped for household necessities. The moving men who hauled furniture into our house were pleasant and deferential to a fault. Neighbors showed up to introduce themselves and drop off bottles of jam or canned fruit. Before we had even left Cambridge, our Utah Mormon congregation had gotten busy assigning two men (our "home teachers") and two women (my "visiting teachers") to ensure that our move proceeded safely and comfortably. You could live in

Cambridge several lifetimes without experiencing half the helpful good-will that greeted me my first day back in Provo.

All of this would have been true no matter where I'd been born, or to whom, but I probably received an extra dose of kindness because of my lineage. Lineage matters in Mormonism. A lot. The pioneer Saints origi-nally organized Utah as a literal theocratic kingdom, with the Mormon prophet crowned king. That changed when the leaders of nineteenth-century Utah opted for inclusion in the United States, but to this day the social structure of the Latter-day Saint community is more aristocracy than democracy. Descendants of the early pioneers enjoy a subtly but dis-tinctly higher status than new converts and are more likely to be pro-moted to high rank in the Church's lay ministry.

All worthy Mormon males twelve and older are ordained into the priesthood—in fact, the word *priesthood* is used as a synonym for the word *men* or even for one individual man (hence the slightly salacious Mormon woman's comment, "I hold the priesthood every night"). Men are "called" to serve in positions of leadership, most of which are tempo-rary. The exceptions are the very high officers who are paid by the Church and serve for life. Everyone starts out as a foot soldier, even the very top officials, the Quorum of the Twelve (also known as the twelve apostles), the president (who is also God's prophet), and the president's "counselors." These are the true celebrities of Utah society, revered, prayed for, honored, adulated. On the occasions when top-dog leaders came to my childhood home (which happened a lot more to me than to most Mormon children), it was as though Elvis Presley, the president of the United States, and the pope had been rolled up in one and deposited in our living room.

Almost every Mormon man holds some office, and the higher the rank, the greater the cachet of celebrity. As in any aristocracy, this carries over to relatives. Since the early leaders were polygamous and deeply committed to grand-scale reproduction, they have lots and lots and *lots* of relatives. In the nineteenth century, when the Mormons were first gain-ing a foothold in the Utah Territory, young men were advised to marry as many women as possible, since this increased the likelihood of their being appointed to high Church offices. As a result, there's still an enormous amount of royal blood coursing through the veins of today's Latter-day Saints.

I myself am not quite royal, but in Mormonism I am definitely of noble birth. One of my great-grandfathers was presiding bishop of the Church (a General Authority position much higher than the rank of local bishops, who preside over individual congregations). Sadly, my great-grandfather topped out at a paltry three wives, and his genes are therefore rather thinly represented in Utah's present population. Another of my progenitors was the personal dentist of the prophet Joseph Smith himself, though he held no official position (as a Jew—the first to join the Mormons—he was probably doomed to low rank from the get-go). This great-great-grandfather also instructed Brother Joseph in German, Hebrew, and Jewish mysticism. Under his tutelage, the prophet began spicing up his speeches and proclamations with concepts from the Kabbalah. This still pleases me, in a perverse way: I know a lot of people who claim that their families are weirder because of Mormonism, but I am one of a much more select group who can justifiably claim that Mormonism is weirder because of my family.

Which brings us back to my father.

By the time I was born, when my father was fifty-two, he had already established himself as an intellectual warrior who served eagerly and well at the behest of the highest Church authorities, vigorously counterattacking scholars and writers who cast aspersions on the Mormon belief system. Utah is chock-full o' pedestals, and by virtue of his singular skill as an apologist, my father was given a high one. His wit and eccentricity, combined with his bloodline and his pivotal role in defending the Church, made him almost legendary. Some of my earliest memories are of adult strangers crowded around me, quizzing me about my father: How many languages could he read? About fifteen, I thought. How many books and articles had he written? I'd lost count. Did he really buy secondhand clothes? Yes. Was he truly so absentminded that he often lost the family car? Yes. Why did he always wear sunglasses outside, no matter what the weather, and frequently inside as well? I wasn't sure.

As a child, I hadn't understood exactly why my father was so revered, but I enjoyed basking in his reflected glory. On the other hand, being related to a local celebrity carried the same disadvantages in Utah that it does anywhere else. I felt compelled to be an upstanding citizen, since people I'd never met knew me on sight as my father's daughter. Classmates noticed and resented the extra attention I got from my teachers. In elementary school, I created a tempest in a teapot—well, more of a tempest in a teaspoon, really—by becoming best friends with the only Catholic girl in the student body, instead of avoiding her as my teachers blatantly suggested I should ("Now, Martha, considering who your father is, don't you think you can find other girls to play with?"). You'd think I had chosen to play pat-a-cake with the local leper.

So I'd breathed a sigh of relief when I went off to Cambridge. True, Mormon strangers still stopped me on the street to say, "My testimony of the Gospel is *so much* stronger because of your father's writings!" (a "testimony of the Gospel" refers to an individual's belief in the veracity of the Church). But these groupies were very rare in Cambridge, and I forgot what it was like to feel like a goldfish. By the time I moved back to Utah, I figured people would long ago have stopped recognizing me. I figured wrong. Before the end of my first day in Provo, a half-dozen new acquaintances had introduced themselves, chatted a moment, then inquired with barely disguised fascination about my father's health, his daily habits, his latest book. I answered with reflexive politeness, scolding myself for the knee-jerk inclination to tell these folks they needed to get out more. It was like entering a time warp, a seamless continuation of a social role that had changed not one whit during my years away from Zion (by which the Saints mean any territory they dominate) and my adventures in Babylon (which is what the Saints call the non-Mormon world).

All of this—the baby-friendly infrastructure of Provo, the exquisite neighborliness of its residents, the homage I received as part of my genetic heritage—made the Latter-day Saint community around me seem strangely unreal. I felt as though I were seeing all of it at a great distance, from the cheap seats of a movie theater where some Disney cartoon kingdom was being projected onto the screen. I remember wondering, during those first few days in Utah, whether Walt Disney's Mormon wife helped him dream up all those fairy lands where the houses were sweetly domestic, the people pink-skinned and kind, the commoners respectfully obsessed with the lives of the aristocracy.

It troubled me that, glad as I was to be back, I still didn't feel I fit in. I was a young Mormon mother, but I was other things, too—things that made me feel like a stranger in a strange land. Part of my mind was back at Harvard, chewing on ideas for my doctoral dissertation. (Wouldn't it be interesting to study the Mormon response to the feminist movement? That way I could just watch myself, write up my journal, and call it sociological research.) I unconsciously applied various sociological models to Utah's cultural structures, unthinkingly cracked cynical jokes. The discomfiture of my first day in Provo brought back an entire childhood of being a round peg in a religion full of square holes. As I bounced Adam in his strap-on front pack and told the incredibly nice moving men where to put our furniture, I remembered designing another house, when I was nine or ten years old.

Back then, all Mormon children attended a special midweek meeting known as Primary, which I suppose stood for Primary Religious Education or something. The meeting began with all the children in one room, singing an anthem that began, "The primary colors are one, two, three: red, yellow, and blue." For some reason, I couldn't bear to sing this correctly; even when I joined in the chorus, I'd shout out substitute colors, like "puce, fuchsia, and beige," which frustrated my young-lady Primary teachers to the point of tears.

On the occasion in question, the girls in my age group were in for a real treat: we were going to decorate gingerbread houses. My sweet twenty-something teacher had spent hours baking and assembling the basic structures, which we nine-year-olds were to finish with white icing and all manner of confectionary notions. The teacher had brought wonderful decorations, not just colored jimmies and gumdrops but tiny picket fences, brown licorice to make miniature outdoor woodpiles, and even shiny, minuscule toy axes to lean against the wood. She encouraged all of us girls to re-create a house from one of our favorite storybooks. So I did.

While the other girls in my class set to work creating Sleeping Beauty's cottage or the cabin from *Little House in the Big Woods,* I covered my gingerbread house with a thick layer of frosting, piled more white in huge drifts around the structure, and leaned a few brown licorice sticks against the walls, hoping they'd look like rough-hewn structural supports. Then I used black gumdrops and toothpicks to assemble a gorilla-like figure, which I positioned on the roof, staring down the chimney. I was putting an ax in the figure's upraised right hand when the teacher came to check on my progress.

"Uh, that's . . . very interesting, Martha," she said. "What . . . exactly . . . I mean, what . . . ?"

"It's Hrothgar's mead hall," I explained. "You know, from *Beowulf*. That's Grendel—the monster Grendel—on the roof." I dripped red food coloring around the mead hall's entryway. "Blood," I explained. I found a length of red string licorice and draped it over one of the beams. "This is somebody's intestines." The teacher looked as though I'd hit her with a board. During my childhood, I'd seen that look on the faces of more Mormon teachers than I could count, but this time I felt suddenly ashamed. I began hiding in the shrubbery when it was time to go to Primary, and thenceforth was known as something of a rebel.

Now, years later, as I observed my own reactions to the Provo environment, I could see why my sassy behavior had upset other Mormons so much. My childhood teachers, like most Latter-day Saints, were so earnest, so guileless, that they had virtually no defense against cynicism. They were as vulnerable to snide comments as the American Indians had been to smallpox and syphilis. I'd been the kind of brat who delighted in upsetting them, and I could tell the trait still ran in my veins, incongruously blended with my noble Mormon blood. In retrospect, given the entirety of my childhood, not just the part visible to outsiders, this perversity seems reasonable. Of course, I wasn't thinking about that when I returned to my homeland. I just told myself I was a grown-up now, and I should do better. If I were going to have a spiritual rebirth, I'd have to play by the rules.

So I told the moving men to arrange our house exactly as I thought an ideal Latter-day Saint mother would have it. I suppressed even mental snappy comebacks to the kind Church members who inquired about my father. I opened myself to the sweetness, the innocence, the profound good intentions of my native people, promising myself I would never second-guess or criticize their way of living and thinking, ever again.

Oh, well.

CHAPTER 6

The Work

Thump, thump, thump. My father's fine-boned fingers are still tapping the upholstered arm of his chair. I'm not sure how to proceed. The conversation is going nowhere, but there's still so much I want to say. He hasn't answered my question, the one about what God feels like to him. Perhaps I should drop the subject, but after all, this meeting is not exactly a flowerbed of social niceties, and I'm deeply curious.

It's not as if I have a memory full of daddy/daughter chats to establish protocol. My father rarely conversed with me while I was growing up, and when he did he often used languages other than English. I could follow his French reasonably well, especially after I started studying it in middle school, but when he spoke Russian or Arabic or even German I was completely in the dark. Even now, the words he is murmuring under his breath sound alien. I think they might be Greek.

For my whole adult life, I've been chastising myself for failing to communicate well with my father. Now I remember why I never managed it. Trying to talk to him is like playing one of those carnival games—the Coke bottle ringtoss or dart the balloon. It looks ridiculously easy, but when I actually try it, the Coke bottles and balloons become bizarrely evasive, and I always miss. During my adult religious phase, when I'd just moved back to Utah, this had baffled me. I kept trying to talk to my religious-icon father about God, only to become more frustrated than ever when he switched languages, left the room, or went into that blank, dissociated stare.

Once, I'd invited him to go with me on a drive into the mountains with Katie and Adam. My father loves nature, and he'd consented to accompany us, but my plan for filial bonding didn't go far. My father spoke not a word of English on the thirty-minute trip to a small mountain lake. We got out to walk by the lakeshore, and I awkwardly, hesitantly tried to tell him about my search for faith. Before I'd spoken two sentences, my father literally turned and ran away from me. I remember standing there in somewhat wounded puzzlement, holding Adam and watching this eighty-year-old man in stained clothing and heavy sunglasses bound through the forest like Bambi's mother. Of course, now I know why. If I were in his position, I probably could have set a world record in cross-country distance running.

At the moment, my father looks as though he's about to bolt again. This may be my last shot at the Coke bottle ringtoss of connecting with him, so I decide to try another tack, one that might put him more at ease.

"You know, when I came back to Utah after Adam was born, I checked out every book about religious experience that I could find in the BYU library." Brigham Young University, where my father taught religion throughout his distinguished career, has one of the biggest libraries in the country. Many of the books it contains are there at his recommendation.

He isn't looking at me. Thump, thump, thump.

"I was pretty much obsessed with it—wanted to know every spiritual practice from every culture anywhere. I checked out all these obscure books on shamanism and mysticism and religion. And a lot of times, when I signed my name on the check-out card in the back of the book, there was only one other name there. Yours."

I smile at my father, and though he only sees me peripherally, this seems to set him somewhat at ease. He risks a small chuckle. "Well," he says, "isn't that something."

"I think so."

He's still not exactly relaxed, but I'm encouraged by his response. If I act genial enough, maybe he'll see that I mean him no harm. Perhaps then he'll be willing to bridge the gap that yawns between us.

"It's fascinating to me," I say, "that so many different people, in so many different cultures, came up with the same spiritual practices. It's almost like a technology of the spirit, you know? Like using a magnifying lens—look through a telescope, you'll see the moons of Jupiter; learn to meditate, you'll see your spirit. And other people's. Maybe even God's."

I look straight at his eyes, which skitter sideways to avoid mine. Nevertheless, I think I really am making some kind of contact. My father's expression brightens, and he sits up straighter in his chair.

"Oh, yes," he says. "Yes, indeed. Of course. That's why this book is so important."

I have to think for a second. "You mean the book you're writing?"

I don't remember a time when my father wasn't writing a book. He's finished many—all scholarly defenses of Mormon doctrine—but the one he's working on now seems to elude completion. He's been working on it for over a decade. It has to do with an Egyptian papyrus once owned by the prophet Joseph Smith. I've read passages from it, and to me they were all incomprehensible trails of circular reasoning. My father's mind seems to be caught in the Egyptian stuff like a rat in a blind maze.

"Yes, yes," says my father. "This book is the big one. This is going to knock their socks off."

"Really!" I make my smile broader, encouraging him to keep talking. I feel as though I'm on the verge of having an actual conversation with the man. After all, I'm a writer myself now. Maybe my father and I can meet on the common ground of authorship.

"So, are you nearly finished?"

"Very nearly," he says briskly. He fastens his eyes on the middle distance several feet to my right, but his next words are downright animated.

"You know, I gave an address from the book last week. To an entire conference of seminary teachers."

"No kidding!" In Mormonism, seminary classes are recommended for every teenager and taught by laypeople who have been trained in the Church Education System. "Seminary" is separate from Sunday school, a daily class added to the school day at high schools, taught in separate small buildings near the schools, but located just off school property to avoid breaching the constitutional wall between church and state. Seminary students learn extensive—though carefully edited—information about Mormon history, scripture, and doctrine. The teachers tend to be particularly well versed in my father's work and particularly worshipful in his presence.

"I was supposed to start speaking at 7 a.m.," he says. "Can you imagine? Such a ridiculous hour! Of course I thought no one would be there, but when I got to the hall, they were standing in the aisles. Hundreds of them! At seven o'clock in the morning! And when I was finished—well, you should have heard them! They cheered! They actually cheered!"

My father's eyes are shining. A slow wave of understanding breaks over my mind, and with it, an awful pity. Oh, my goodness, I think. All my blather about the technology of the spirit must have been as opaque to him as his recent writing is to me. What sustains my father is the cheering crowd, the adulation, the approval. I suspect this is the closest he has come to feeling unconditionally loved. I recognize the symptoms, because I've been there.

It's a terrible place.

Before I can even comment, my father segues to another story. I seem to have tapped some sort of conversational vein.

"Yes, this work is absolutely fundamental to the Gospel. I met with the brethren about it last month." The brethren, in Mormonism, have nothing to do with the Supreme Court. They rank far higher than that. They are the highest of the General Authorities, and include the prophet of God's true church, his counselors, and his twelve apostles. The prophet literally communicates God's words to the human race, not through historical documents but through direct revelation. The apostles are considered to be equal with Jesus' original gang of twelve. Together, these men constitute the highest authority on earth, and any Mormon who meets with them has bragging rights for life. My father rubs shoulders with the brethren on a regular basis.

"They told me there's really no one else who can do what I'm doing. No one else who can defend the Lord's work in this particular way, you see."

Again, that dry, self-deprecating little laugh. My father is not immodest, but the fact is that at ninety-one, he's still a vital bulwark in the defense of the one true Church. No wonder he seems so spry. How many nonagenarians feel that needed?

"So," he says, "I suppose that's why I'm still here. The Lord's work must go on!"

I look at him through a haze of irony so thick it's almost visible, considering the price my father and I both paid for his willingness to do "the

Lord's work." I remember a joke I heard not long ago, from another apostate like myself. I'm sure the original joke had to do with lawyers or politicians, but the way it was told to me, it was about a Mormon man destined to become one of the brethren. In it, the devil appears before a promising young Mormon and says, "I'll give you all the fame and glory you can imagine—I'll convince people that you speak for God Himself. And all I want in exchange is your soul."

The young man contemplates Satan's offer for a long moment. Then he says, "Okay. So what's the catch?"

CHAPTER 7

Valhalla

Sometime during our first days in Utah, I loaded my children into the car John and I had just purchased and drove down to see my parents. And I do mean *down*.

In Provo, social status correlates directly with altitude. The higher a house sits on the mountains, the more respectable its inhabitants. The decent Provo neighborhoods begin in the lower foothills just east of Brigham Young University, where most of the professors—including John's father but not mine—raise their families. A few hundred feet up you'll find the grander homes of the doctors, lawyers, and business-people who practice the Seven Habits of Highly Effective People (including the author of *The Seven Habits of Highly Effective People*). Higher still are the estates of the techno-tycoons who started the computer companies that thrive in Utah Valley. The Osmonds own a whole gated lane at an altitude so exalted that postal workers probably need bottled oxygen just to deliver their fan mail.

Me, I'm a valley girl. The house where I grew up is located on the dead-flat bottom of the dried-up lake that once flooded Utah Valley and hence the dead-flat bottom of the Provo social ladder. Even in the world beyond Zion, the one profession that garners high prestige but very low wages is that of a college professor. Brigham Young University, where my father is a tenured professor emeritus of religion, is owned and operated by the Mormon Church, and its funds come from the tithing dollars of faithful members, each of whom must donate 10 percent of his or her income in order to remain in good standing. Naturally, this money is to be used sparingly, so BYU pays its employees even less than many other universities. In other words, despite my father's local fame, he made very little money to support a family of ten.

In a strange way, my father enjoys his nearly impoverished status. He has always loathed wealthy people, believing deeply in an economic system known as the United Order, pioneered (pun intended) by early Mormon prophets. The United Order was basically theocratic communism: each member of a community donated work and took whatever money was necessary to sustain life and health. During the early years of colonizing Utah, the Mormons set up a few cities (the most famous being the town of Orderville) that operated according to this principle. I grew up hearing my parents discuss how these experiments had failed only because the communities worked so well, and other cities, populated by jealous closet capitalists, sabotaged their continued success. My father seemed determined to live the United Order in the midst of what he saw as a satanically materialistic culture. His thrift-store clothes and dilapidated little house were political statements, and he was proud of them.

His children, at least early in life, were not.

Growing up, I avoided letting friends even see my house, much less come inside. The location was shameful, the exterior even more so—I mean, who paints a brick house swimming-pool blue?—but the inside was the real stunner. The rooms were set up with careful bilateral symmetry, having been built by a fair-minded pioneer to give equal space to each of his two wives (with one bathroom squarely in the center, to maximize the effectiveness of the plumbing). My parents had added an upstairs, with one more bathroom and four tiny bedrooms. The ten members of our family not only lived in this cramped space, but filled it with decades' worth of flotsam and jetsam. It took me years to realize that we were poor, because although we had very little actual money, I grew up surrounded by a wild abundance of stuff.

There were bookshelves in every room of the blue house, all of them crammed with books at least two deep, extra volumes crammed in horizontally and spilling onto the floor. I turned five before I was taller than the pile of unmatched socks in our unfinished concrete basement. I could find pretty much anything in the mounds of stuff that filled every available surface. Archery equipment? A butter churn? Fright wigs? If I just dug deep enough, I knew they'd be there. And of course, there were lots of things you could find nowhere else *but* in our house, like the alarm clock my brother made out of a sundial and a magnifying glass (you posi-tioned the device so that at the appointed hour, the magnifying lens concentrated the sun's rays onto a fuse, which ignited, burned, and ulti-mately fired a small cannon). It was as though Santa had set up his work-shop in the city dump.

At the center of this remarkable edifice was the kitchen, where we'd spent many a long summer day canning fruit and making jam. To save money on canning equipment, we never threw anything away. Every empty pickle jar, every used piece of aluminum foil, every disposable plastic cup was stored for future use. These things had consumed all the available cupboard space long before I entered the picture. Bottles, condiments, and food crowded every kitchen surface. We cleaned the table (though not very often) by lifting these items, wiping the tabletop beneath them, then replacing everything in its original location.

This was what my mother was doing the morning I brought Adam for his first visit. Katie had been to the blue house before, so she knew what to do: she went directly to a pile of stuff and began digging for toys, or possibly live animals. My mother gave her a smile, a cracker, and a pat on the head before turning her attention to the baby.

"There he is!" she crowed, lifting him out of his baby carrier. "There's Adam!" Her soft face brightened behind her glasses but not with your typical Hallmark card commercial, doting grandma, swooning ecstasy. First of all, Adam was not my mother's first grandchild. I believe he was her sixteenth or seventeenth, somewhere in there. And then, of course, there was the Down syndrome. I shifted nervously from foot to foot, studying my mother's face, trying to read in her expression the true ex-tent of my baby's abnormality.

I needn't have worried. My mother held the new addition to her family just as she would any infant, with the confident assurance of a world-class expert. Which she was. She had borne nine children, eight of whom survived to adulthood, all of whom weighed over nine pounds at birth, meaning that my mother's small-framed, zaftig, rather fragile body had personally ejected over eighty pounds of human being into the uni-verse. She feared nothing baby related—not colic, not diarrhea, not any brand of exotic infant virus, and apparently not Down syndrome.

"Are you going to wake up and say hello?" my mother crooned. Adam opened his eyes, crossed them, and uncrossed them again, trying to focus on his grandma's face.

"Oh, he's a sweet baby," said my mother. "He's a good baby." She tucked Adam expertly onto one hip as she poured Diet Dr Pepper from a can into a goblet made of thick blue glass. The Dr Pepper was her favorite vice, a beverage strict Mormons won't drink, since it contains caffeine. The goblet was another indulgence, one of the few things my mother had always reserved as her personal property. I remember the day she threw caution to the wind and bought it for herself, blowing fully $1.99 at Smith's Food King. The moment she'd pulled it from the grocery bag was one of the few times during my childhood that my mother seemed almost happy.

As she finished lunch, we chatted about Adam's birth, her health problems, my father's work. Katie came into the kitchen, knees gray from playing on the dirty carpet, and my mother gave her another cracker. I felt a little dizzy. It was strange to see my mother through adult eyes. She was so different from my childhood memories. Not dangerous at all. Not a force of nature who would scare you into hiding for hours at a time. She was, in fact, a very nice person.

· · ·

This, let me tell you, was an amazing paradigm shift for me. My mother was the reigning terror of my childhood. I both loved her desperately and found her infinitely horrifying, like the Hindu mother-goddess Kali, the source of essential nourishment and malevolent destruction. I didn't understand that she was probably profoundly clinically depressed, that her behavior was perhaps the result of circumstance rather than innate personality. I only knew that my mother often went for days without changing out of her nightclothes, that she almost never laughed or went outside, that she spent almost all her time lying on her bed, crying. Things were even worse when she got up, erupting from her room like lava from a volcano, screaming with fury, tearing at the hair she usually wore in a teased-up beehive.

I was never sure when this would happen, but I was certain that when it did, it would be my fault.

To this day, I can't figure out exactly which of my behaviors tripped my mother's trigger so intensely, but my impression that I was her scapegoat was borne out by the way my siblings used to warn me to lay low. When they said she was on the warpath, I'd climb the tall fir tree next to our house, or bury myself under the sock pile in the basement. Sometimes this gave her enough time to calm down, but usually there was still hell to pay—the occasional slap, but far worse, my mother's scalding words. I never seemed to grow enough emotional calluses to tolerate my mother's shouted accusations that I was an ungrateful, selfish brat. As I grew into adolescence, I tried frantically to please her by doing well in school, but this seemed to make her even angrier. When I got into Harvard she was so furious she barely spoke to me for two weeks. I'm still not sure why. But by the time I brought Adam to meet her, I thought I'd figured it out.

I'd now read enough feminist literature to believe I understood my mother. After all, Harvard hadn't even accepted women when she was college age. While the world had opened up for girls of my generation, my mother kept grinding away at the one occupation recommended for Mormon females: breeding well in captivity. She was good at this; she just didn't like it. I could certainly identify with that.

Since my marriage, while we weren't what you'd call intimate, my mother and I had established a sort of uneasy détente. I had learned to be deeply grateful to her for sacrificing her body and life to the Mormon tradition of high fertility, because in doing this, she gave me the most wonderful gift I could possibly receive. Seven gifts, to be exact: my four brothers and three sisters. Thanks to my siblings, I was raised not so much by a depressed mother as by a village of half-grown Vikings. To outsiders, we were probably a litter of mangy, indistinguishable, nearsighted blond urchins. But to me, my brothers and sisters were quite simply the walking definition of love.

It wasn't that we were a demonstrative bunch—far from it. The only emotional expression we allowed ourselves was laughter, and a lot of it. But I was sure no one else had brothers so strong, creative, and large-hearted that they would include my one-year-old baby sister in their football games (they played her in the only position she could really handle—the ball—and responsibly chose not to punt, although there was a lot of handing off and some spectacular long passing). No one else had sisters who could win beauty contests *and* outscore all their male schoolmates on every test. When my siblings were in it, our weird, shameful home became something altogether more noble, a lofty place where pain was ignored and nothing was too sacred to ridicule. It wasn't just a polygamist's hand-me-down. It was Valhalla.

.   .   .

Mommy, look!" Katie ran back into the kitchen, holding a sharp wooden sword straight out in front of her. I recognized the sword—in fact, technically I owned it. One of my brothers had whittled it for me as a birthday present when I was six, just before he taught me to joust. It was much more dangerous than a store-bought toy—I knew this, because I once accidentally rammed it a considerable distance into my own knee.

My mother and I saw the sword at precisely the same moment and reacted with precisely the same expression: that of a mother assessing whether one of her children is about to accidentally gouge out a sibling's eye. Again, in that moment, I saw my mother as an equal, and was stunned by the immensity of all she had given me: life itself, her limited strength, the gang of rowdy misfits who raised me.

The sword zoomed in, aimed directly at Adam's unsuspecting face. My mother's expression never changed, but at the last possible instant, she threw a deft, empty-handed parry that deflected Katie's lethal weapon into a pile of rewashed disposable cups. The cups scattered helter-skelter over the kitchen floor, where they looked right at home.

"Don't stab your brother," said my mother mildly. "Go back into the living room and stab something there." She didn't mean it as a joke. My mother rarely meant anything as a joke.

But you could see she had a streak of Viking in her, just the same.

CHAPTER 8

The Camel

I t took me several weeks to disengage from the frantic, pressured mind-set I'd always used at Harvard and settle into the gentler rhythm of life in Utah. In most ways, my new situation was idyllic.

I spent the mornings working with Adam, putting him through a variety of strange exercises meant to minimize his disability by stimulating his brain, a process known as "early intervention." With Katie's help, I'd strip Adam to his diaper and roll him in the grass, jingle keys and spoons in his face, half bury him in a tub of dry beans, and make him do a baby bodybuilding routine—sit-ups, push-ups, leg presses, and so on. It seemed odd to spot someone through biceps curls when the biceps in question were only as big as my thumb, but Adam worked hard enough to impress Arnold Schwarzenegger. Little by little, his floppy limbs became stronger, his motor skills more controlled, and his gaze brighter.

Once Adam finished working out, I'd take both kids to a playground or over to my parents' house to visit their grandma. My mother and I were getting along better than I'd ever hoped. This was largely due to the fact that I'd put my academic career on the back burner and was trying my hardest to be a respectful daughter and a good Mormon homemaker.

It was all part of my desire to realize God. One of the books I'd been reading—a Buddhist description of an Islamic text—described every spiritual quest as having three stages: the camel, the lion, and the child. "In the camel stages of awakening," the author said, "we make ourselves available to the spirit through humility, prayer, repetition, and manual labor." In a Zen monastery, this might mean submitting to the famous two-step "chop wood, carry water." A Catholic, like Mother Teresa, might volunteer to serve the poor and the sick. Mormon culture is pretty clear about the disciplines recommended for women who hope to win

God's favor. Basically, they're supposed to act a lot like Martha Stewart, minus the money, the attitude, and the prison time. So, as a seeker at the "camel" stage of development, I threw myself into housekeeping as a religious discipline.

For the first time in my adult life, I actually used the skills I'd been taught during all those years in Primary. I washed, mended, and ironed, picked flowers from the garden and arranged them in pretty vases for the kitchen table, made peach pies from scratch. As the summer waned and the raspberries in our backyard ripened, Katie and I picked them and used them to make jam, which we ate on bread we'd kneaded and baked ourselves.

For me this level of domesticity was absolutely unprecedented. Nevertheless, I still fell far short of the standards set by really dedicated Latter-day Saint housewives. Did you ever hear the comedian Roseanne Barr joke about her desire to be called a "domestic goddess"? Well, she grew up in Utah, among my people (whom she called the "Nazi Amish"). The phrase she quoted to make audiences howl with laughter was used quite seriously in guides for Latter-day Saint homemakers of my generation. To enter the domestic goddess league, I would have had to go far beyond mere jam production. I would have gathered and canned windfall apricots, pears, and cherries. I would have ground raw wheat into flour for my homemade bread. I would have pressed the flowers from the garden, using them to decorate family scrapbooks, instead of letting them wilt and then tossing them out. I was never more than a mediocre homemaker by Mormon standards, but throughout that summer I kept trying.

John thought all this was a little strange. I'd expected him to be delighted. His mother was a virtually perfect Mormon woman, who cleaned her *ceilings* on a weekly basis and cooked gorgeous, nutritious meals several times a day. But though John loved his mother dearly, it turned out he didn't want me to behave just like the girl who married dear old Dad. He wanted me to act like *me*—a neurotic bookworm who kept irregular hours, rarely sat down to eat, and had no housewifely inclinations whatsoever. One day he came home with an automatic bread maker that closely resembled R2-D2, the robot droid from *Star Wars*.

"Look," John said, opening the dome-shaped lid. "You put the flour and stuff in here, turn it on, and it does everything for you—kneading, rising, cooking, everything."

I was pleased but perplexed. I'd always been taught that despite the advent of feminism (or perhaps because of it), what every man wanted was a wife who baked like a brick oven, day in, day out.

"That's great, John," I said, "but . . . I mean . . . don't you want Katie to learn how to cook?"

"No," said John. "I want her to learn how to hire help."

"Really?" It was as though he'd burst the buttons on a very tight nineteenth-century corset I'd been wearing for dress-up. I could feel myself breathing easier.

"Really," said John. "Look at it this way, Marth: While that thing makes bread, you can finish your degree. But if you spend your time baking, it can't get a PhD for you."

He had a point.

So as the summer cooled and the morning air began to drop subtle hints about its plans to become autumn, I stopped thinking bread and started thinking school.

I'd left Cambridge still lacking one of the course credits I needed for my degree. I wasn't sure how I was going to finish, but ever-resourceful John concocted a plan. He was still working for a Boston-based consulting firm that required him to travel frequently, sometimes to the East Coast, sometimes all the way to Asia. During the previous year, he'd literally commuted from Boston to Singapore every couple of weeks. This meant that John thought of traveling across a continent the way other people think of walking to the mailbox, and also that he had more frequent flier points than God. Airline employees probably would have carried him through airports on their backs, if he'd thought to ask. This, ultimately, is what saved my graduate education.

When September arrived and Adam was old enough to stop nursing, I weaned him and enrolled in a Harvard seminar on socioeconomic development that met once a week, on Wednesday. Every Tuesday night, I'd take a red-eye flight (purchased with John's frequent-flier points) from Salt Lake City to Boston. I'd hop a cab to Cambridge, attend class, head straight back to the airport, and fly home, arriving less than twenty-four hours after departing. It may sound complex, but it was actually far less stressful than trying to live in Harvard Square while raising children.

I studied like a maniac that fall, not because I had an inordinate amount of course work—I got most of that done on airplanes—but because I was still trying to be an obedient spiritual camel. All the pressure Harvard could dish out was nothing compared with the pressure coming from within me, the feeling the medieval author of *The Cloud of Unknowing* called "the soul's naked intent toward God." The overwhelming, bittersweet longing I'd felt since Adam was born never seemed to weaken, let alone disappear. It was like the drone of a bagpipe, the steady, single tone that underscored the changing melodies of my daily actions. Please, I begged, not knowing exactly what I wanted. Please, please, please, please . . .

I didn't know whether my spirit was trying to regain some genuine Paradise Lost, or whether my glimpses of heaven were hallucinations— and I didn't care. I just wanted that sense of peace and wholeness to come back. Day after day, as my children grew, the bread maker baked, and I climbed on and off airplanes, that indescribable hunger ached inside my soul. *Please, please, please* . . . Sometimes I managed to distract myself but never for long. If nothing else, my son was always there, his sweet strange face and floppy little body reminding me that I needed some deeper reason for living than I could find by earning degrees or writing books.

Reading books, though—that seemed to be a productive occupation for a spiritual camel. That's why most of my study time wasn't focused on the socioeconomic dynamics I was studying for my degree. Instead, I was busy reading anything and everything about religious experience. At night, after John and the children fell asleep, I pored over accounts of Native American sweat lodges and Ghost Dances, the altered states achieved by East Indian gurus and yogis, the mystical visions of medieval monks and abbesses, the experiences of ordinary individuals who'd been declared dead during accidents or illnesses but unexpectedly survived.

It was comforting to read that such people often experienced both elation and depression following mystical experiences. On one hand, they described the inexpressible joy of spiritual communion; on the other, their subsequent disenchantment with their ordinary life, which seemed miserable by comparison. *Please, please, please* . . . Sometimes I'd run across a description of this yearning that resonated so completely with my own experience that I'd cry like a baby, partly from the comfort I was not alone, partly from the desolation of unfulfilled longing.

But I wasn't just studying mysticism to store up information. I was looking for actual methods, those pragmatic steps that, years later, I would describe to my father as "spiritual technologies." What could I actually do to invite, invoke, induce some sort of mystical state? I was willing to try anything. I would happily have taken peyote or hallucinogenic mushrooms, but these were described in the literature as unpredictable, and I had no idea where to get them in a metropolitan area that had one hundred thousand people and only one bar. So I focused on strategies that didn't require props. Fasting was a common mystical practice, so I did it for days at a time, even while I was nursing. It made me gaunt and haggard but never brought God into close range. I prayed incessantly, using every format and ritual I could find in books. It never seemed to have any effect on my inner life, which remained stuck on just one vague prayer, that agonized mantra: *Please, please, please, please* . . .

Of course, I read and followed many religious texts by Mormon leaders, but I was much too needy to stop there. I also researched and practiced the disciplines of other religions, and faiths that weren't necessarily religion at all. Since I'd lived in Asia and studied both Chinese and Japanese, I was particularly drawn to Eastern philosophy. I loved Taoism, with its image of a vast, inchoate, benevolent Way flowing through all things. Zen appealed to me with its spareness, Chinese Buddhism because of its emphasis on erasing delusion, as opposed to adding knowledge. All these traditions focus heavily on meditation, a practice that was also recommended (in a Christianized form) by some Mormon leaders. And so I added meditation to the reading, praying, and homemaking that filled my religious-camel calendar.

The first time I tried to meditate was a clear, cold night in October. I was sitting in our living room again, tired and hungry from chronic overdoses of studying, child rearing, fasting, and housework. My physical neediness was making my spiritual neediness even more pronounced than usual, which is saying a lot. The drumbeat of *please please please* from

52   MARTHA BECK

my heart sounded so loud in my own ears that I was amazed it didn't wake the neighbors.

I'd just finished reading a Buddhist text that recommended a simple form of meditation, basically just sitting still and focusing on one's breath. I put the book down, sat on the floor, crossed my legs, and tried to let all thoughts leave my mind. The whole idea of Buddhism, as I understood it, was to achieve detachment from all desire. But I knew perfectly well what was going to happen once I stopped actively thinking, and I was right. With no analyzing, planning, or remembering to occupy it, my brain filled with nothing *but* desire. The drone note filled my whole consciousness: *Please, please, please, please . . .*

The grief, the sense of loneliness and isolation, was almost unbearable. It made me angry. I began mentally shouting at the Tao, the Buddha, the Messiah, or whatever other power was in charge of the universe. Where the hell *was* it? Why wouldn't it come back for me? How come, no matter what I did or how hard I tried—I mean, I'd been *baking bread,* for God's sake—how come I couldn't feel anything but this endless, unfulfilled need?

As I tried to release these thoughts from my mind ("Gently," the book said, "as though you are brushing away a cloud"), something happened. The skin all over my body suddenly felt very warm, as though I'd been dropped into a perfectly heated bath of some fluid much softer than water. The sensation was delicious, so pleasurable that my breath caught in my throat. The warmth seemed to soak into my skin, then *through* it, into deeper and deeper layers of muscle, bone, and gut. The need in my soul became even more intense, like a magnet pulling itself toward metal: *Please, please, please . . .* The waves of feeling from inside and outside strained toward each other. I had a sense that I was about to experience some tremendous epiphany. And then, just before that wonderful comfort could fill up my body entirely,

WHAM!

My eyes flew open and I literally leapt to my feet. By the time I was fully aware of what had happened, I was standing with my back pressed to the wall, trembling violently, my hands extended as if to ward off a blow, my heart rattling like a snare drum. I was absolutely terrified, more afraid than I'd ever felt in a very fear-fraught life. I had no idea why.

For a few minutes I just stood there, panting, shaking, waiting for my heart to slow down. Then I put my hands over my face and slid down the wall to the floor, where I burst into tears. I was horribly confused and utterly frustrated. I didn't understand what had just happened. It felt as though I'd almost been granted the thing I prayed for night and day: a sense of connection with the divine energy in the universe, a unity with unconditional love. But just when this was about to happen, something slammed closed in my mind, locking me back in cold and darkness, severing me from the warmth and light I had almost reached. And maddeningly, it felt as though the part of me doing the slamming was the very same part that longed so desperately for communion with God.

I didn't know what any of this meant, whether the experience was caused by spiritual dynamics or physical stress or mental illness. My books weren't good enough; I needed to connect with people who understood what it was like to be on a spiritual quest. I needed soul guides, mentors, amanuenses. Immersed as I was in motherhood, school, travel, and obsessive-compulsive religious study, I hadn't really shared my spiritual quest with a community.

So as I crouched on the floor, chilled, tired, famished in body and spirit, I decided to fling myself wholeheartedly into the practice of organized religion. I wouldn't just be a perfect Mormon housewife, I'd be a perfect Mormon, full stop. It was a camel's decision, well meaning and submissive. And in a way, it worked. My plan would eventually lead me to the happiness I wanted, to the peace that passeth understanding. But it would take me there by a route my camel self would never, ever have chosen.

CHAPTER 9

Oak Hills Fourth

My pledge to find a religious community was easy to keep, because once it became clear that John and I were in Utah for an indefinite period, my parents-in-law decided to build a new home for their retirement and sell us the house where John had grown up. I loved the house, and for John, it was a veritable womb with a view, as comfortable and familiar as his own skin. Moreover, he told me, it happened to be located in the best ward in all of Mormonism.

A Mormon "ward" is a congregation of about three hundred people who live within a designated geographic area. In parts of the world where Latter-day Saints are scarce, a ward might encompass hundreds of square miles, but in Provo ward boundaries cordon off areas of only a few blocks. The people in each ward gather together for church meetings on Sunday, and often for different activities—sports, craft workshops, inspirational speeches—on other days of the week. They know each other intimately, partly because of all the interaction and partly because they're always being "called" to official Church positions, which require that they serve one another. Every ward community is staffed with ordinary Latter-day Saints, all "called" by the authority just above them in rank. It is unheard of to refuse a call, especially since a lot of social currency accrues from one's ward rank. From the top-dog rank of bishop, to the mid-prestige senior Sunday school teachers, to the lowly child-care specialists in the junior Sunday school, ward members are assigned to care for each other in sickness, teach each other in health, and communicate a mutual sense of belonging and respect on a continual basis.

The congregation in which I grew up is what Mormons call a "newly-wed and nearly dead" ward, because it was in a zone of low-cost housing owned by young families and impoverished senior citizens. As a result, I never experienced the sense of social integration John got in his ward. Furthermore, though my body attended church as a child, my mind had always been somewhere else, lost in a carefully concealed paperback book or occupied with one of the time-killing games passed down by generations of bored, pew-bound children. (My favorite was going through the hymnbook and appending the phrase "in the bathtub" to every song title: "I Stand All Amazed in the Bathtub"; "I Know That My Redeemer Lives in the Bathtub"; "Behold a Royal Army in the Bathtub.") So, although I'd attended a lot of Mormon church services in my lifetime, my memories of them were a strange collage of pulp fiction and madcap washroom antics, set in a quasi-religious milieu in which my parents and siblings occupied the full length of a long pew.

This had led to a lackadaisical attitude toward church attendance, one that, despite my good intentions, persisted for some time even after I became a devout spiritual "camel." For our first months in Utah, before we moved into John's home ward, I rarely made it to the three-hour spate of Sunday meetings, and my contact with ward members, though pleasant, was usually brief.

All that changed the first time I attended the Oak Hills Fourth Ward. It was a cool late-winter morning, the sky a downy blue, snowdrifts melting in bright sunlight. Our house was within walking distance of the chapel—every house in Provo is within walking distance of a chapel—so we set out for meetings with Katie in her stroller and John carrying Adam in the crook of his arm. John, who usually couldn't care less how our children were dressed, had taken unusual pains that morning to make sure they were presentable. Katie looked adorable in a lacy dress with white patent leather shoes, and Adam was decked out in a blue suit and silk tie that would have looked very corporate if they hadn't been small enough to fit a hand puppet.

I was bemused by John's combination of anxiety and excitement, but as we walked toward the chapel I began to understand it. Churchgoers were emerging from virtually every one of the well-tended homes in the neighborhood, and all of them reacted to John as if he were their own long-lost son. He might as well have been; all our neighbors were around the age of John's parents and had raised children within shouting distance of each other. Some of that second generation, like us, had settled in the area as adults. There were virtually no strangers.

As we walked along, waving to the people who waved to us, John reminisced about how he'd helped Brother and Sister Boyle's two sons dig a large, unauthorized hole in the Boyle backyard, how he'd fallen off the roof of Sister Erickson's garage into a flowerbed, how a whole gang of neighborhood kids had staged a mock Beatles concert in the basement of the Holts' split-level home. But none of these stories quite prepared me for the rush of affection that engulfed us the minute we entered the chapel itself. The foyer was filled with milling church members, practically all of whom turned toward us as we walked in.

"Look! It's John!" cried an exultant voice. "And Martha, and Katie, and little Adam!" I never knew who the speaker was, because as soon as the words rang out, a swarm of Latter-day Saints converged on us like a defensive line rushing the passer. There were women in modestly frilly dresses, smelling of talcum powder and lavender; men in conservative suits, like extremely friendly FBI agents; and children who just got swept up in the hubbub. Dozens of voices cheered our presence. Dozens of hands reached out to squeeze mine or pat me on the back. I had no clue who most of these people were, but I'd never felt so welcome.

If they seemed thrilled to see me, the ward members' reaction to John was off the charts. "Oh, you're so grown up!" said one elderly woman, pulling him forward in a fragrant hug, then wiping tears from her eyes.

A man concurred. "Seems like just a minute ago you were in our kitchen, eating peanut butter sandwiches."

"And now you're *back!*" someone else caroled. "With your own little ones!" Katie was lifted from her stroller by eager but gentle arms, to be passed around, along with Adam, for adoring inspection.

"Oh, they're beautiful children, just *beautiful!*" a woman in a pink jacket told me. "And how is Adam doing?"

"Uh . . . he's . . . fine," I stammered. Now that I thought about it, it seemed perfectly natural that Faye, my mother-in-law, had kept the ward well informed about the events in John's life. Still, I was astonished by how much these people remembered about me and, even more, by how much they seemed to care. My own father could never remember my children's names, but these strangers knew all about them.

"We were so worried about you when this little one was on his way," said the lady holding Adam.

"Yes," another voice agreed. "You were in our prayers every day."

My eyes filled with tears as I remembered the long, cold months when I had felt so isolated in my illness and grief. All that time, though I never knew it, these gentle people had been silently sending me their support. With them, there was no need to explain Adam and his condition. My Harvard acquaintances had reacted to newborn Adam by wincing painfully and then ignoring him, as though he were a large, infected scab. Here in Oak Hills Fourth, his extra chromosome made him a star. Everyone else was going to have to earn a place in heaven, but Adam was a shoo-in.

• • •

Despite the intoxicating warmth of our welcome, I expected to be bored during the worship service. Because of Mormonism's lay ministry, all sermons are delivered by ordinary church members, chosen in rough rotation by leaders in the ward. Listening to them is a kind of low-stress Russian roulette. You never know if the sermon will be delivered by a fascinating word master (not likely) or by some poor schmuck with the vocabulary of a sea cucumber and a paralyzing fear of public speaking (a pretty good bet). To make matters worse, our first Sunday at our new ward was also the first Sunday of the month, known as Fast Sunday because good Mormons fast for twenty-four hours on these days, donating the money they save on food to the general welfare. On Fast Sundays, the church service is a special procedure called testimony meeting. This is a sort of Quakerish open-mike affair, wherein everyone sits silently in the pews until somebody feels moved to "bear testimony," the Mormon phrase for announcing one's belief in the Church.

The problem is that in every ward, there's at least one person who *lives* for testimony meeting. These people are often slightly deranged, if not flat-out certifiable, and once they take the floor, good luck getting it back. In my ward growing up, the resident loon was Sister Alice Muirhead, who lived across the street from us in a huge, bizarre "apartment house" she and her husband had patched together from discarded plywood and old nails, which was condemned by the city approximately every fifteen minutes. Each Fast Sunday, my whole ward would cringe as Sister Muirhead grabbed the mike, heaved herself up on her hind legs, and began another diatribe about her war with the city zoning department and the welfare of her grown children, Ernest and Alice Jr. Even with my books and word games ("He Is Risen in the Bathtub," "Come, Come Ye Saints in the Bathtub"), Sister Alice's testimonies were almost unbearable.

So I anticipated that our first meeting at Oak Hills Fourth would be a tedious marathon of child hushing. Given these low expectations, I was more than pleasantly surprised by the meeting. The first person to speak, an English professor, gave a brief, thought-provoking account of a mild epiphany he'd experienced while reading Faulkner. Next we heard from a professional violinist who thanked the ward for helping her through a grave illness, using a wry, intelligent tone that had everyone laughing, even me. One after another, ward members discussed their life experiences and spiritual beliefs with thoughtfulness and warmth.

Most startling of all, there were a few impromptu talks that made the hair bristle all over my body. Dogen, the Zen teacher whose twelfth-century writings I was reading at night, once commented that years of hearing about the taste of watermelon can't teach you as much as one real mouthful. Since becoming an obsessive spiritual camel, I'd heard many people discuss their own metaphysical experiences, but all of them sounded to me as though they were trying to describe watermelon without ever having tasted it. That morning in Oak Hills Fourth Ward was the first time I'd met people who actually seemed to have had experiences similar to my own. The way some of them talked about compassion, hope, joy, forgiveness—there was no mistaking it. Without hearing a single woo-woo story, I became convinced that these people had felt the exquisite touch of that other dimension and longed to reunite with it as much as I did. It wasn't like getting to go home, but it was like meeting friends who understood exile.

Of course, nothing is perfect. Toward the end of the meeting, the Oak Hills Fourth Ward's microphone was seized by a craggy old man with a terrible comb-over, whose name, let's say, was Peter B. Deiter.

"My dear brothers and sisters," Brother Deiter began, "I thank our Father in Heaven for allowing me to be here with you this day, for I feel that the time has come for me to speak about a subject that is terribly important to each and every one of God's children. I suspect you know what I mean." He paused for emphasis, then said, "Beneficial nematodes."

The entire chapel rustled slightly as everyone gave a tolerant sigh, and I saw that the majority of the ward expected this sort of thing from Brother Deiter. I also saw that they accepted him anyway. In fact, by the time we left the church that day, I'd learned that (1) a beneficial nematode is a parasitic worm that coexists symbiotically with some plants; (2) Brother Deiter's obsession with horticulture featured in every testimony meeting; (3) the old man kept a huge compost pile in his driveway, which had once become so frantic with bacterial activity that it had burst into flames; and (4) the entire ward, though perpetually embarrassed by the unsightly Deiter lot, had rushed to put out the blaze so that the fire department wouldn't condemn Brother Pete's home.

In short, John was right. We had just joined the best "ward family" in the world, a congregation filled with kindness, affection, and real striving to know God. I'd read that to succeed as a spiritual camel, one must push past emotional reservations and open completely to the fellowship of tradition and community. Now I'd stumbled into a congregation where I knew I'd be able to do just that. It felt like a miracle to be so welcome and so safe. It was clear that the compassion these sweet people were offering me was real and spontaneous, that nothing I could ever do would set me outside the circle of their acceptance.

Looking back over the various illusions I've harbored during my lifetime, I would have to say that this was one of the very, very best.

CHAPTER 10

The World of Allusion

I t's the darndest thing," says my father. "Every day, people come to my office, asking what they should do with their lives."

Having described his speech to the seminary teachers and his conferences with the brethren, he has moved on to discuss the other aspects of his public life.

"Just yesterday, a very wealthy man came to see me—said he'd read my books, and now he's going to give away all his money. He asked me what I thought he should do with it."

For the third or fourth time in just a few minutes, I have that odd sensation that my life is following my father's pattern, as though our careers are coded in our shared DNA. I spent considerable time trying to be a good academic, but my students began hiring me to advise them outside of class, and I ended up writing self-help books and becoming what the newspapers call a life coach. I wonder if my father and I secrete some kind of pheromone that causes people to believe, against all reason, that we give good advice.

"So, what did you tell him?"

"Eh?" says my father, whose attention seems to have turned inward.

"What did you tell the man he should do with his money?"

"Oh, well. Of course I said he should give it to the Church—after all, that's the covenant he made in the temple."

I nod again. That's one of the things I haven't mentioned about the Mormon temple ceremony (mind the entrails, please), but it's true. No one gets out of the building without promising to give everything— every bit of money, property, time, and talent—to the Church. They don't tell you you're going to make this vow when you go in: They spring it on you after you're already in so deep, having mimed your own death and all, that it's pretty impossible to say no.

"He told me I've made all the difference in his life," says my father, chuckling. "Made him a better person."

I'm surprised by how open to emotion my father seems—much more so than during my childhood and adolescence. There was a time when he would have been alarmed by anything as sentimental as the conversation he's just described.

When I was growing up, my father seemed to abide by the general rule that emotion was a bad idea. When one of my sisters (the most overtly emotional person in our family) was about ten, my father took her to see a photography display at Brigham Young University. It was very rare for him to single out one child in this way, so my sister concluded that this must be a special outing, with a special purpose. She was right. My father took her straight to a portrait shot of a man whose face was completely disfigured with huge, grotesque warts.

"Do you know what causes that?" he asked.

My sister shook her head.

"Nerves," said my father, slowly, with heavy emphasis. "It's a nervous condition brought on by too much emotion." He paused to see if she'd really gotten the message, then added, "You need to control yourself."

Of course, the very fact that my sister told me this story is evidence that she didn't buy it. In fact, she thought it was hilarious. Even as a child, she had enough psychological clarity to be appalled and amused by my father's fervent belief in total emotional repression.

Not me.

Partly because it was so much easier than feeling anything, and partly because I wanted desperately to please my father, I spent my early years almost completely oblivious to my own psychological state. He approved of this. I think. The problem is that when two people commit to a mutual ideal of total emotional repression, it's damn hard to figure out whether anyone approves of anything.

As I grew into adolescence and my older siblings started moving out, my father and I were stuck in each other's proximity more and more often. So, in addition to his occasionally addressing me in foreign languages, we developed a roundabout way of communicating about our feelings. I called our method Dueling Allusions. To use it, you simply allude to a passage from literature that reflects your emotional state. If a passage is too directly emotional, quote an innocuous segment of the surrounding text, knowing that the other person will complete the quotation in his or her mind and thereby understand what you are trying to say. In dire circumstances, it is also permissible to leave entire books where the other person can find them.

Of course, the problem with this little conversational crabwalk is that you can never be really sure the other person is taking your allusion exactly as you meant it. For example, when I was a teenager, I joined the enormous ranks of girls my age who were obsessed with weight loss. I was different from most anorexics in that I acknowledged my real dieting objective: death. I'd been considering suicide on and off since the age of six. I remember eating a bowl of Alpha-Bits and wondering how to kill myself when my legs were still too short to reach the kitchen floor. I had no idea this was unusual; I assumed everyone felt that way: sad, lost, and empty, certain only of death. I never wondered whether other people considered suicide, I just wondered how one went about it. It was a question I pondered often as I went through a particularly gloomy puberty. By the time I was old enough to understand—perhaps even execute—the mechanics involved, I had become stymied by the fear that poison or bullets really were sins for which I would be sent to outer darkness. By contrast, starvation seemed so nicely passive as to be irreproachable, and I set out to accomplish it.

Let me just say that from the standpoint of physical comfort, starving is even more unpleasant than you might think.

After four hungry years, when I was eighteen and so emaciated that the skin had rubbed off the jutting points of my elbows, vertebrae, and pelvis, my father gave me a book for Christmas, entitled *The Doctor's Diet for Teenage Girls*. In hindsight I believe he must have thought the book would recommend a healthy *increase* in my calorie intake. But it was written for parents whose teenagers were morbidly obese, and I concluded that my father was as horrified by my portliness as I was. To please him, I followed every weight-loss hint the book contained, and managed to reach the stage of starvation at which a downy coat of lanugo hair appeared on my shoulder blades—at least on the flat part of the bone, where it hadn't been rubbed skinless.

My father and I did speak once—in English!—about my anorexia and suicidal obsessions. This occurred shortly after one of my brothers (always the informal surrogate father for us younger siblings) began taking me to a therapist. My brother's actions probably saved my life but made my actual father overwhelmingly nervous. He all but stopped sleeping and began to spend the nights walking around and around the block in our quiet Provo neighborhood. One day he finally initiated a conversation with me. I was hunched in a chair in the living room, reading Sartre and wishing I could just *think* myself dead, when my father entered the room and sat down in his big brown armchair.

" 'Cast thy nighted colour off,' " he said (quoting *Hamlet*). " 'Let not your heart be troubled' " (this from the New Testament). "That's an order!" This last phrase, delivered in a jocular tone, was his own.

I stared at him listlessly, which is about all you can manage when you're that hungry. Finally I picked a line from *Hamlet* for myself. " 'Oh, that this too, too solid flesh would melt, / Thaw and resolve itself into a dew,' " I said.

" 'Or that the Everlasting had not fixed / His canon 'gainst self-slaughter'?" My father finished the line, knitting his brow and making his voice a question.

I nodded. I was touched that he would ask.

" 'Oh, God, God,' " he went on, " 'how weary, stale, flat and unprofitable / seem to me all the uses of this world.' "

I nodded again.

"Well," he said, "we all feel that way from time to time. But the Lord commands us to rejoice and be exceeding glad." This quotation was from the Book of Mormon, the sacred text that ranks right up there with the Holy Bible in the Latter-day Saint lexicon.

I didn't answer for several seconds, because I would never have voiced the snotty, nihilistic, adolescent thought that popped into my head—namely, that "the Lord" could go screw himself if he existed, which he didn't. Life is a bitch, and then you die. How's that for a quotable quote, Daddy?

My father picked up one of his books, a musty volume written in

Coptic, and began to mutter as he read. He often read aloud to himself, in a very soft whisper, when he was having trouble staying focused. The conversation could have died right then, but for some reason I decided not to let it.

" 'The tempest in my mind,' " I said, " 'Doth from my senses take all feeling else / Save what beats there.' " This was from *King Lear,* and I meant it to convey that I suspected I was going mad, as Lear had done. My father's head jerked up.

"Filial ingratitude?" he asked, since this was the end of the line I'd quoted.

I shrugged.

"Surely not," said my father.

This time I was the one who looked away, because my eyes had filled with tears. He had practically said I was a good daughter. He had practically said he loved me.

•   •   •

Twenty years later, after nearly a decade of silence between us, I sit in a hotel room and grope for an allusion that will convey to my father the many conflicting emotions in my heart. He's still marveling at his effect on the people who read his books and listen to his lectures.

"I never would have thought so many people would end up coming to me for advice," he says. "Ridiculous, isn't it?" He aims a bright-eyed smile at the coffee table. For a moment I consider talking about my own writing and coaching career, but I'm not sure my father knows anything about this, and I'd rather discuss something more fundamental. The Dueling Allusions quotation that comes to mind is from Robert Frost.

"Well, 'when at times the mob is swayed,' " I say, smiling back at my father. I know he will remember the entire line: "So when at times the mob is swayed / To carry praise or blame too far, / We may choose something like a star / To stay our minds on and be staid."

My father's smile fades like a chastised child's. "Yes, yes," he says, instantly ashamed at having complimented himself. "Of course."

I want to explain what I mean, to tell him that I don't begrudge him the smallest iota of his success and that I wish with all my heart that sometime during his childhood, almost a hundred years ago, he'd developed a healthy dose of self-esteem. I scramble for a quotation that can express this indirectly. Then I remember: I can just talk to him. I can say exactly what I meant when I quoted Frost, use my very own words. It's so crazy, it just might work.

"To me, the 'something like a star' is God," I say. "Or the true self, if there's any difference. It's not that there's anything wrong with praise or blame, it's just that they come and go. Part of the world of illusion, I guess a Buddhist would say. Do you know what I mean?"

"Oh, mm, indeed," he murmurs, staring at the floor. As I look at him my internal Allusion Manager brings up a phrase from the philosopher John Locke: tabula rasa, a blank slate. My father's face has become just that. He's not firing back another allusion. I have only the foggiest idea what might be written on the part of his mind that only he can see.

CHAPTER II

Miracles

Adam was about fifteen months old when John and I decided to have a third child. We loved our son to distraction, but both of us felt that his birth was like an unresolved chord; we hadn't stopped wanting the typical baby we'd expected before his diagnosis. So we decided to let nature take its course, which it did in about half an hour. Infertility was one of the few childbearing problems John and I never experienced. I think we could have conceived a child just by sending each other enthusiastic e-mails from separate continents.

Welcome as it was, this pregnancy hit my body like a wrecking ball. I didn't know that I was having an immune response to the fetus, as though it were an incompatible transplanted organ. The reaction got worse with every day I spent carrying a child. During my third pregnancy, I was almost too sick to raise my head, which took all the fun out of continuous vomiting. A few times I ended up in the hospital, taking fluid through a tube in my arm, as I'd often done when Adam was on the way.

Other than that, though, this pregnancy couldn't have been more different from my ordeal in Cambridge. There, I'd felt not only sick but alone, cold, and seriously short on resources. Being pregnant in Provo meant I was surrounded by kindness and comfort. John hired a pretty, patient, sweet-natured Brigham Young University student to be our family's Mary Poppins (we advertised in the campus newspaper for a "regular babysitter," because we were told that "nanny" was forbidden—Mormon women are expected to raise their own children). John also spent more money than we really had to wire our bedroom with remote-controlled stereo and television, which eased my boredom and took my mind off the nausea.

Other helpers showed up all by themselves. My beloved sister-in-law, a nurse, came to the house every single day to give me an injection of vitamins and change my sheets. One of my best friends from high school, who worked with John, made it her business to come over every day at lunchtime, bringing assorted groceries in case there was something I could hold down. Through diligent research, we discovered that chicken had the best staying power. Thereafter, my friend appeared at the bedroom door every noontime with a small roasted fryer from the deli section at the grocery store. She'd stand at my bedroom door, raise the chicken high above her head, and announce, in a stentorian voice, "Bird of Paradise!" Then we would both laugh until I threw up, and she'd entertain me while I forced myself to eat.

As if this weren't enough pampering, members of our "ward family" amazed me with their kindness. They left casseroles on our doorstep for John and the kids, flowers for me. When autumn arrived, we often woke up to discover that someone had raked the leaves off our lawn well before sunup, and during that year's long, cold winter our sidewalks were as perfectly and mysteriously clear as if they'd been shoveled by a troupe of fairy-tale elves. While I was in the hospital for refills, I'd open my eyes between spates of exhausted unconsciousness to find random members of the ward stationed by the bed—just sitting there, patiently, hoping their presence would cheer me, even though I usually felt too weak to follow a conversation.

· · ·

When I wasn't being ministered to by all these earth angels, I lay in my bed and tried to contact heavenly ones. Illness and fear have a remarkable power to focus one's mind on connecting with a higher power, and I was both sick and scared. I knew that, having borne one child with Down syndrome, my odds of having another were much, much higher than those of a typical twenty-seven-year-old woman. John and I decided against amniocentesis, since we wouldn't have aborted the baby even if it did have an extra chromosome, but I was far from serene. I had dreams in which I bore quadruplets, all with Down syndrome, and even the thought that I could now field an entire Special Olympics basketball team failed to make this gratifying.

But even as fear assailed me, I knew that this third child would be "normal." I knew it in the same way I'd known that Adam would be different, at a level much deeper than logic, deeper even than emotion. I found that when I allowed myself to trust this odd, illogical, unemotional knowing, my nausea retreated a little. For a spiritual seeker at the camel phase, this was incredibly educational. I learned some of the most valuable lessons of my life lying there week after week, watching the room spin. For instance, touring the mental pathways of catastrophic fantasy (which had always been one of my favorite pastimes) made my body tighten up until I puked like Vesuvius. When I trusted the things I knew in my heart of hearts, I felt much better and could relax completely. I doubt that any more motivating form of biofeedback could possibly exist.

My ability to center myself and calm my body came in handy when, five months into my pregnancy, I suddenly began to hemorrhage. The same thing had happened, at the same point in gestation, when I was carrying Adam. On both occasions, I was suffering from what doctors call a placental abruption, in which the placenta tears away from the wall of the uterus. It's a dangerous condition, one that can kill both mother and child, and only a miracle (either that or a whopping dose of placebo effect) had saved me the first time it happened. Busily bleeding out in our Cambridge apartment, I'd asked for the help of the spiritual beings around me, and to my dazed astonishment I'd felt what seemed to be unseen hands touching and soothing me. The bleeding had inexplicably stopped, without any official medical treatment at all.

So halfway through my third pregnancy, when I saw the blood on my underclothes (yes, that would be maternity garments), I was perhaps not as alarmed as I should have been. I did call my obstetrician, who had me come in right away for an ultrasound exam. John drove me to the hospital, half carried me into the obstetrician's office, and sat holding my hand while the doctor prodded my abdomen, asked me questions, and looked at the fuzzy, unrecognizable image on the ultrasound screen.

"Well," he said, with an apologetic grimace. "I have to tell you, it doesn't look good."

The room spun a little faster. "Is the baby in danger?" I asked.

He put his hand on my shoulder. "You're young," he said. "You have lots of time left. There will be others."

Two years earlier, this gently discouraging answer would have sent me into a panic. Not this time. I'd been down this road once already and found help waiting where no doctor would ever look for it. It never occurred to me that this baby wouldn't get the same miraculous help Adam had—especially since I knew the obstetrician was wrong: I did not have more pregnancies in my future. I was pushing the envelope of my physical capacity as it was.

The doctor was talking with John about the advisability of performing the quick abortion that could keep the situation from becoming lethal for me. As far as the baby was concerned, I could tell that the doctor thought of it as a goner. But I could also tell that John didn't agree. He hadn't supported me through my previous pregnancy for nothing. John believed in miracles as irrationally as I did.

"Look," I said calmly, "what should I do to give the baby the best possible chance of making it?"

The obstetrician shook his head a little, giving me a sad smile. "Well," he sighed, holding his hands up in surrender, "I don't think it will work, but for what it's worth, you should try to lie completely still. We can catheterize you, so that you don't have to get up at all. Don't even move your arms, if you can help it. Maybe that'll slow things down. But if you're still bleeding in a couple of hours, I want you back here, and we'll go ahead with . . . the procedure." Doctors in Utah talked about abortion much more reluctantly than doctors in Massachusetts.

So John and I went home, and he carried me into the bedroom, and we asked the Force for medical assistance. John even went so far as to perform Mormonism's ritual for healing the sick, which can be done by almost any Latter-day Saint male in good standing (remember, virtually every boy is ordained to the priesthood, though it's more a mark of good standing than a special office). John dabbed a drop of specially blessed oil on my forehead, put his hands over the spot, and prayed for me and for our baby.

They say you don't remember the feeling of labor pains until you're in the middle of them, and I have found this to be true. The same can be said of another sensation: that of being miraculously healed in the midst of a placental abruption. As John prayed, I felt a rush of comfort, similar to the comfort that had arrived inexplicably two years earlier, when Adam and I nearly bought the big condo in the sky. Every muscle in my body went limp at once, as though someone had cut the strings of a marionette. Within seconds I fell into the deepest sleep I've ever experienced. John couldn't wake me up when he finished his prayer. For thirty hours, I lay absolutely motionless, so still that he kept anxiously checking my pulse and breathing. He also checked for more bleeding, only to find that it had stopped, abruptly and completely. When I woke up in the middle of the next afternoon, I felt better than I had in months.

·   ·   ·

Sometime later, when that particular fetus had become a voluble, chubby-cheeked three-year-old, we took her out trick-or-treating for the very first time. John and I waited in our next-door neighbors' driveway while Lizzy, looking very tiny in a pink and gray mouse costume, accompanied Adam the pirate and Katie the dinosaur up to the front door. We watched as the kids rang the bell, recited "Trick or treat," received their candy, and thanked the neighbors. Then Lizzy turned and came back down the driveway at a flat-out sprint, screaming, *"It worked! It worked!"*

That's exactly how I felt when I awoke from my prayer-induced coma in the winter of 1990, and knew in the most irrational way that once more, my baby and I were safe. I realized that I might be experiencing a psychological effect, that my belief in miraculous healing might have been enough in and of itself to create a beneficial reaction in my body. But for whatever reason, this little bit of spiritual technology had done just what John and I so desperately hoped it would do.

It worked. It worked.

CHAPTER 12

Elizabeth

After my dramatic recovery from the placental abruption, my fear about having another child with a disability almost vanished. I began to trust my intuitive hunch that this baby would be fine. I even mustered the energy to resume working on my PhD dissertation, lying on my back with my knees up and a laptop computer resting on my thighs. It seemed a suitable position in which to write about my topic: the sociological ramifications of changes in women's roles, as seen in the unusually patriarchal context of Mormonism, the largest indigenous American religion. This subject turned my geographic location from a disadvantage to an advantage and allowed me to chat with pretty much anyone in Utah and call it research.

I developed congenial telephone relationships with a few of the sociology faculty at Brigham Young University. I'd met many of these people already, and they were graciously generous with advice and information. I began to think of them as friends and colleagues and called some of them frequently to ask questions about the Mormon Church's response to feminism, a topic that was getting a lot of play in the national news at that time. Mormonism had been considered by many to play a key factor in the failure of the equal rights amendment, which the Church of Jesus Christ of Latter-day Saints had staunchly opposed, and reporters were still interested in the way its self-proclaimed "patriarchal order" was dealing with women's lib.

I was surprised and flattered the first time a reporter from the *Los Angeles Times* called to ask me about Mormonism and the women's movement. The reporter said he'd gotten my name from someone in the BYU sociology department, who had refused to tell him anything else. Looking back, I remember that a tiny alarm went off in the back of my mind when I heard this bit of information. But my wariness was drowned out by the happy, pompous thought that reputable professionals in my field considered me a quotable expert in something. I willingly chatted with the reporter, discussing what I knew about Mormon culture, about the conflicting pressures on Latter-day Saint women, about the fact that, while virtually all Mormons agreed with the current prophet that mothers should not work under any circumstances, most Latter-day Saint mothers were already employed outside the home.

As soon as the *Times* piece ran, I became serious press bait, fielding calls from reporters several times a week. Though terribly busy lying in bed staring at the ceiling, I somehow made time to discuss my sociological perspective, often at great length. After all (thought Pandora, loosening the lid of the box), what could it hurt? I became such a willing source for journalists, such a Mormon-feminist quote whore, that when I was eight months pregnant, a local news team actually trooped over to my house to do an on-screen interview. I draped myself in an enormous sweater that I'd bought during my last pregnancy, propped myself up on the couch, and agreed to the interview on the condition that the news cameras promise not to show any part of my body except my head.

The next week, a day after Adam turned two, I went into labor. John and I buzzed down to the hospital, where we were assigned a homey labor room with flowered wallpaper and a pretty carpet, completely unlike the cold industrial setting in which Adam had been born. Between contractions, we watched the television that was mounted on the wall. Within a couple of hours I was in "active labor," a term doctors use because "excruciatingly and continuously painful labor" tends to put people off.

At this point, a couple of labor nurses came in to say that their names were Jennifer and Bethany, and that it was time for them to perform a certain hygienic indignity designed to facilitate childbirth. I won't tell you exactly what they did (sounds like "enemy"), but you can trust me when I tell you they did not do it to my face. So I was propped up in a position similar to what yoga practitioners call "downward-facing dog" when John glanced up at the television and saw—me! The news interview I'd taped a week before was airing at that very moment, and the TV in the labor room just happened to be tuned to the right channel.

"That's Martha!" John told the nurses, excitedly.

They looked at him in confusion. They weren't paying the slightest attention to the television, and the side of me they were looking at wasn't the side I'd let the reporters film. They thought John was talking about the woman on the table, not the one on TV.

"Yes, sir," said Bethany, "we know."

"I mean, that's my wife!" John crowed, still hyped on the adrenaline of childbirth, astonished at the coincidence. "There she is!"

I saw the nurses exchange worried looks. "Brother Beck, we believe you," Jennifer said in a soothing tone.

"But that's her head! That's my wife's head!"

"Do you think we should send him out?" Jennifer whispered to Bethany.

By this time, I'd caught a glance at the TV myself, so I explained the situation to the nurses as best I could. "Uhnrrrgaaaah," I said. "Wooonggphahhh."

"Just breathe," Bethany advised me.

And so things went for several minutes, until suddenly I was ready to push. The nurses weren't even finished with their procedures; I had to inform them of my condition by flailing at them like a mammoth trapped in a tar pit.

Nothing in this scenario bothered Bethany and Jennifer, not even the deranged husband, because as I've mentioned, Utah Valley Medical Center is a veritable geyser of human infants. Any nurse who's worked there more than a week has seen babies come out right side up, backside first, and sideways. Add to that the fact that these two nurses were Mormon, and you'll begin to get an idea how unflappably sweet they were. After Adam's birth, which had the general cheerful ambience of a nuclear weapons test, the hominess of a Utah delivery was absolutely euphoric.

At the last possible moment the obstetrician came in, with the casual deportment of a short-order cook getting ready to flip a pancake, and Elizabeth came out. From her first lusty squall, I knew she was, as the doctor put it, "Normal, normal, normal." He cut the umbilical cord while Bethany and Jennifer wiped her off and wrapped her in a blanket, commenting on her thick curly hair and terrific muscle tone in voices that were sweeter to me than any music I'd ever heard. Then they put

Lizzy on my belly, warming us both with heat lamps while the doctor de-livered the placenta.

I'd forgotten how newborns without Down syndrome look, all wrin-kled and wizened where Down kids have smooth, tiny features. I was struck by how much Lizzy looked like her grandma Beck. This was a good thing, because John's mother was a beautiful woman, but I have to say that you don't know the meaning of the word *surreal* until you've seen a bright red, football-sized version of your mother-in-law trying to crawl up your torso. It's the closest I'd ever come to an acid flashback.

A few hours later, after John had bonded with his third child and gone home to tend to his first two, I was finally alone with Elizabeth. I felt drenched in bliss. My body was free from nausea for the first time in many months, and my family felt sweetly complete.

I was also in a kind of spiritual rapture.

After Katie was born, I felt as if I'd been hit by a hurricane of love and protectiveness. But I'd also been nagged by guilt that I'd brought yet an-other human into a cold and difficult world and by fear that I could never protect her from life's inevitable pain. "Born astride the grave," said the Allusion Manager in my brain, quoting Samuel Beckett. "Born astride the grave, and a difficult labor." I was happy, but also very scared.

When Adam arrived, I was just starting to believe that there might be some larger purpose, some kinder intelligence that had sent him. With Lizzie, I was in full-bore religious mode, so I gave myself permission to feel all the dazzling spiritual wonder of birth. As I held her, brushed her fuzzy head, kissed her tiny hands, my Allusion Manager sent up a quota-tion from Wordsworth that bore no trace of fear or nihilism:

> Not in entire forgetfulness,
> And not in utter nakedness,
> But trailing clouds of glory do we come
> From God, who is our home   . . .

It seemed Down syndrome wasn't the only reason for the divine en-ergy I'd felt around Adam when he was born, because it was here again, with Lizzy. That meant Wordsworth might be right: The glory of God might accompany every single one of us into this life, born astride the grave though we are. For the first time in my adult life, I began to really think about the concept of God as a parent.

Mormons believe in a literal Father and Mother in Heaven. (In fact, a whole bunch of heavenly mothers, since the Father is supposed to be impressively polygamous. Each Mormon man, if exalted after death, is supposed to be given his own worlds—that is, planets—to populate. You can't do that working with just one woman, so the more chicks per man-God, the better.) Female figures that are important in other religions, such as Mother Mary, aren't given divine status; Mother in Heaven is a vague and bashful figure in Mormonism. One is not supposed to discuss her too frequently or in any detail, lest her tender feelings be hurt. Some Latter-day Saint feminists are known to have prayed to Mother in Heaven, despite being sternly admonished to stop it. At any rate, the image of heavenly parents of either gender never appealed to me as a child, and I'd rejected it completely as an adolescent. It would have meant that the universe was ruled by an awe-inspiring but utterly distracted male deity and a female counterpart who wanted to smack me upside the head.

But what if God felt about me the way I felt about my own children, about this tiny person I held in my arms? What if the force that ruled the universe adored me *this much,* accepted me without reservation, would protect me no matter what the cost?

These thoughts were so new to me, so emotionally seductive, that they almost felt like blasphemy. Still, I longed to relax into them—almost did, in fact. But when I tried, WHAM! Something in me slammed shut, exactly as it had in my living room the night I started meditating. Once again, just as I felt ready to connect with some transcendent realm, part of me recoiled violently, as if I'd reached for a handful of wildflowers and grabbed a snake instead.

If I hadn't been so crazy about my new baby, I might have died of frustration. I had a sickening feeling that at the moment I really felt the presence of God as a loving parent, something else—something awful—would come into my consciousness with it. I had no idea what that something might be, but even acknowledging that it was there brought on a spasm of unexpected horror. So there I lay cuddling Elizabeth, my mind contemplating the idea of a loving God, my heart unable to feel it. It was like being able to chew but not swallow.

I was so overwhelmed by my welter of feelings—joy, gratitude, awe, fear, frustration, and longing—that I took an easy way out: I popped two of the codeine pills my doctor had prescribed to dull my postpartum contractions. I love chemistry. In a matter of minutes, my emotional confusion and spiritual angst all but disappeared, leaving me with the simple, blessed joy of getting to know Elizabeth. She already impressed me as one of the finest people I'd ever met.

·   ·   ·

After a while, Nurse Bethany came to take the baby back to the nursery so I could rest. Hah, I thought. Over my dead body. Since giving birth to Adam, I'd lost my awe of medical personnel and ceased following their instructions when I didn't want to. At the moment, I was too tired (not to mention stoned) to get up and run away from the nurse, so I pressed the "elevate" control on the hospital bed until my mattress had risen all the way to her eye level, where she couldn't easily get hold of my baby.

"I'm not going to drop her," I assured Bethany. The bed had bars on the sides, like a truncated crib, so Lizzy and I were well squared away.

"Sister Beck," said Bethany, using the Mormon form of polite address, "you could fall asleep and roll over on her and smother her. Do you want that to happen?"

"I appreciate your concern, Bethany," I said, "but I just gave birth. It would take a forklift to roll me over right now. We'll be fine, I promise. Thank you. Bye."

Bethany stood there for a moment, fuming in an incredibly nice, Latter-day Saint sort of way. Then she seemed to decide to wash her hands of this entire strange family. She walked out of the room, and I lay back snuggling my baby, high in every sense of the word. And there I stayed. Every minute during the next two days, I kept Lizzy in my arms and the bed up as far as it would go. It drove the nurses crazy, but until I was good and ready I refused to descend from the small heaven where we cuddled together, me and my bright red daughter and her clouds of glory.

CHAPTER 13

The Lord's University

I started teaching at Brigham Young University a few months after Lizzy was born. Owned and operated by the Mormon Church, BYU was founded to provide young Latter-day Saints with fine academic educations while inculcating the values of Mormonism into their very plasma. The opportunity to work there part time while I completed my doctoral research was a godsend, since I needed the money and an academic environment to help me finish my dissertation.

Mormons consider BYU "the Lord's University," and in many ways it is more central to Latter-day Saint culture than the governing offices in Salt Lake City. It's where young Saints meet and marry, where they often bear their first few children, where they're taught the official Mormon perspective on human knowledge. When I was growing up, admission to BYU was almost automatic for a Latter-day Saint student, but it's since become quite competitive, and the students are both intelligent and sensitive, able to learn about things like, say, evolutionary theory while simultaneously disbelieving them. The campus population—around thirty thousand souls, all told—is Mormon to the furthest possible degree, because anyone either enrolled at or employed by BYU is allowed to stay only if they follow the Church's code of conduct. The vast majority, of course, are Latter-day Saints, but the occasional non-Mormon enrolls, mainly to flesh out the university's impressive athletic programs.

Supposedly, all these people keep the rules: No alcohol, caffeine, or tobacco. No extramarital sex or even serious petting. Women may not wear shorts or miniskirts. Men's hair must not be long enough to touch their ears or collars, and beards are permitted only to those who have a doctor's note saying their skin is too sensitive to shave. Men must also wear socks, on the premise that the hair on human ankles can be thought of as an extension of pubic hair (I don't know what group of anatomical analysts made this determination, but whoever they are, I never want to see them naked). All females, it goes without saying, shave their legs—underarms, too, though these are concealed by required sleeves (it's unclear to me whether armpit hair is also suspected of having pubic origins, but I wouldn't doubt it). If a student or faculty member regularly misses church, the authorities are notified, and that person's status at the school is placed in serious jeopardy.

In the spring of 1990, I found this quaint and amusing, like Amish hats and buggies. As I trudged from the part-time-faculty parking lot to the social science building for my first day of work, I couldn't help but be impressed by the sparkling cleanliness of everything at BYU. Though the sidewalks swarmed with thousands of people, not a footprint marred the emerald lawns. The buildings glistened as though they had just been washed (probably because they *had* just been washed—an administrator once told me that the windows and floors were cleaned up to six times a day). The students heading to class looked like an endless procession of newly minted Ken and Barbie dolls. For sheer tidiness, BYU made Harvard look like a homeless shelter.

I headed up to the eighth floor of the social science building and found the venue for my first faculty meeting. It was a conference room near the department offices, with a long table stretching its entire length. About fifteen faculty members were already seated at the table when I came in. I felt a spasm of self-consciousness—the newbie meeting a group of seasoned pros—and was trying to come up with a clever-yet-humble way to introduce myself when this turned out to be unnecessary. Several people I'd never met greeted me cheerfully by name as the department chairman waved me toward an empty chair and I sat down.

"So, Martha, how's your dad?" said a beefy professor, whose rumpled suit and elbow patches managed to give him the sartorial flourish of an academic while still meeting BYU's dress code.

The room suddenly hushed. Everyone looked at me, waiting for my answer.

"He . . . uh . . . he's fine," I said, a little flustered. I'd been in my Harvard mind-set, forgetting that on this campus, I was almost a celebrity, the child of a legend.

A young professor in a red bow tie chimed in from his side of the table.

"When's his next book coming out?"

"I don't know," I said. "I don't think anytime soon."

"Oh, well," said Bow Tie. "I won't be able to understand it anyway. Your dad's smarter than ten of me."

There was a general chuckle of good-natured agreement, and then the department chairman stood up, bringing the meeting to order. He passed around a written schedule of the sociology curriculum, showing who was teaching which course. Some of the faculty grumbled about their assignments, but I wasn't one of them. Though I'd worked as a teaching fellow at Harvard, I'd never designed and taught a course all by myself. I was only too happy to be assigned to teach an introductory class and a course on the sociology of gender, where I'd be on familiar turf. Once we'd covered scheduling, the chairman moved on to other agenda items.

"I'm sure you're all aware," he said, "that the brethren in Salt Lake are asking BYU faculty to refrain from publishing in any journals that are considered 'alternative voices.' "

It took me a second to recall that "alternative voices" was the label applied by Latter-day Saints to any publications not approved by the Church authorities, from the *Christian Science Monitor* to *Hustler*.

"Naturally," the chairman went on, "we in the sociology department will follow these . . . uh . . . guidelines."

"We will?" said the young professor in the bow tie. "I assumed we were going to ignore them—everyone here's been doing it for years." I suddenly remembered that I'd met him at Harvard, back when I was an undergraduate. He'd been there on a Fulbright or something.

The chairman sighed wearily, as though he'd been expecting this. "Look, Scott," he said, "up to now, the brethren were just uncomfortable with the 'alternative voice' publications. As of this year, they've banned them. It's official now."

"But that's ridiculous!" Scott exclaimed. "Where are we supposed to publish? Nobody takes church journals seriously. I mean, *I* don't take them seriously. They'll never let us tell the truth."

The whole room rustled and then seemed to harden, going from sweet and mellow to sharp and brittle like syrup crystallizing in ice water. A tiny lightbulb went on above my head as I recalled something I'd seen in the newspaper earlier that summer: A group of BYU professors had gone public with protests that the Mormon Church was limiting "academic freedom." The phrase went back to the Middle Ages, when Galileo was excommunicated by the pope for claiming that the earth revolved around the sun, contradicting the belief that the Holy Roman Empire was the center of the universe. I thought it was a bit ridiculous for a few miffed professors in Utah to put themselves in this august company, but every faculty needs something to gripe about.

"Calm down, Scotty," said a gruff-voiced professor sitting a few places to my left. "The brethren have made their decision, and we have to abide by it." Professors at BYU know that a choice between current academic thinking and the dictates of the Mormon General Authorities really is no choice: the Authorities speak God's words and, if you want to get cynical, also sign his checks.

"And you can publish anything you want in the Church's journals," said one of the three women in the room, in a soothing voice. "They're very open to whatever—"

The chairman interrupted her. "Um, I don't think so."

Everyone looked up, a flock of bright-eyed crows watching a shiny object.

"I've had several phone calls from Salt Lake recently," said the chairman. "They want us to avoid . . . um . . . sensitive research. There are some subjects that aren't suitable for publication. We . . . well, we probably don't want to study those topics at all."

The faculty members were gazing at the chairman intently, as though he were a mess of goat entrails from which they were trying to divine the future. It reminded me of something, some other group I'd seen with precisely that guarded, quizzical expression, but I couldn't remember where.

"What does that mean?" said Scott. "What topics are 'unsuitable for publication'? And what are they going to do if we learn about them— fire us?"

Silence.

I suddenly remembered where I'd seen people act this way: in the

People's Republic of China, where I'd gone to do research in 1984. I re-called an interview with some factory administrators, who, assuming I spoke no Chinese, had a frank discussion right in front of me about what lies they should tell in order to make sure nothing damaging got back to the party. It occurred to me that although the Mormon Church wouldn't endanger these professors' lives, it could definitely take away their living. Once academics have spent several years at BYU, most other universities won't touch them; rightly or wrongly, they're seen as religious loonies who prefer fundamentalist doctrine to academic process. The place was a dead end. These people had to keep their jobs.

"Oh, for crying out loud!" said Scott, grabbing his hair in both hands. "Are you saying they're going to fire us if we *know* too much? We're *schol-ars*. We should be fired if we know too *little*."

"Well, now, nothing's been stated explicitly except for the alternative voices ruling," said the chairman, looking utterly miserable. "But yes, I think it was implied that . . . I just think it's advisable that we avoid certain issues altogether."

"What issues?" That question came from me. Confusion and curiosity had made me bold enough to break my silence. The answer came from half a dozen voices, all over the room.

"Evolution."

"Mormon history."

"American archaeology."

"Feminism."

This last one got my attention. I knew that the other topics men-tioned might lead to fields of knowledge that contradicted Mormon beliefs—some Saints are firmly creationist, historians are known for dis-covering unsavory details about early Mormonism, archaeologists stub-bornly refuse to verify what Mormons claim are the Jewish origins of the American Indian—but I didn't happen to be writing a dissertation about them.

"We're not supposed to study feminism?" I said.

The woman who had already spoken shook her head. "It's the other f-word. We don't even say it."

"What grounds could they possibly have for firing sociologists who study feminism?" I said, wondering how I was supposed to teach Sociology of Gender without f-ing up. "Scott's right, we should be fired if we *don't* study it. I mean, it *is* one of the most dramatic social phenomena of the twentieth century."

There was another beat of that hard-edged silence, and then someone said, "You haven't been here long, have you?"

I agreed that I hadn't, silently adding that I was grateful to be a Harvard student with a part-time job, rather than someone whose family income depended on a BYU faculty position. From this safe haven, I judged that the mood in that faculty meeting was probably way overblown. After all, many of the top Church leaders had visited my father at home when I was younger, and they all seemed intelligent and good-hearted. Extremely so. I was sure they were exactly the kind of thoughtful, well-educated spiritual masters I hoped to become. Such people would never be afraid of simple, factual truths. I also knew that social scientists are notorious crusaders, always scapegoating the nearest authority figure, so I figured the members of BYU's sociology faculty were making a mountain out of a molehill. I liked them immensely anyway.

• • •

Later that day, exhilarated by meeting so many amiable colleagues and teaching my first solo class to ninety sparkly clean Kens and Barbies, I headed for the library to do a little dissertation research. BYU's library is massive, one of the biggest in the country, containing over a million volumes of literature from every discipline. I walked into the lobby and past a row of distinguished-looking black-and-white portraits: the winners of the BYU Professor of the Year Award for each year since the honor was created. The first picture was of my father. A few portraits down was John's dad. I planned to bring my children to see the wall when they were old enough to know how proud they should be.

I flashed my faculty card to gain access to the periodical section, then entered the enormous glass-enclosed room that held the microfiche images of major newspapers from all over the world. I'd reached a point in my dissertation where I needed to discuss the case of one Sonia Johnson, a Mormon woman who had been excommunicated by the Church in the 1970s for championing the equal rights amendment. When I mentioned my dissertation topic to people at Harvard, Johnson's name popped out of their mouths almost reflexively, because her case had received an enormous amount of national press attention. Sonia Johnson herself had made her battle against Mormon policy into a major story, offering interviews to practically every newspaper in the country. I'd been an oblivious teenager when she was all over the news, and my Harvard advisers found my ignorance about the whole saga inexcusable.

There weren't many academic articles or books about Johnson's struggle with the Mormon authorities, but the BYU library had microfilm of most large newspapers, extending back to a time well before the equal rights amendment was proposed, so I could learn about Sonia Johnson and her feminist efforts from primary sources. I had just two hours to do research before my babysitter went off duty—not nearly enough time to closely read everything written about Sonia Johnson in every newspaper—but I was prepared to speed-read through the more important articles, getting a few crucial facts and an overall picture of the way the American media had dealt with the story.

As it turned out, I had more than enough time to read everything about Sonia Johnson in the BYU library, because not a single reference to her showed up on the library's retrieval system. Puzzled, I checked the references I'd gotten from books, the ones that quoted specific articles in major newspapers. I found the correct papers, dates, and page numbers, then scrutinized the microfilm screens with the care of an art restorer examining a painting. And what I found, while insignificant in the scheme of things, troubled me just a bit.

The articles were simply missing.

All of them.

Someone in the BYU library had spent an enormous amount of time and effort to excise every single reference to Sonia Johnson that had ever appeared in print. Whatever splash she'd made in the non-Mormon world, in the microcosm that was the Lord's University, it was as though nothing about Johnson—not the angry, quixotic woman herself, nor her doomed political quest to assist the passage of the equal rights amendment, nor the Church's disapproving response—had ever existed at all.

People really do underestimate the capacity of things to disappear.

CHAPTER 14

Dad Faces Death, Part I

Clearly, I'm not going to be able to help my father relax. The situation in the hotel room is too weirdly stressful, his position too much like that of a hostage. Seeing that I don't have a prayer of making him comfortable, I decide to make him even more *un*comfortable. But in a good way. A way, I tell myself, that will later make him glad.

My Harvard professors and classmates often told me I was too ingratiating, almost obsequious, in class discussions (New English intellectuals tend to be terse and frank, sparing with both their time and their patience). When I came back to Utah, on the other hand, people described me as "blunt," which, translated from the Mormon into regular American English, means "audaciously bitchy." Even using the word *blunt* is uncharacteristically blunt for Latter-day Saints, particularly the women, who, if asked to describe Charles Manson, might say in a tone of sweet, meaningful understatement, "Well, he's . . . different." During my camel phase, I worked hard to overcome the forwardness I'd learned at Harvard.

But here in this hotel room, after apostatizing and then spending ten years at a job that includes pushing people past their usual limits, I am back to being a blunt object.

"So," I say to my father, who has begun to hum very softly, "do you ever think about death?" I use as friendly a voice as I possess.

"Hm?" His eyes fly open momentarily, and he braces himself in his chair as if it's on the deck of a ship that just hit rough water.

"Death," I repeat. "What do you think it'll be like?"

This is one of the main things I've come to ask. Though it's not a question one usually poses in polite conversation, I expect that my father will be able to handle it with aplomb. Anyone his age, with his enormous religious faith, must have spent years coming to terms with his own mortality.

What I want to know is, how does my father plan to explain the darker moments of his life to God, who saw it all happen?

During the end of my stay in Utah, I became obsessed with this question, and not just in regard to my father. By that time, everyone and everything around me had begun to feel as slippery and unstable as the flecks of light in a kaleidoscope. I developed an almost physical hunger to have people treat *me* bluntly, to say what they really meant, describe what they'd really seen, go where logic really took them.

I used to spend the hours when I couldn't sleep visiting a mental sanctuary I called Truth Island, a tiny, fictional stretch of rocks in the North Sea, where a sharp, clean wind always blew and the only structure was a square one-room cottage with windows that had no glass. In the room were two wooden chairs. Nothing else. I could go into that house with anyone and ask all the questions I wanted. Here's the thing: on Truth Island, anyone who lied, even a little bit, even unconsciously, turned blue—powder blue for small lies, periwinkle for naughty fibs, cobalt for outright deception, and so on to deep navy.

During the time I was leaving the Saints, I visited this imaginary island so frequently, with such intensity, that whenever I conversed with anyone, I'd automatically estimate the exact shade their skin would be on that rocky little slab of stones. Some people would stay rosy or brown in my mind's eye, while others took on a slight cerulean tinge at certain moments, and still others walked around as blue as indigo all the time, even when they weren't talking. Now I'm eager to see what shade my father turns when he tells me his expectations about death.

He's staring at me with one eyebrow up, the other down. The effect is a superior, critical expression he often wears when challenged.

"Oh," my father says, in a tone of intellectual ennui. "I know exactly what death will be like."

"Really?" I'm genuinely fascinated.

"Certainly. I've experienced it, as far as that goes."

"You have?" I thought I vaguely remembered hearing that my father was a near-death-experience survivor, but of course I could never ask. Even at the height of my Dueling Allusions capabilities, I could never have addressed him so directly, gotten him to discuss something so personal.

"Yes, often." He shrugs. "It happened just the other night."

"You're kidding. What was it like?"

His arched eyebrow goes down, and he grimaces. "Well, my whole body was ice cold—I could feel the grave, the dirt pressing against my face, going up my nose, the whole thing." He shivers a little. "But my work is not yet done, as I said. So here I still am." He offers a nonchalant chuckle.

It takes me a minute to process this. As part of my obsession with all things spiritual, I've read dozens of reported near-death experiences, related by people who were considered physically dead, yet say they continued to experience consciousness along with a variety of interesting events. I'm sure you've heard the stories, too. Many of the resuscitated say they heard an unpleasant buzzing sound at the moment of "death," felt themselves lifted out of their bodies, watched medical personnel trying to resuscitate them, passed through a long dark tunnel, then encountered deceased loved ones and/or a Being of Light, who emanated love and joy. I'm so used to this litany, and so firmly locked in to my belief in my father's spirituality, that the story he's just told takes me completely by surprise.

"You mean . . . ," I stammer, "you mean you felt what was going to happen to your *body* after you die?"

My father cocks his head a little, like a curious squirrel. Now *he's* puzzled, as though to him, any normal discussion of death would focus on the physical sensation of being entombed. I'm amazed. Mormons are absolute suckers for a juicy life-after-death testimonial, and my father, a Mormon's Mormon if there ever was one, is talking more like Stephen King.

On the other hand, I remember that Mormons also believe in the literal resurrection of the physical body. Latter-day Saints never cremate their dead, because on the morning of the first resurrection, when Jesus appears (in Jackson County, Missouri, if you'd like to get your tickets right away), all the graves of the truly righteous Saints will fly open, and they'll be raised up to meet Christ with their original flesh and bone (but, intriguingly, no blood) reanimated and restored to excellent condition, like a preowned Lexus. I have at least one friend who spent years in therapy just to get over learning this doctrine as a child, and many more are haunted by technical questions: What if you lose a limb years before death—do you get it back in the resurrection? If a soldier dies, say, in Afghanistan, will he pop back to life all the way over there, and have to make the trek to Missouri on his own? And what happens to people who just get blown to bits? If a jackal eats part of you, will your flesh be reclaimed from the animal's?

"But apart from your body," I say to my father. "What do you think will happen to your spirit? You know, your consciousness? Do you think it goes on?"

He laughs, apparently recovered from the fit of willies he got pursuant to feeling grave gravel in his sinuses. "What a question!" he says, in a voice that would be completely scornful if it were not also amused. "Of course the spirit goes on! The Gospel tells us that, if nothing else!"

"So, do you think it's really set up in the Mormon way? The afterlife, I mean."

"Of course," he nods emphatically. "Joseph Smith described it very clearly." I'm trying to remember all the details of Latter-day Saint doctrine pertaining to life after death. As I recall, it's all about kingdoms. Sinners end up in the telestial kingdom, which is like earth, only nicer, sort of like a Holiday Inn. Virtuous non-Mormons get much cozier accommodations in a four-star environment called the terrestrial kingdom, and righteous Saints in the sublime celestial kingdom, where the streets are paved with gold. There are further divisions within each kingdom— for example, the celestial kingdom has a central zone called the kingdom of the firstborn, reserved for Mormons who live the "true and eternal principle of plural marriage" (polygamy). Each man in this kingdom gets to rule his own planets, populating them by copulating with his many wives, who give birth in the spirit world to infants "as numberless as the sands of the sea," who will later be incarnated on Dad's personal real estate throughout the universe.

The most important rule of the Mormon afterlife is that people are allowed to visit anyone in their kingdom or lower, but no one can "visit up." In other words, if I go to the terrestrial kingdom, I can visit friends and relations in the terrestrial or the telestial kingdom but not in the celestial kingdom. Of course, I don't have to worry about these logistics, because I'm going to outer darkness: no visiting hours, no parole. John calls this the Chutes and Ladders version of heaven. He's going to outer darkness, too. There won't be many of us—only apostate Mormons— but at least we'll know all the same people. Most of us, after all, will be from Provo.

I reel my mind back from these ruminations and ask my father, "What do you expect the hereafter will be like for you?"

"Well," he says, blowing out a long breath. "Joseph Smith said that if we could see how glorious the telestial kingdom really is—even the telestial—we'd all be committing suicide just to get into it."

It's an enigmatic answer. Perhaps he's just being optimistic in a modest way, implying that he doesn't presume to think of himself as worthy to live in the celestial or even the terrestrial kingdom (it's a bit of a catch-22, since claiming perfection would be pride, which is a sin, which would rule him out of all the best kingdoms by definition).

Or maybe . . . maybe he remembers everything. If so, he knows that by Mormon rules, he can only get into the celestial kingdom by confessing to a religious leader in this life, then taking the punishment the Church would dish out: excommunication, probably, followed a year later by rebaptism, but forever blotting his reputation. Maybe he's decided that settling for bottom-dollar salvation is better than enduring such hideous shame in mortality. After all, whatever else my father did, he never lost the faith, never left the Church. At least he's not outer darkness material.

"So are you afraid?" I say, blunt as blunt can be.

My father makes a sharp puffing sound, a whispered "pah!" "Of course not," he says. "Never have been. Nothing to fear."

I squint at him, because in my mind's eye, the skin all over his entire body has just turned as blue as his eyes.

The thing is, I know he's afraid of death. I remember noticing, when I was still a small child, that the fear of death stalked my father everywhere, slid into his mind and swam in his wake like the ticktocking crocodile that stalked Captain Hook in *Peter Pan*.

A quick montage of memories plays rapidly in my head: My father, his face almost as white as his hair, stopping to check his pulse every few steps as he walked up the hill to his office at BYU. The way he sprinkled an abstemious two or three grains of salt on his food at dinner, determined to keep his blood pressure low. The nauseating smell of the beverage he drank each morning, a brew of hot water, apple cider vinegar, cod liver oil, brewer's yeast, crushed eggshells, and anything else he'd read might extend his life span.

One morning, when I was six or so, my father took my little sister and me for a brief hike in the mountains near Provo. My sister was skipping along a ridge of rock when something (a screaming hawk? the smell of pine? I'll never know) seemed to hit a tripwire in my father's mind.

"*Get down, you damn fool!*" he screamed, running at my startled sister. As he neared her, he hunched down strangely, scuttling like an injured dog. He was almost doubled over when he finally knocked her off her feet.

"*Never!*" he yelled, dropping to the ground next to my sister. Then he stopped, gasped for breath, and continued in a voice that was softer, but trembling. "Never never *never* walk on the horizon. They'll shoot you just for target practice if they see you on the horizon. You might as well paint a bull's-eye on your head."

My sister looked at me, with those same blue eyes my father has, and I could see that even at the age of four, she knew what was happening as well as I did. Daddy wasn't even talking to us. Daddy was still in the war. We'd heard our mother and our older siblings talking about it, every time he had one of his "five o'clocks." He would wake up, always at about five o'clock in the morning, shouting about Germans and foxholes and bullets and the end of the world, and it would often take days until he seemed fully himself again.

The five o'clocks made me love my father more than ever. I knew that he was horribly afraid of death not because he'd never faced it, but because he'd faced it in huge, mind-numbing, senseless quantities. People think a six-year-old can't understand these things, but I did. So did my sister—even at age four—as she lay on her scuffed knees and prickled face in the pine needles, promising my father that she would never walk on the horizon, ever again. We went on with our hike without talking any more about it, knowing more deeply than ever how much our father loved us and how terrified he was of dying.

"Me, afraid of death!" says my father now. "Ridiculous."

He shakes his head in scorn, rolling his eyes to demonstrate his utter fearlessness. But we both know that he only does this so that he can flick the subtlest of glances at the corner of the room, where the crocodile—ticktock, ticktock—takes another sly step toward him.

CHAPTER 15

Nightmares

I was beginning to suspect that there was something seriously wrong with me. On the surface, my life looked closer to perfect than I'd ever expected it would: I had a husband I adored, three darling little kids, a beautiful home, an enjoyable job, two academic degrees with another on the way, and a close-knit religious community that supported me both physically and emotionally. Most of the time, in appreciation of all this bounty, I managed to act as happy as I should have been. I was pretty successful at hiding from everyone—even John and the kids—the fact that beneath the surface, I was a slow-motion train wreck.

My growing unhappiness seemed to be intertwined with my obsessive spiritual hunger. Immediately after Adam's birth, when my taste of spiritual reality had been fresh, I'd thought that my yearning to keep it (*please, please, please, please* . . .) would fade as time passed. It turned out that this was like expecting to get less hungry the longer I went without eating—a strategy, by the way, that actually works for a while, but then backfires like a bazooka. I did have periods of numbness that temporarily dimmed the sense of longing, but these made life simply bearable, not satisfying, and they were getting shorter. As the days went by, it became all I could do to wait until the kids were asleep before I fled to the darkened living room, curled up in a chair, and dissolved in tears, surrendering to the craving that shook my heart like a rag doll.

My emotional life was the thing that hurt most, but I was also doing plenty of good old-fashioned physical suffering. For no reason doctors could ascertain, I was plagued by constant pain that virtually immobilized various areas of my body. If you've ever had a really awful sore throat, one that makes you put off swallowing as long as possible, you know the sensation. The pain suffused the muscles of my upper legs and

lower back, making it agonizing to stand, walk, or sit. The same condition affected my hands so severely that I could use them only as clubs or
claws. Just holding a pencil was problematic, and writing a check, on
days when I could manage it at all, was so painful it brought tears to my
eyes. I'd been affected by these symptoms on and off for a decade. Now,
at the age of twenty-eight, I was very nearly bedridden by them. I'd been
to specialist after specialist, submitted to test after test, all with no diagnosis. "It must be simple muscle strain," the doctors would say. "Just rest
until it goes away."

But though I spent most of my time lying down, the pain never went
away. It just ebbed and flowed, growing slowly more intense and pervasive over time. I adopted many coping mechanisms, cleaning my house
on hands and knees (I couldn't bend to pick up objects) and working on
my dissertation by taping pencils between the fingers of my nearly useless
hands and pressing the computer keys with the eraser ends. Even so, trying to do an ordinary amount of work was so exhausting that after a few
hours I had to lie down and focus on nothing but tolerating the pain.

Perhaps because I couldn't move much, I had a very difficult time
making myself eat. At five foot seven, I weighed under a hundred pounds
for the first time since my anorexic days, making me fashionably thin by
magazine standards, but so weak and atrophied I could barely lift my toddlers. My fingernails stopped growing. My hair started falling out. Despite the wealth of self-pity I could wring from these ailments, the
"queen for a day" glory was no real substitute for well-being.

Bothersome though it was that my body was going AWOL, none of
that worried me as much as what was going on in my head. For starters,
I was terrified all the time. Though I craved rest, I couldn't doze off without experiencing horrible nightmares. I'd struggle awake, gasping and
sobbing with fear, as though sleep were a suffocating shroud with static
cling. I'd suffered from nightmares my whole life, but these were
humdingers, grand mal scare-fests. You'd think I would remember every
detail of something so frightening, but I rarely recalled even a part of my
nightmares—except for one, which was slightly less terrifying than others. It returned night after night, with only slight variations.

The dream began pleasantly enough. I'd find myself on the foothills of the Wasatch Mountains, looking over the valley where I lived. Then I'd catch a tiny flicker of movement in the corner of my eye, and turn to see that a rockslide was beginning on a mountain slope several miles distant. I'd watch the dirt avalanche, fascinated, hoping that nothing in the valley would be disturbed—and then, like the soft pitter-patter of raindrops, I'd hear pebbles rolling across the ground at my feet. Before I had a chance to realize what this meant, it became horribly clear: The earth beneath my feet began to heave and surge. I'd run helplessly over disintegrating terrain, looking for shelter, knowing there was nowhere safe to go. Then I'd wake up.

A few times, this dream had an odd variation, which wouldn't make sense to me until later. As I was scrambling for cover, hiding behind a tree or bush, a car drove up and parked nearby. The driver climbed out, apparently unconcerned by the shattering, sliding instability of the earth. She was a middle-aged acquaintance from our ward. In real life I knew this woman just well enough to remember her name, which, let's say, was Rosemary Douglas. She seemed nice enough, but I'd never really spoken to her. In the dream, Sister Douglas stood in the midst of the tumult, not showing the slightest fear, and called to me.

"Don't worry!" she yelled. "You don't need to hide! It's safer in the open!"

I never quite believed her, but when I awoke from this version of the dream, I wasn't quite as scared as when Rosemary didn't show up. I'd lie awake sweating and tense, but at least I didn't scream.

Screaming had become such an ordinary part of my nightly activities that it probably counted as regular vocal exercise. If John accidentally touched me during the night, I'd wake up totally disoriented, screaming as though I'd brushed against a huge scorpion. Sometimes I wasn't fully conscious until I was standing across the room, hands outstretched as though to hold something back. John was amazingly kind during these episodes. He often spent hours calming me back into trembling sleepiness. Finally, to ease my back pain and spare John so many rude awakenings, I took to sleeping on the floor beside the bed. Actually, I felt safer *under* the bed, but when I slept there, my leaping startle reaction often made me smash my head against the springs.

John and I talked about all of this, of course, but we were at a loss to explain what was happening to me. We considered physiological problems—a chemical imbalance, genetic tendency to depression—but none of the medical doctors we consulted could diagnose or change my condition. We wondered if my constant spiritual seeking was somehow opening me up to an unhealthy wavelength in the cosmic ether. (Had I been wearing the protective regulation temple garments night and day? Actually, yes.) But religious explanations for my night terrors and pervasive despair didn't ring true for me, either. My sense was that I'd begun to play with my impressive collection of mental blocks, bumping into some sort of psychological barrier to inner peace.

.   .   .

You'd think I would have figured out the whole problem sooner, because I was supposedly trained to understand the mind. In fact, I was even training other people to understand it. John and I had begun teaching a group psychology course at BYU, a reprisal of a class John had taught as a fellow at Harvard. It met twice a week. Every other meeting, I played sidekick as John led a discussion, explaining the dynamics of what shrinks call "group process." On the other days, I'd go behind a one-way mirror with a rotating group of three students, who observed everyone else in "free discussion." During free discussion, John sat quietly, not offering any structure, content, or direction. The group chatter was apparently aimless, but as those of us behind the mirror could always see, the group fell ineluctably into typical, predictable patterns of interaction.

The longer free discussion continued, the more the students revealed about themselves. About halfway through the semester, the discussion would invariably turn to deeply personal, sometimes tragic episodes in the lives of the group members. I'd read the research and theory describing this process, so when I showed up for class one particular afternoon I was fascinated to see if that day's free discussion would follow the expected pattern.

"Watch," I told the three students who had joined me in the observation chamber. "This week people are supposed to go into some really serious personal history. Trauma, betrayal, loss, that kind of thing." Looking forward to a little drama, the four of us picked up our pens and prepared to take notes that would either validate or disconfirm our hypothesis.

The theory was right. After a little small talk, the class discussion suddenly turned to difficult issues in the students' personal lives. Since I was taking notes, I have a record of the conversation (though I've changed identifying details here). The first person to discuss something mildly revealing was a young man I'll call Ben, who had the most dominant personality in the group.

"I'm sick of everyone telling me I should turn out like my father," he said. "Everyone loves him, thinks he's perfect. But he's always been a jerk to my mom."

"Mm-hmm," said a perfectly accessorized coed named Stephanie. "My dad hates my guts. I don't care anymore, but when I was little it really sucked." She threw a quick, nervous glance at John, probably wondering if saying "sucked" was against BYU rules. It was, but John just smiled.

"You guys, think of the Third Commandment," said a twenty-one-year-old returned missionary named Eric. "Honor thy father and thy mother, you know? Every family has problems. I used to be mad at my parents, but I forgave them." He sounded as though he were giving one of the standard, memorized "missionary discussions" to yet another family of Peruvian villagers who were too polite to kick out the gringo Mormons; teaching them the Plan of Salvation with the aid of a Spanish-language flipchart and his fervent teenage faith. "You know," he added, "when you truly forgive, you don't even remember what the other person did to you."

A mousy little teenager named Mary, who dressed like a pioneer and rarely said a word, spoke up for the first time that hour. "I must be the champion forgiver of the universe," she said. "I don't remember anything that happened before I was, like, eleven. I just kind of . . . *woke up* in sixth grade. Everything before that is, like, a total blank." She chanced a nervous smile at the other students, then withdrew into her usual cautious silence.

Stephanie coughed and shifted in her chair.

"Um, Mary, don't you think that's sort of . . . odd?" she said.

"Well, yeah, kind of." Mary nodded.

"Why do you think you don't remember?" asked Ben.

Mary twisted the long ash blond braid of hair that usually hung straight down her back. "I . . . well, I think I maybe wasn't such a good kid. Like, I did a lot of things wrong. Bad things."

She fell silent again, but those of us in the observation chamber knew by the group's body language that the discussion wasn't going anywhere without Mary. The whole class just sat there, looking at her with varying degrees of curiosity.

"You don't seem like a bad person to me," said Ben. There was a murmur of agreement. "What could you have done that was so bad?"

Mary had gone very pale. She absentmindedly put the end of her braid into her mouth. "Oh, you know . . ." She couldn't look up. "You know, like . . . sex and stuff."

The three observers and I, still scribbling notes, raised our faces to give each other meaningful glances. Though she could have been very attractive, Mary dressed and acted about as sexual as a sack of mud.

"Before you were eleven?" said Eric. "Why would you think that?"

Mary had begun to cry softly. "I don't know," she whispered. "I really don't know, I just feel like . . . like I was bad. That way."

Behind my glass partition, I began to feel bored. For some reason, little Mary was annoying the hell out of me. Besides, the observation booth was small and hot, and I hadn't gotten a good night's sleep for weeks. Maybe months.

After a few long seconds, a student named Barbara, the class beauty, cleared her throat and spoke in a shaky voice, though she was clearly trying to act nonchalant.

"I got date-raped once."

Through the amplifier that connected the classroom to the observation chamber, I could hear the whole class draw a sharp breath. The students next to me took notes furiously, writing down each person's body-language reaction to this little bombshell. My annoyance was growing into outright anger. My hands, which had been hurting intensely all day, began to feel almost paralyzed. My pen fell out of my fingers and clacked to the floor. It hurt like hell to pick it up.

"It was my high school boyfriend," Barbara went on determinedly, her voice shaking even more. "I was fourteen; he was eighteen. I thought I was in love with him. He wanted to have sex with me, and when I wouldn't he just did it anyway. "

Mary was riveted, her reddened eyes staring at Barbara "Wow," she breathed. "Did you confess to your bishop?"

"She was *raped,* Mary!" exclaimed Eric. "She didn't have anything to confess."

My hands felt like sponges dipped in acid, soaked in pure pain. I was intensely, horrifically angry at all the students, and the observation booth, with its close air and crowded space, was driving me absolutely nuts.

"Yeah, but . . ." Mary sounded doubtful. "I mean, he was her boyfriend. She probably sort of let him, you know. She could have stopped him."

"I couldn't," said Barbara, but there was doubt in her voice.

"Maybe you could," Mary insisted, "if you had just—"

"Mary. *She couldn't.*" This from a student named Joanne. There was a rasping edge in her voice and the whole class swiveled to stare at her. She, too, had gone pale. "He was just too strong," Joanne whispered. Then she put her head on her desk and began to cry.

I wondered if the climate control in the observation chamber was working at all. The air around me was disgusting, hot and rank. I could hardly breathe. My hands were killing me, and now my back was going into spasm as well. I was *furious.*

"Geez," Eric said on the other side of the glass. "I didn't think that things like that happened here. In Utah, I mean. At least not to Church members."

Mary was still looking at Barbara. "Well, *I* think you could have done something to stop him," she said, sounding just like the Church Lady on *Saturday Night Live.*

I had a sudden, intense urge to tie Mary's long pioneer braid to a doorknob and bat her head around like a tetherball. But I couldn't, because now I'd lost any vestige of control over my hands. They weren't just immobilized; they were twitching convulsively, like dying spiders. Then my back went into a full-blown, excruciating spasm, so painful it took away my breath and didn't give it back. I didn't have time to figure out what was happening. I just knew I had to get out: out of the observation room, out of the building, out of the country, if possible. I stood up and lunged for the door, shoving the three students out of the way.

As I opened the door, it finally hit: the *real* pain, the pain for which back spasms and hand convulsions were only a tiny teaser. I felt a horrendous ripping sensation between my legs, so intense that (thank God) I couldn't scream. I couldn't even whimper. I just lurched into the corridor, grabbed the wall as if it were my very best long-lost friend, and slid, unconscious, to the sparkling clean linoleum floor.

CHAPTER 16

The Light

My doctor was worried. He'd just finished examining me after John (assisted by our fascinated students) had picked me up off the floor of the psychology building, loaded me into the backseat of our car, and placed a call to our medical clinic. The doctor had found a large lump in what I will call the gynecological region of my body. He feared it might be a malignancy. He phoned several hospitals looking for one that could perform exploratory surgery on me immediately.

In the meantime, John went home to relieve our babysitter, and returned bringing the children with him. By then, the doctor had managed to locate an OR where I could get treatment that night. It was in Salt Lake City, about forty-five miles away. There was no telling how long the operation would take. It would depend, the doctor said uneasily, on what the surgeons found.

I was so scared that I did something I'd sworn I would never do: I called my mother, explained the situation, and asked her if she'd watch my kids while I was in surgery. I knew this was the wrong move when I heard the tension in her voice. "I have to make dinner for your father," she said, sounding about eight years old. I kicked myself, withdrawing the request. In a Mormon context, what I'd just done was like calling the chef for the White House and asking him to rustle up some chicken nuggets for my rug rats while he was busy cooking for the president. John finally phoned his sister, who kindly agreed to juggle our brood for the night. I kissed them good-bye as calmly as I could, wondering if the next time I saw them I'd be announcing some horrifying news about my impending demise, disease, or disability.

John and I didn't talk much in the car; I was in a haze of pain, and he was too frightened to speak. We were both grateful to find a surgeon waiting for us at the emergency room door. Before I knew it, I was lying on an operating table with an IV tube in my arm and an unattractive blue paper hat on my head.

A small circle of doctors and nurses ringed the table, discussing how to proceed. The lump that was causing me so much pain could be a tumor growing from either my digestive or reproductive organs; they weren't sure which. After poking me gingerly, they decided that the answer was B: reproductive. They agreed that they needed a gynecologist on the team, but they weren't sure where to find one. They decided to scatter throughout the hospital and simply grab any gynecologist they could find roaming the halls. I've never before or since seen medical personnel act so down-to-earth, so genuinely interested in a patient's welfare. I was touched, but before I had time to thank them, they rushed off, leaving me alone with the anesthesiologist.

This doctor had a balding head beneath his surgical cap and a beard behind the mask that covered his lower face. From the gap between them, his brown eyes looked at me with sympathy and concern. He sat silently near my head for a minute or so. Then he said, "Are you in pain?"

"A little," I said, and smiled bravely, like the princess trying to cope with the pea. Then it occurred to me that for anesthesiologists, the question "How are you feeling?" may not be rhetorical, so I corrected myself. "A lot, actually."

"I've been thinking about pain for years," said the anesthesiologist. "There are a lot of ways to handle it."

I said nothing.

"Meditation, for example," the doctor went on. "Do you know how to meditate?"

"I've been trying," I said, thinking about the WHAM! that always interfered with my attempts to calm my thoughts.

"Here," said the doctor, as though he were handing me one of his instruments, "I'm going to teach you a good meditation technique." For the next few minutes, he had me close my eyes and visualize a series of curtains with numbers on them, each one pulling away to reveal another behind it. I went along with it—I was hardly in a position to resist—but I suspected it was only a matter of time before the good doctor started reading my aura and teaching me to resist alien abduction.

Fortunately, at that moment the swinging doors opened, and the head surgeon came in with a gynecologist he'd managed to waylay at the end of her shift. The rest of the surgical team followed, and the whole group spent a few more minutes prodding my lump. Finally the lead surgeon nodded to the anesthesiologist like a symphony conductor telling the soloist it was time to begin.

"All right, we're ready," the anesthesiologist told me. "You'll feel a little sting when the juice goes in, and then it's nap time, okay?" I nodded. He leaned down and added in a whisper, "You really need to start meditating. I mean regularly."

I murmured, "Okay," and dropped off the edge of the earth.

I don't know how long I was completely out. When I became aware again, the surgeons had already cut deep into my tissues and were poking around for the lump. I know this, because I sat up and watched them. This did not surprise me at the time, nor did I feel any fear. It seemed perfectly natural.

"Look at this," said the head surgeon. "Is there a cyst in there?"

"Not that I can see," said the gynecologist, peering into the incision, pulling it open to get a better view. "There's just a lot of bleeding. A *lot* of bleeding. Strange."

I turned to look at the anesthesiologist. His attention was flitting back and forth between my body, the IV drug supply, and the instruments showing my vital signs. He looked as focused as a race-car driver at two hundred miles an hour.

It wasn't until that moment that I began to wonder what was happening. Wait, wait, wait a minute, I thought. I'm lying on the table. My eyes are closed. What the . . . ? I seemed to lie back again, prostrate, but I could still see. Eyes closed, I scrutinized the complex geometry of surgical lights and medical instruments and wondered why I wasn't afraid. In fact, I *couldn't* be afraid—I tried, and it simply wouldn't happen. I knew the surgery was going well. I also knew that the doctors were puzzled and worried, and I felt an urge to tell them I was fine. But before I could figure out how to go about this, something else happened. Something that captured every iota of my attention.

It was just a ball of light. Sounds like nothing, when you say it that way. I myself had never understood the obsession near-death survivors have with the Being of Light they say they encounter during their experiences. I mean, we've all seen balls of light—it might just as well be the sun, or one of a billion electric bulbs that illuminate every building in the civilized world. So what?

Now I get it.

The problem with describing the light that appeared during my surgery is that I seemed to perceive it with several senses I usually don't possess, all of them specially designed to experience beauty beyond anything words could ever convey. It's like describing a sunset to someone born blind, or strawberries to a person who has never had the ability to taste or smell. I can give you a visual description, tell you that the light was spherical, about the size of a golf ball when I first noticed it, and that it was far, far brighter than the glaring surgical lights. I can tell you that instead of blinding me, it seemed to make my eyes more able to tolerate brilliance, so that I could see an intense, soft luminosity in everything around me. I can describe how it began to expand outward, saturating objects rather than reflecting off them.

I can also tell you that as it grew, it touched me, flowed into my material body, and that this was the most exquisite physical sensation I have ever felt. I sometimes wonder if it's like the feeling crack cocaine or heroin gives to drug addicts; I think it must be the authentic sensation they are pursuing with artificial means. I'd felt it briefly when I was pregnant with Adam, flirted with it on several occasions since, but only in tiny, flickering moments of faith. Now it poured right through me, and there was no need to have faith anymore. There was no need for anything. Only the vivid, drenching, infinite presence of love and peace and joy. It was . . . home. I was home.

"What's the matter with her?" I heard a surgeon say, his voice sharp with worry. I realized without embarrassment or concern that I—my body, that is—had begun to cry, tears streaming down my temples and dripping onto the sterile paper cap that covered my hair.

"Is she in pain?" asked the gynecologist, as worried as the other surgeon.

"Okay, I'll . . ." said the anesthesiologist, and then went silent. I saw him settle back onto the stool by my head. "She's okay," he said to the other doctors. "She's fine."

He was wrong; I was so, so, so much more than fine. I was wrapped in the arms of Love itself. Time no longer existed, so it was self-evident that every dear thing I had ever lost or thought to lose was mine again, forever. Every bygone sweetness was still present and always would be. Every bitter moment was there, too, but touched, healed, and comforted by the light, the light, that indescribably beautiful Light, with which I was utterly and eternally in love. The world I had thought I inhabited— born astride the grave, and a difficult labor—was nothing but a brief, dark dream.

I could feel enormous delight and amusement, joyous hilarity, flowing back and forth between my own heart and the limitless compassion that held me. We were best friends sharing a joke: "Oh, my God, can you *believe* I thought all that crap was *real?*" "Yeah, you were totally buying it for a couple of decades there." Gales of laughter, from both of us. "Remember how I was always thinking, 'Oh, no, there's pain everywhere and we're all gonna die, we're as doomed as doomed can be . . .' " More laughter, bubbling over, filling the universe. "Kid, you were freaking *out!*" "God, I *know!*"

God.

I know.

For a while I simply drank comfort, drank life, like the desert drinks rain. Then I somehow noticed that the Light was not there just to visit but to deliver a message, too—which was easy, because we were really the same being, the same consciousness. My bizarre, delusional belief that I had ever been separated from it was part of the bad dream from which I'd just woken up. But I also knew—the Light seemed to tell me this—that I would soon be back in the dream again, and that it would feel almost as real to me as it had before. *Hey, kid,* the Light said, still laughing but also very serious, indescribably tender. *There are some things you'll need to remember.*

And though they were not described in words, the things I would need to remember were as clear as if this Being of Light had written them down in bullet points, memo-style, like this:

1. *I am here. Always. I am always right here.*

2. *The way we are now, this being together, being one, is not the way you are supposed to feel after you die. It is the way you are meant to experience life.*

3. *The one place you can find me is the one place you have been afraid to go: your own heart.*

4. *It will not be easy for you to go there.*

5. *I will be here. Always. I will always be right here.*

Then I was coughing and choking and straining my sticky eyelids open in the recovery room. My throat was bone dry, my crotch felt like a war zone, I needed to vomit, and I felt better than I ever had in my life. Before I was fully awake, I began sobbing great gulping sobs of pure happiness, pure relief. The first person I saw was a pockmarked teenager in gang clothing who must have been fulfilling a term of court-appointed public service by cleaning hospital floors. It's a good thing I was crying too hard to get up, because I felt such a flood of love for that boy that I wanted to struggle off my gurney and throw my arms around him, buy him a car, marry him. He looked at me for a moment with widened eyes, then rushed out of the room and returned with a nurse. She came over and took my pulse, mainly, I think, to give me the comfort of her hand on my arm.

"There there," she murmured, patting me, tucking in my sheets. "It's all right. It's okay."

"Do a lot of people cry like this?" I croaked, my eyes spouting like lawn sprinklers.

The nurse thought about it. "Well, sometimes," she said. "Surgery is very traumatic."

"No, no," I said (though it came out "Doh, doh"). "Do they cry because they're happy?"

She looked puzzled. "Maybe. I guess. Say, if it's an exploratory surgery, and things turn out all right."

It was clear to me that my overwhelming happiness wasn't a universal side effect of surgery. I thought about telling the nurse what had happened, but it felt too precious. Instead I asked to speak with the anesthesiologist. She went to get him. I thought I would float right off the gurney on a cloud of joy by the time he came into the recovery room.

"You wanted to see me?" said the anesthesiologist. His voice was beautiful. Everything was beautiful. The world was a beautiful, beautiful, beautiful place.

"Yes," I said, snuffling hard, trying but no doubt failing to appear marginally sane. "I was wondering if you could tell me whether there might have been any side effects from the anesthesia you just used on me."

He raised his eyebrows and rubbed his salt-and-pepper beard. "Well," he said, "there's often some residual numbness around the injection site. Nausea is pretty common, too. And—"

"No," I said. "During the operation."

His brow furrowed. "What do you mean?"

I opened my mouth, trying to think of some way to quiz him about the hallucinogenic effects of the anesthesia without telling him what I'd actually experienced. Nothing came to mind. Perhaps my powers of deceit had been weakened by contact with Truth.

The doctor pursed his lips for moment, then nodded slowly, as though he'd made an important decision.

"Listen," he said. "Why don't you tell me what happened in there?"

I regarded him warily, wanting and not wanting to talk about it. The anesthesiologist looked around for nurses, saw that they had gone back to their stations, then spoke in a hushed, embarrassed voice.

"Before the surgery, when we were waiting for the others, I got this strange feeling that I *had* to teach you how to meditate," he said. "It was so peculiar, as though something was pushing me. I mean, I've thought for years that meditation may help with pain control, but . . ." He shook his head. Then his voice dropped even lower.

"Maybe I wouldn't have thought much about it," he said, "but then we were right in the middle of surgery, and you started crying." He drew an index finger down the side of his face to show the path of my tears. "We thought you might be in pain, and I was trying to decide whether to up the dosage—which can be dangerous, but we didn't want you suffering—and then . . ." He leaned toward me. "This . . . this *voice* told me not to do anything. It said that I shouldn't worry. It said you were crying because you were happy. And the weird thing is, I believed it. I didn't do a thing." His eyes were beseeching now, as if he were terrified he'd made a mistake. "What happened?"

His kindness, even more than his story, made me dissolve in tears again. I still didn't know what to say, but I gestured for him to come even closer, then whispered in his ear, "I've been trying to find God all my life, and . . . in there . . . well, I think what happened is that God found me." Even in my weakened condition, I thought this sounded overly dramatic and probably delusional. But the doctor didn't bat an eye.

"I thought maybe that was it," he said, and to my astonishment I noticed that there were tears in his eyes, too. Then he said, "In thirty years of practicing medicine, do you know how many times this kind of thing has happened to me?"

I shook my head.

"Once." He leaned forward and kissed me very softly on the forehead. Then he was gone, before I remembered to ask him which drugs he had given me, what they might have done to my brain, and whether I could please have some more.

CHAPTER 17

Dad Faces Death, Part II

My father and I have been talking for a half hour now, and I am becoming more and more relaxed, almost boldly inquisitive. "So, how do you think you'll do on your life review? I mean, assuming the near-death people are right about how death works."

I'm amazed how free it feels, just talking to my father, speaking my thoughts without editing or censoring or invoking Dueling Allusions. It's like the first time I went scuba diving, the astounding liberation of being able to move in three dimensions, up and down as well as backward, forward, left, and right. Throughout my childhood, through continuous indirect communication, I learned that a good Mormon girl doesn't ever travel in the dimension of *direct* communication. I feel almost giddy letting myself cruise along this forbidden trajectory.

"You know what I'm talking about, right?" I ask. "You've heard about people who say they see their whole lives at once, and have to sit there evaluating themselves right there with the Being of Light?"

"Of course," says my father, his eyes sharp but a little squinty, like the eyes of a confused eagle. I know that expression from my years at Harvard; it's the look of a smart person trying to appear familiar with something that has escaped his memory.

"You know, those near-death people," I explain. "They flatline or whatever, and then this Being of Light shows up, and that's when they have the life review. Sometimes they see the effects of their actions— ripples going through the entire world, all because of what they did or didn't do."

His eyes suddenly stop squinting, open wide. "Yes, yes, I know," he says impatiently. "That fellow came to talk to me about it himself, you know. Raymond Moody."

"Really?"

I'm enthralled. Raymond Moody is the author of the book *Life After Life,* which launched the common knowledge of near-death experiences into mainstream American culture. I'm not sure why he would have spent time with my father, but it's easy to believe he did. For a long time, the brethren in Salt Lake were prone to arranging visits between my father and any visiting intellectuals who showed up in Utah. I suppose the presumption was that his vast knowledge and over-the-top IQ would impress the visitors and thwart potential criticism aimed at the Church.

"Yes, of course. He came to Utah just after he published that book of his."

"Cool!" I say, meaning it. "What did you talk about?"

"Well, his work, naturally." My father picks up his battered hat, which has been sitting on the chair arm, and darts a nervous glance at the door. I think this is my cue to say good-bye with courtesy and grace, but I can't seem to muster much of either. So I just sit there and gaze at him until he starts talking again.

"Of course, we've known about all that stuff for years and years. Joseph Smith saw it all, much more clearly than anyone else could. He couldn't talk about all of it, of course, but he visited those realms. Often."

Another pause.

"And, as far as that goes," he finally says, "it happened to me, too."

"You had a near-death experience?"

"Well, yes, I guess they call it that. While I was having my appendix out. In the army. During the surgery, you know. It was all just the way Moody described it."

This is spellbinding. For years I've ached to talk about the white light, how life-changing it is to see it, how hard it is to walk through the ordinary world afterward, when you *can't* see it, at least not with your eyes. And now, of all people, my long-lost father turns out to have shared the experience.

"Tell me about it," I almost beg.

"Well," he says, settling back into his chair, casting his gaze up and his mind back, "it was during the surgery. I rose up out of my body, detached from it, and went up toward the ceiling, just as they say. And then I went through the dark tunnel."

I hold my breath for a moment, until I just have to ask, "Did you come out the other end?"

"Oh, yes."

He falls silent, tapping the arm of his chair.

"And?" I say.

No response for a moment. Thump, thump, thump. Then: "Well, it was huge. Infinite."

I nod, transfixed. I remember that sense of unlimited presence, of being connected to the whole vast universe. It had made me feel so whole, so loved, that I knew nothing up to and including death could ever really harm me.

"Didn't it feel wonderful?"

Those piercing eyes look right at me, for once. They blink.

"What?"

I kick myself for asking a leading question. I was trained to do non-directive sociological interviewing, and I've just broken the rules, projecting my own experience onto my father instead of waiting for him to articulate it himself. I hurry to rephrase the question.

"What did it feel like when you came out of the tunnel?"

My father's brow furrows, as though this is the first time he's ever considered the issue. Finally he says, "Oh, it was very empowering, I suppose. Yes, I felt very powerful."

"Really?" This intrigues me, because it is exactly the opposite of what I felt in My Most Mystical Moment. For me it had been like melting into eternity, surrendering all thought of personal power. It's another way of looking at it, I guess.

"What kind of powerful?" I asked. "Empowered in what way?"

"Well," says my father. "I could do any mathematical equation whatsoever."

Now I'm the one with the furrowed brow. Mathematical equations? My internal Allusion Manager sends up a line from a sonnet by Edna St. Vincent Millay: "Euclid alone has looked on Beauty bare." Maybe my father saw the intricate fractal geometry of things, got a sense of the mathematical perfection inherent in creation. But it's so different from my own experience that I'm taken aback.

"And that made you feel good?"

It sounds like a stupid question even as I say it, but I can't shake my fixation on the *feelings* associated with metaphysical experience. For the first twenty years of my life I was almost totally unaware of having feelings, but since then I've come to consider them far more useful and important than most thoughts (so much so that if my father's view of emotion were empirically correct, I'd be totally disfigured by warts).

"Well, of course it did," he says. "Because there had been times when I doubted my capacities in that area. But no—I saw that I could solve any equation as easily as the greatest mathematician. I had no deficiency at all."

I nod, wait. There's another awkward silence. Then I blurt, "Did you see the White Light? The Being of Light?"

"Hmm?" says my father. "Oh. Yes. That, too." He shrugs.

Well, now, there you go, says my Allusion Manager. The best laid plans of mice and men . . . I've had a plan, see, without even knowing it. Ever since my own White Light experience, I've believed that when my father encountered the Being of Light he'd be flooded with the kind of unconditional love I'd felt when I saw it. I fantasized that this experience would instantly pull all the skeletons out of his closet and transform them into healthy living things, like the righteous dead on the day Jesus makes it back to Missouri. I thought he'd understand in a flash that there is never any need to fear truth, that nothing we do can ever separate us from God's love, and that therefore everything—everything, everything, everything—is fundamentally safe. Once he had a brush with the Light, I imagined, my father and I would be right on the same wavelength.

Apparently, that hypothesis is a dog that just won't hunt.

My brain, which has already tossed many assumptions during this conversation, scrambles to come up with a new theory. It occurs to me that if our conscious identities do in fact continue after death, we actually *can* take things with us: Ideas. Thoughts. States of mind. What if I'd gone into my own surgery believing, as my father seems to, that emotion is dangerous and the intellect is God? The Being of Light was completely accepting—there's no way it would have forced any reality upon me—

so maybe I would have experienced it not as a torrent of love, but as the parts of Truth and Beauty that are wholly intellectual, rational, devoid of emotion: in other words, mathematical equations.

This is a new insight for me, but it trashes my plan to bond with my father. I'm not sure how to create an equation that will describe why I need to speak to him, why I hope we can find some common ground. Moreover, he doesn't seem nearly as rapt by contemplation of his experience as I will always be with mine. He's fidgeting with boredom as he talks about his brush with the beyond. So, I think, feeling sheepish not to have seen this before, God has a whole bunch of wavelengths, and my father and I, white light or no white light, are still on different ones. I knew I should have taken that extra course on fractal geometry.

"Well . . . ," I say, still a little disoriented, "then what happened?"

"I came back to my body, obviously," says my father. "I still had my mission to fulfill. My work to do. Always the work." He grabs his hat again and plops it on his head. "So!" he says in a voice full of hearty finality. "Time to get back to it now! Shoulder to the wheel, nose to the grindstone!"

Even in the non-Mormon world, common courtesy would dictate that I wrap up my end of the conversation. The man is old, he's tired, he's uncomfortable, and he's already shared more with me during this brief meeting than he did in my entire career as a devoted daughter, prior to the most recent decade. I'm sure any patient, high-minded, enlightened person would let him go right now.

Me, I'm just getting started.

CHAPTER 18

Blast from the Past

Two days after my surgery, I was still goofy with joy. Not only had I gotten a chance to connect with the Force, but I'd received a clean bill of health from the doctors in Salt Lake City. They didn't know exactly what had happened, but it wasn't anything to worry about. I had a lot of scar tissue in my female parts, and for some unknown reason a spontaneous tear had opened inside it. The lump they'd thought might be a tumor was actually pooled blood from the internal wound. The surgeons had drained it and left it open to heal on its own. It hurt, but that was no big deal. In fact, I was thrilled to have it, because it had taken me to the Light, the Light, the Light! My heart had a new drone note, not *please* but *thank you thank you thank you thank you* . . .

I was buoyantly praying this prayer when John came home from teaching in midafternoon. Despite my good mood, he seemed a bit nervous. The whole episode—the fainting in class, the surgery, my euphoria ever since—had unnerved him. I'd tried to tell him about the Light, but I could tell he didn't really understand. He made every effort to follow what I was saying, but my powers of description were hopelessly inadequate.

"How are you?" he asked me cautiously, putting down his briefcase.

"Fine." I smiled at him.

"You're limping. Do you feel okay?"

"John, I'm *fine*."

"Well, don't bite my head off."

"Sorry. I didn't mean to."

"Why are you so angry?" John persisted.

I frowned at him. "What do you mean? I'm not angry."

"Well, you look angry. You sound angry."

I was genuinely baffled. I didn't know what John was talking about. But when he walked up and tried to give me a hug, I realized I actually *was* feeling sort of irritable. I didn't want to be touched. I let him put his arms around me anyway.

"You want to talk about it?" he said.

I rolled my eyes. "John, I'm all right, got it? And I'm not angry."

Instead of hugging him back, I put my hands on his chest and tried to push him away. But John wouldn't be pushed. He stayed right there, his face concerned, his arms encircling me. Suddenly, I found this completely unbearable. I *was* angry now—very angry, in fact. I pushed him as hard as I could, but I was very weak at the time, and John could easily bench-press three times my weight. I've since asked him why he didn't let go of me at that moment, and he said it was because my expression showed so much rage he was afraid to let me loose, for fear I'd run wild. So he kept holding me like a boxer in the clinch, and I kept pushing him.

And then the universe exploded.

My brain seemed to erupt like a volcano, spewing up a memory that was both incredibly vivid and absolutely incomprehensible.

· · ·

I am five years old, my hands are tied, and my father is doing something that feels as though it's ripping me in two. I am stretched out on my back, legs spread, like a frog on a dissecting table, unable to see or understand what is happening, focusing as hard as I can on the cord around my hands, because it distracts me from what is happening elsewhere. A rush of strange words bounce around in my head, words my father is saying: Father Abraham. The Book of the Dead. The Book of Breathings. The prophet Joseph. Amut the Destroyer. The prophet Joseph Smith. Sacrifice. Abrahamic sacrifice. I have a dim idea that my father has been commanded by God to do what he is doing, the way Abraham was commanded to sacrifice Isaac. None of it makes any sense.

That first horrific flashback was like a nuclear detonation. It felt nearly as real as if I were actually experiencing the original event, as though the nerve impulses for perceiving it had frozen into the tissues of my body, never reaching the level of conscious awareness, and were now finally completing their long-delayed journey. Gouts of fresh blood poured from the wound between my legs. My hands went white and numb, dancing their weird, spastic tarantella (this is happening again as I write—it has happened on each of the rare occasions I have told this story—and I have to say, it makes typing really problematic).

John tells me I screamed and struggled, trapped in the circle of his arms, for about three or four minutes. He knew something monstrous was happening to me, but he had no idea what it was or how he should react. So he just held on while my memory blasted me like a fire hose. When the intensity eased to the point where I could control my own behavior again, I leaned into his chest, sobbing. The only thing I could say was, "No one's going to believe me. No one's going to believe me. No one's going to believe me."

I mean, *I* wouldn't have believed me, if I'd had a choice. The images were as real as anything I'd ever remembered, but they were stranger than anything I could have imagined. I had no idea what to make of the religious words and phrases. It was almost impossible to describe the whole thing to John, since I remembered only the disconnected, confused sensations and impressions of a terrified five-year-old. I stuttered out what disjointed explanations I could, but none of it—none of what I remembered, none of what I said—made any sense at all.

Except that it did.

My analytical mind had prudently taken a vacation to a galaxy far, far away during the bizarre tumult of the flashback. It returned when John let go of me and I began rapidly pacing the house, room to room, gasping and shaking my head like a wounded animal trying to outdistance its pain. This seemed to let my gray matter start functioning again, and more ordinary memories, things I'd never repressed, began popping into my head. They were all anomalous experiences, bits and pieces of my life I'd never quite understood. Suddenly, they all began to make sense. It was as though I had stumbled over the combination for a very complex lock, and all the tumblers were simultaneously falling into place.

•   •   •

I'm five years old, playing outside in my one-piece sunsuit, seeing blood on my thighs, feeling sick with worry—not because I'm bleeding, but because someone might have seen me, and now they'll know . . . what? My brain suddenly goes blind, and I feel the world retreating from me as though I've developed an invisible shell.

Still five, on another day, wearing another outfit. I want to play on the neighbor's swing set, but I can't because of the pain between my legs when I sit down. I know I have to hide this problem, because if anyone finds out about it, no one will ever marry me. I'm not sure how I know this, but oh, boy, do I know it.

I'm ten years old, trying to sleep, knowing the night will probably consist of several sleepless hours, followed by horrible dreams. I'm conducting the ritual I've developed to ensure that God won't make me perform an Abrahamic sacrifice. I don't know what an Abrahamic sacrifice might be, but for as long as I can remember, the fear of them has kept me awake at night. I say a long, complicated prayer, all in one breath, trying to time the "amen" so that it comes out at the exact moment the space heater turns on. I do this kneeling by the bed, even though it's cold, because it's no good to pray under the covers. Tonight I do the ritual perfectly. Even so, my heart sickens because I know it probably won't work.

I'm sixteen, and I've fallen asleep while studying on my bed. The sun has set when my father, uncharacteristically, comes to wake me up for dinner. I feel his hand on my shoulder, hear his voice, and suddenly, I'm scrambling to my feet on the bed, backing into the corner with my hands out, sobbing, "No! No!" He doesn't ask what's wrong or try to calm me down. Instead, he looks at me with an expression of the most profound despair, his shoulders slumping as though weighed down by some enormous burden. He turns around and walks out of the room, muttering. I stand there on my bed, wondering what just happened, and listen to him as he goes down the stairs, saying over and over, "I'm a terrible father, I'm a terrible father, I'm a terrible father."

I'm seventeen years old, a college freshman, and I've come to the student health services to get a prescription for a yeast infection. An intern parks me in those dreadful stirrups, performs a pelvic exam, and writes me a prescription. Then he says, "So, what are you using for birth control?"

I feel myself blush. "Don't need it. I've never . . ."

The intern gives a snort of cynical laughter. "Oh, please."

"It's true," I say, perplexed and a little offended. "I haven't."

He rolls his eyes. "I could prescribe a diaphragm for you. If not, then at least use condoms."

"Use them for what?" I say. "I don't even have a boyfriend." I guess the world outside of Utah is so jaded that doctors can't believe there's such a thing as a seventeen-year-old virgin.

"Whatever," says the doctor. "But you're being really irresponsible." I'm baffled but also very anxious. After all, this guy has just boldly gone—or at least boldly examined—where no man has gone before. Aren't doctors supposed to be able to tell? Why doesn't he believe me?

Flash forward to another doctor's office, eight years later. I'm twenty-five, and now I do need birth control, because Adam has just popped out of the oven, and I'm not in the mood for more baking just yet. But the real reason I'm visiting this obstetrician is sheer paranoia. Since producing a baby with an extra chromosome, I'm afraid of everything related to childbearing, and it seems to me that there's something weird going on Down There. I'm afraid I might have, I don't know, vaginal polyps or something.

(I must interject here that I realize that there is only one thing less appealing than mentioning one's own intimate body parts in public, and that is mentioning them in conjunction with the word *polyp*. But, like the national networks reporting on a U.S. president's colon cancer [albeit with a much less important story], I feel I have no choice.)

The obstetrician listens to my concerns, then inspects the evidence. "Naw," he says. "Those aren't polyps. You've just got a lot of scar tissue."

"Oh, great." I sigh in relief.

"Did you have an at-home delivery?"

"No. Hospital."

The doctor looks surprised. "Well, someone was asleep on the job, let-
ting you tear like that and then not even repairing it." To my relief, he
sits up and talks to my face. "See, when you tore, it pulled the tissue
apart like cloth—you get a lot of ragged edges on a vaginal tear. Your
doctor should have clipped off the ragged edges and then sewn you back
together."

"Uh-huh," I say, not really listening, just thrilled that I'm not dying
of polyps.

"I can't believe your ob-gyn didn't clean you up," the doctor contin-
ues. "You healed with all the ragged stuff sort of attaching to itself every
which way—that's why there are skin tags all over. I could go in there
and clean it up for you surgically, if you want."

"Nope," I say. "I'm fine."

. . .

And I was. I didn't even think about this examination again until
three years later, as I confirmed with John that I'd never torn during
childbirth; with each delivery, I had a tiny, tidy episiotomy, a small cut to
ensure that I *didn't* tear. Doctors two and three had specifically told
me that they would cut over the previous scar, so there would only be
one. The doctor who discussed my scar tissue with me said that it was
largely internal, with only a few obvious wounds visible upon cursory
inspection.

What suddenly seemed even stranger than the presence of ragged
scar tissue was that I had never, not for one single second, wondered
where or how I got it.

John was following me through our house, still confused, but slowly
becoming less so. As he digested what I was saying, his face took on the
look of someone who has just figured out the plot to a particularly
baffling murder mystery.

"That's why you space out when I touch you," he said. "That's why
you scream in your sleep. That's why you can never really relax. And all
those surgeries—do you think they were connected?" Along with his
words, another grab bag of recollections popped into my mind: fissures
and abscesses, lesions and adhesions, all in body parts you're never supposed to mention in polite company.

• • •

I'm twenty-six, lying in another damned emergency room. The doctor has just told me that I waited so long to seek treatment for an abscess in the tissues of my perineum (look it up) that he's afraid infection might enter my bloodstream any minute. There's no time to put me under general anesthesia, so he gives me a shot of Novocain in a very private place, then hands me a clean washcloth and tells me to bite down on it. "Please don't hate me," he says, and starts operating.

Numbed by the local, I don't even feel the first incision. But then he sticks a pair of scissors into it, and the pain is just absolutely incredible. I've never felt anything this bad, not in childbirth, not when a dentist accidentally drilled right into a nerve. I am positive that I've hit the limit of my pain capacity, that nothing could possibly hurt more than this. Then the doctor opens the scissors inside the incision, and I realize I was wrong. And then, oh, Lordy. Then he starts to cut.

• • •

Out of all my medical misadventures, this memory stood out most in my mind the day of my first flashback—not just because the injury was related to those badly healed scars, but because the pain my body felt during that surgery was the only thing I could compare to the pain my mind and heart felt when the flashbacks started. It wasn't simply the agony and degradation of being raped but, more, the absolute horror of a five-year-old who has just learned that the universe is ruled by an evil god and that this god seems to have commanded the most beloved and powerful figure in her life to destroy her in a manner much more devastating than death. "We all have our little sorrows," said my Allusion Manager, quoting screenwriter Ronald Harwood even at this awful pass, "and the littler you are, the larger the sorrow."

But that day, right after the flashbacks started, my inner adult wasn't coping a whole lot better than my inner child. There was nothing, *nothing* I could possibly have dreamed up that would have devastated my entire life as completely as believing that the memory I had just experienced was real. I didn't want to believe it—God, did I ever not want to believe it—but I couldn't stop the corroborating evidence from popping into my mind, the rapid click click click of more mental tumblers falling into place.

. . .

I'm twenty-three and have just become a mother. I'm chatting with my oldest sister, my mentor in parenting matters. She's repeating some-thing I've heard her say over and over: that once your children reach the age of four, you must stop touching them except when it is absolutely necessary—no hugs, no cuddles, no kisses. My sister explains that this is because to any child over four, all touch is sexual. I'm wondering why this piece of advice, which is conventional wisdom in our family, never shows up in any of the parenting books I read. I suppose it's something psychology has yet to discover.

. . .

And so it continued all day long, my grotesque trip down memory lane. Both John and I were way too freaked out to work; instead, we talked all afternoon until it was time to pick up the kids, then rented a cartoon video for them so that we could talk all evening, then put them to bed and talked most of the night.

I was overwhelmed by horror, shame, and fear, but at the same time I felt a sense of relief and clarity like nothing I'd ever experienced. Aston-ishing, titanic surges of grief shuddered through me, but for the first time ever the sorrow seemed to flow out with my tears. The sense of poison draining from my mind was as clear and real as the feeling of blood drain-ing from my physical wound.

Around 5 a.m., with an exhausted John snoozing beside me, I fell asleep for maybe a half hour. I woke up slowly, and only when I was fully conscious did I notice that I was lying in a very strange position. I'd kicked off the covers and scooted way down to the middle of the bed, where I lay on my back, my hands stretched above my head, crossed at the wrist, the right hand over the left. My knees were bent, the soles of my feet pressed together, and my legs shoved out sideways at a very awk-ward angle, like a butterfly's wings. They pulled my lower back into a deep arch. It was a very uncomfortable position, and I lay there some-what amazed that I could even achieve it.

Then I noticed something even more surprising. For the first time in months, the searing, sore-throat tenderness in my back, hips, and hands had disappeared. It was as though my body had decided to send me a message by posing this way, so it no longer needed to tell its story through pain. *Remember what happened to me,* it was saying. *Never forget again.*

How many times since that night have I woken up in exactly this position? A thousand? Two thousand? Whatever the number, the night before I began writing this chapter it happened again: I blinked awake from a thick black oblivion to find myself, once more, in the position of a frog about to be dissected. It was weirdly reassuring. Well, here I am again, I thought. Without my knowledge or consent, my body has once more arranged itself in this bizarre position. This isn't something I do on purpose. It isn't something that happens for no reason. It isn't something I made up. *Never forget again.*

This is what I remember.

CHAPTER 19

Ran Dori

*R*an dori, which literally means "chaotic fighting," has always been my least favorite part of the martial arts. I'd started studying karate in my thirties to get over my paralyzing fear of being physically attacked, so it was very strange for me to stand across the dojo from my karate buddies and realize that *I* was expected to attack *them*. I had no idea what to do; the thought of running up and whacking somebody felt about as natural to me as standing on my head at a cocktail party. Now it's my father squared off against me, across a hotel room instead of a dojo, and though my only weapons are words, it's still hard to make myself use them on someone who isn't taking the offensive.

"I know you'd like to get going," I stammer, sounding ambivalent even to myself, "but I want . . . I mean, there are a couple of things I need to ask you first."

His face tenses into an expression that looks like annoyance, but I recognize it as fear. How do I get him to understand that one of my major objectives is to *free* him from fear, not mire him in it even more deeply?

That was the other difficult thing about *ran dori:* it required fighting without hurting. Nothing is easier than unscrupulous combat; just grab a big rock, wait until your opponent's back is turned, and clobber him. But rendering someone harmless without causing any harm yourself—now, that's a pisser. It requires an enormous amount of training, restraint, athleticism, subtlety, and to be perfectly honest, luck. I was never very good at it.

"Here's what I want to know," I say, deciding on a direct frontal attack. "What were you doing with all that Egyptian stuff? I mean, when you were performing your 'Abrahamic sacrifices' on me?"

The blow lands right on target; my father flinches, his face flashing an expression that tells me a great deal. It isn't just frightened. It certainly isn't confused. It's *knowing,* in a way that both chills and reassures me. It tells me that while I can't trust him, I can trust my own memory.

"What do you mean?" my father asks, his voice cracking a little.

"Oh, come on," I say. "There's no reason to pretend. We were both there."

In this I feel completely secure. I needed all my martial arts training, plus a battery of hidden loved ones, to muster up the nerve to sit in a room alone with this little old man. But in one way, I can have more confidence in him than in anyone else on earth: He's the only person who knows for a fact that I'm not making anything up. He's the only person I don't have to worry about convincing.

"I remember you talking a lot about Abraham and a lot about Egypt," I tell him. "The first part I understand—the sacrifice of Isaac and everything—but that Egyptian stuff . . ." I shake my head. "I just don't see how it tied in."

He takes his hat off, begins rotating it between his hands as he stares at the floor in front of him.

"Really," I make my voice soft. "I just want to understand."

"Never happened," says my father.

"Dad, I've got the scars. I remember."

He twirls his hat faster for a moment, then abruptly stops.

"This was prophesied, you know," he says.

My father is a talented sparring opponent, I'll say that for him. He really knows how to throw me off balance.

"What?"

"Yes," he says, "it was prophesied that Satan would take from me even my most beloved child. Anything to stop my work."

Goodness, he's using moves I never even knew he had. "It was prophesied" is unquestionably weird, bringing Satan into the discussion even weirder, but at least both these approaches are in character for my father. The phrase that really startles me is "most beloved child." During my acquaintanceship with my father, words like *beloved* only came from his mouth firmly ensconced in quotations. In my wildest dreams, I would never have expected him to use that word to describe me. It's a surprise he's been saving for nearly forty years, apparently restraining himself from expressing affection or initiating connection through conversations, phone calls, letters, or other means.

I remember, with an ignominious surge of self-pity, the only time I called my father on the phone. It was a very dark night when I was a seventeen-year-old college freshman, diligently trying to starve myself to death. I'd collapsed during a long run, six or seven miles away from my dorm, and after lying in the snow for a while, realized that I probably wasn't going to die that night. I couldn't figure out why the hell not—I hadn't eaten for three days, my ears were ringing, I was light-headed to the point of delirium, and I was seriously underdressed for the subzero temperatures. Devastated by the suspicion that I would survive the night, I finally surrendered to it and crawled into a phone booth for protection from the wind. The presence of the phone, along with my urge to seek comfort, overwhelmed my better judgment. I called home, collect. My father answered, and when the operator asked if he would accept the call my teenage reserve buckled under the weight of my neediness. "Please, Daddy," I sobbed over her official-sounding voice. "Please talk to me!" All my father said before he hung up—speaking to the operator, not to me—was, "Of course not."

"My most beloved child"? Where the hell did *that* come from? Then a thought occurs to me, and I feel the click of yet another tumbler locking into place. My Allusion Manager dredges up the famous story from Genesis "God did tempt Abraham, and said unto him, Abraham: and he said, Behold, here I am. And he said, take now thy son, thine only son Isaac, whom thou lovest, and get thee into the land of Moriah; and offer him there for a burnt offering."

"This is how Satan works," my father continues. "And he's always taken a special interest in me, I can tell you that." He shakes his head mournfully. "It's the price you pay for defending the Gospel."

I'm suddenly reminded of an acquaintance who was a missionary in Japan when the local Mormon authorities decided to print up glossy English-language brochures, using them to lure prospective converts with the promise of English lessons. Unfortunately, they left one letter out of the word *Satan* and handed out thousands of leaflets informing the confused Japanese that someone named Stan was trying to drag them down to hell.

"This isn't about the devil," I say to my father, "it's about posttraumatic stress disorder. I think you've got it—from your childhood and the war and who knows what else—and you passed it on to me. In your own wacky way. One of those family gifts that keeps on giving."

My attempt to lighten the mood goes over like a pregnant pole-vaulter.

"Yes," my father mutters, his eyes oddly fixed, almost glazed. "He's tried to destroy me every way he can."

I assume he's talking about Stan, and I think he's expecting me to be shamed or frightened by the implication that I'm colluding with the devil. He's wrong; as a Mormon apostate, I've been considered the vilest kind of sinner for years, and I block the strike, disbelieving him completely, without a second thought.

I'm contemplating my next best move when my father takes the initiative and launches a new attack, leaning forward and raising his eyes to a place just a few inches right of my face. When his voice comes out, it's different, harsh and low, almost guttural.

"You and your trendy illnesses," he says. "Depression, that anorexia thing. Very fashionable, aren't you?"

He really is good. This time I don't even counter, just sit there in desolate surprise. Until this moment, I didn't know my father was familiar with the word *anorexia,* much less aware that I've had it—the weight-loss guide for teens he'd given me was hardly a clear signal. I remember the endless years of slow starvation, the physical and emotional agony, the slow-healing wounds on my wrists from "hesitation cuts," which helped me get through the days but which I never had the courage to turn into full-fledged suicide. I always thought my father was simply oblivious to it all. Now I realize he might actually have noticed. What a concept.

"And now you have this false-memory syndrome," my father continues, spitting the words as though they are a particularly infectious sort of phlegm.

The words don't scare me, but the rage in his voice does. A lot. My fear makes no rational sense—I'm healthy, comparatively fit, training for my black belt test, and he's about a million years old—but what about this conversation is rational?

"To think that my own child would act in league with Satan . . ." My father's voice quivers with fury.

I'm terrified. I didn't expect this, because I never remember seeing my father angry. That in itself is strange, because my siblings have told me that he always had a violent temper, and that I was one of his favorite targets. They think I made up allegations of sexual abuse because he hit me so much. I don't recall a single blow, but some of them must have been pretty energetic, judging from what my siblings say. I do remember that my father broke my little sister's collarbone in a fit of pique when she was about two years old, and one of my brothers told me about being "spanked" with sturdy wooden hangers so hard and long that on one occasion my father broke three hangers in a row against my brother's body before he calmed down.

"It's revolting," says my father now. "These ridiculous allegations all over the country—and there's no truth to any of them. No evidence whatsoever. Prove one case to me, if you can. All fiction."

The power of his voice to frighten me is almost magical. I literally duck in my chair, brace myself for assault. But that action now triggers a slew of other memories: countless occasions when I've faced an opponent across a rubber mat and made myself move forward instead of retreating. I can almost hear my sensei egging me on, my sparring partners cheering for me even at the moment I manage to throw them. My karate experience is one of the reasons I still love men: their protectiveness, their clear sense of justice, their determination to serve the weak. No one ever tried to hurt me in karate, even though, what with my frequent childhood regressions and all, I had a tendency to bite.

"I really don't know anything about other cases of child abuse," I say to my father. "I imagine some of the accusations are valid, and some aren't. I only have the evidence in this one."

"Do you see?" my father whispers furiously to some unseen audience. "Do you see how she twists things?"

"Really, Dad, don't you even wonder why I've got so much scar tissue that my doctors think I tore in childbirth? Me, your most beloved child?

I mean, Dad, if you love me so much, why doesn't anything I've said make you want to know more? How come you've never talked to me about this whole issue—or, for that matter, about anything?"

This seems to give him pause. It's like watching an actor realize he's been breaking character. Damn, missed a line. What to do, what to do? Then my father's jaw clenches, and he draws himself up to his full height. He speaks as though he has an audience of thousands.

"It's the Salem witch trials all over again," he announces bitterly. "Satan creates these ridiculous allegations, and the Lord's servants are the first targets."

The stentorian voice seems calculated to cow me again, but I'm over that. My father has slipped up so many times during our little sparring match that I'm beginning to think I might be at least as good a fighter. That's more than enough to turn the tide in *ran dori*. Now, instead of shrinking into a terrified five-year-old's desperate combat style, I take a deep breath and center myself in the part of me that's used to fighting: the Harvard-trained sociologist.

"It's interesting, isn't it?" I say. "The whole recovered-memory trend. I've spent a lot of time wondering why so many people are claiming to have memories of abuse. Maybe the American soldiers who had posttraumatic stress from World War II ended up abusing their kids because they weren't treated themselves. Of course we're only talking about a tiny fraction of veterans, guys who were already pretty unstable before the war. But since they had so many children at about the same time, you'd still get high absolute numbers of abused victims in the baby boom generation. They're just reaching the age when repressed childhood memories tend to reemerge."

This approach surprises my father right out of his anger. Suddenly, we're not father and daughter; we're two intellectuals trading ideas. His transformation is visible, vicious Mr. Hyde changing back to the affable Dr. Jekyll. He sits up and cocks his head inquisitively, curious. I love his curiosity. I always have.

"But I think it's more likely that there were always a certain percentage of children being sexually abused, and the late twentieth century was the first time our entire culture began talking about it publicly. People don't talk about trauma when their society is going to react with hostility. They don't even remember it. They start remembering and talking when they realize there might be a chance to find sanctuary."

My father's head is still turned at that inquisitive angle. Someone in there is listening intensely. Not just closely, but eagerly; not with defensiveness, but with desperate hope. I can feel it. And I'd bet my last dime I know who that someone is.

"From what I know, I think you were sexually abused by your mother," I say.

My father's eyes open wide, filled with fear, and now I'm sure I'm right: I've made contact with a small boy who has been waiting the better part of a century for someone to find out, someone to believe him, someone to be *his* sanctuary. I know exactly how he feels.

"You know," I say, "we're really a lot alike. Who knows what choices I would have made, if I were male, if I'd been abused by my mother, if I'd been born when you were? I really have no idea."

This is true. As absolutely as I oppose what my father did to me, as violently as I would physically attack anyone I caught doing it to another child, I know too much to assume that he could have simply controlled himself. I know how stored horror can torture the mind, how utterly despair can shatter the will. I know that my way of thinking really is similar to my father's, and I know how relentlessly pain can dominate it. Ironically, by passing on his genetic makeup and then sending me to hell in early childhood, my father used both nature and nurture to create one of the few people who can really understand him.

Who knows, I think, as my father's ninety-one-year-old face assumes the expression of a devastated child, maybe there is some divine symmetry in this, some way God is trying to transmute even this man's most insane actions into an avenue through which he can be rescued and healed. I believe this is one of God's very best party tricks, the alchemy that transforms evil and suffering into compassion and joy—though I don't believe for a minute that God ordered my father to offer me up as a sacrifice. That's what I remember being told, but it's not something the God of my acquaintance would do. No, that would be my father's own illness, his twisted psychology, his pain. I don't believe in a devil, but I'd guess that my father feels the dark force of his own madness as the Evil One. That's close enough.

Stan, Stan, Stan, I think as I relax a little into my chair, finding to my surprise that I am willing to trust my father—trust him to act completely insane—and convinced for the moment that he isn't going to lunge at me with a wooden hanger. That Stan. Really. What a nut.

Understanding Dad

A week after my first flashback, I'd entered a phase called the flooding stage of dealing with trauma. Intrusive and horrible memories kept forcing their way into my consciousness, at times and places I wasn't able to control. It seemed there were other occasions of abuse besides that first one, though none as strange nor as completely devastating. That's because after the first time, I seemed to have mastered the fine art of dissociation, so that my mind and soul could just go away when unpleasant things were happening to my body.

Even so, the memories were pretty horrific. I felt as though my soul had swallowed some hideous toxin twenty years before, felt queasy and unwell ever since, and was now vomiting up every sickening thing I'd ever experienced. I was barely managing to take care of my children, my weight kept dropping, and I spent virtually all the nighttime hours crying instead of sleeping.

As part of the discipline of a spiritual camel, I'd been in the habit of speaking to my mother quite frequently on the phone, as well as visiting the swimming-pool-blue house a couple of times a week to bring dinner or help with housework. I'd stopped abruptly when the flashbacks started, so I wasn't surprised when my mother called to see what was up. I did feel rather panicky, though—what was I supposed to say to her?

I decided that the wisest course of action was to keep my problems to myself, though I wasn't sure I could sound nonchalant.

"I haven't heard from you for days," my mother said. "Are you all right?"

I closed my eyes and pounded the heel of one hand against my forehead. "Yeah. Yeah, I'm okay." I fought with every fiber to sound normal, but I was terrified. It had only been a couple of years since I'd stopped being the target of my mother's enormous anger. We'd reached a tenuous friendship because I'd finally learned to behave like a grown-up, but now I didn't feel like a grown-up, and my mother's voice had once more become what it was to me in childhood: a signal of looming danger.

"Why don't you come down and see us?" said my mother. "I'm worried about your father. He's not sleeping at all since you stopped calling. He paces all night, and he's taking a lot of sleeping pills, but they don't help. He's even been taking them during the day—I've never seen him like this. I'm not sure what's wrong. Seeing you always seems to calm him down so much."

I took a deep breath. "Um, listen, Mom—Mother. I'm not doing so well. I think I need some time to, uh, be alone."

There was a long silence, and then my mother said, "Is this about something that happened to you when you were a child?"

"Yes." It slipped out, in a whisper, before I could rein it back. I was horrified. It felt like a terribly dangerous thing to say.

"Did your father abuse you? Sexually?"

I was just stunned. After about a week and a half, I managed to stammer, "I think . . . maybe . . . yes."

"You were about five, weren't you?"

"Uh-huh," I said, still dazed and confused. "Five. It stopped just before I turned eight. Because I was baptized. If it happened after I was baptized, the sin would stay with me." I remembered this in my bones, remembered my desperation to "enter the waters of baptism," remembered wondering why, after my ceremonial immersion, I didn't feel as clean as I'd hoped.

"When did it happen?"

"When you were at the doctor with the baby, the first time. All the other kids were at school."

"Ever at night?"

"Four o'clock," I whispered.

"Yes," she said tersely. "That was always the time. How often?"

"I don't know."

I was so nauseated I could barely speak. I was in shock, torn between accepting her support and fearing a backlash. Finally I stammered, "I can't believe you believe me."

"Why shouldn't I believe you?" said my mother in a dead-calm voice. "I know him better than you do."

Within days, my mother would deny that she had ever uttered these words, but they are seared into my memory as if she'd physically branded them on my brain. Though she would soon begin a phone campaign to discredit me, calling everyone she knew and telling them I was a vindictive lunatic, those words were a gift my mother could not take back. She was well into her sixties, totally dependent on my father, so sick in body and heart that for decades, she had barely left her house. But before the overwhelming currents of her life could drag her under completely, she fought just long enough to throw her drowning seventh child a rope, and I will always, always be grateful.

"You know, your grandmother was very strange," my mother was saying. She was talking about my father's mother, who had died before I was born. "There was always something so *creepy* about the way she talked to him. She used to tell me, 'I think he'd be such a fabulous lover.' Something in her voice . . . I don't know, it just made my skin crawl. Once I walked in when she was kissing him—kissing him on the mouth, and not like a mother. He looked paralyzed. Rigid. Like a corpse."

I recalled a brief encounter with a stranger when I was in my teens. A woman sitting next to me at the doctor's office turned to me and said, "I knew your father growing up." I wasn't surprised—strangers mentioned my father out of the blue all the time—but then the woman added, "I knew his mother, too." She glared at me as though I'd committed some kind of crime. I stammered, "That's nice," but the woman shook her head slowly. "No," she said. "She was a monster."

I pulled my attention back to my own mother's voice in the receiver. "That woman!" she fumed. "Did you know she used to put bee venom on his genitals when he was growing up? Said she was doing it for his health, but that was nonsense. It felt like acid burning him. It was torture."

"I know."

I'd been doing plenty of thinking about my father's psychological history, trying to make sense of my own life, and this was a hobby I'd learned from my mother. Throughout my childhood, she'd spent an enormous amount of time trying to figure out her distant, difficult husband by talking over his eccentricities with a few close friends. I couldn't count the times I'd hidden under the kitchen table, picking at the scabs on my knees and listening to her side of the latest phone call as she discussed the latest pop-psych book she'd read, then inevitably returned to a recitation of the many horrific deeds perpetrated by her dearly departed pioneer mother-in-law. My mother clearly knew these stories were unusual and appalling, but the clinical vocabulary of incest—words like *abuse, repression, posttraumatic stress*—weren't yet in popular parlance, especially not in Utah. In light of my new memories, however, these old stories took on enormous significance.

"You know," my mother went on, "once, she told me that when your father was a teenager and she'd go into his room in the middle of the night, he would snarl at her like an animal. I remember thinking, now, why would she be walking into her teenage son's room in the middle of the night?"

Since my flashbacks began, I'd been reading up on the subject of child sexual abuse and had learned much more than I ever wanted to know. It felt very strange, but given my mother's support, I dared to venture a suggestion. "The research says that sons who are abused by their mothers get more mixed up than just about anybody."

My mother let out a long breath through her teeth. "That woman," she said. "She was horrible. I never met a crueler person."

"It wasn't just his mother, though," I said. "I think the war messed him up a lot, too."

I'd come to this conclusion after reading about the dynamics of psychological repression, which allows people to live through unbearable circumstances by dissociating and erasing memory but causes all sorts of disturbing symptoms until the memory is regained and emotionally processed. The syndrome was first noticed in shell-shocked soldiers, and my father seemed to me to be a classic case. He'd spent a lot of time on the front lines, seen death and atrocities. I'd heard that during World War II, American soldiers coined the word *fubar,* an acronym I will euphemistically render as "fouled up beyond all recognition." As I researched the traumatized mind, it became more and more clear to me that if my father's mother hadn't managed to thoroughly fubar his brain, the war certainly could have finished the job.

While I was growing up, if any of my siblings asked our father to tell a war story, he'd usually respond with gruff refusal. But other times he would go into a kind of storyteller's trance, recounting adventures that were exciting to hear about, though they must have been hell to experience. He'd talk about the way everything slowed down in the middle of a battle, so that a minute might seem to take an hour. He'd reminisce about his British buddies, who stopped fighting to have tea at 4 p.m. no matter what was exploding around them. He told us about his Jewish friend, who would flick buttons off captured Nazi soldiers' uniforms with a razor-sharp knife, button by button, as my father interrogated them in perfect German.

The way my father told these stories, you'd think World War II was a faintly comical and very exciting game. But sometimes the content was so grim that even his breezy attitude couldn't mask it. I once heard him describe how he'd been sitting next to a friend on an army cot when the friend blew out his own brains with a service revolver. My father carried an ancient, yellowish leather briefcase spattered with dark rust-colored stains; once he mentioned in an offhand way that he'd grabbed the briefcase from the wreckage of a bombed-out German building and that the rust-stains were human blood. He also told one of my brothers about a time when he'd served with a unit of convicted felons who'd been allowed to fight in Europe rather than finish their prison time in the States. They'd captured a church in France where a wedding was taking place, and several of the Americans had taken turns raping the bride.

The first real conversation my father ever had with John was about the war. They were talking in the Mormon temple on the morning of our wedding, during the part of the ceremony when the men and women were going through separate rituals. My father was sitting to the left of his new son-in-law. Suddenly, incongruously, he leaned over and began whispering to John about a time during the war when he'd discovered a group of prisoners who had been stripped, bound with barbed wire, raped, and left to die of exposure. John thought this a very odd topic for my father to discuss with someone he'd barely met, who was in the process of marrying his daughter. But eight years later, when my own strange memories burst out, it seemed to fit a pattern.

My mother and I talked about all this for a long time, maybe as much as an hour. We discussed my father's five o'clocks, his frequent nightmares, his terror of his mother, his constant psychological dissociation, the load of horrors his artistic, intelligent mind had carried for decades. It seemed to me that life had set him up to have two lives: the child genius hiding the pain of a molestation victim and the sensitive scholar forced to act like a toughened, jaded soldier. He showed the cheerful side to the world, hiding the aftereffects of unbearable torments in the complicated folds of his brilliant mind and eccentric behavior.

"That poor, poor man," my mother said at last. "No wonder he's been so upset. You'd better come down right away, see what you can do to make him feel better."

Despite my analysis of my father's psychological background, despite my sympathy for his situation, this suggestion brought on a violent surge of nausea. The thought of actually encountering my father was almost unbearable. "I'll try," I said, noticing that the burning pain had suddenly returned to my hands and hips.

"It's his birthday Thursday," my mother reminded me. "You could make a cake, bring the kids down."

My head was spinning. At the start of our conversation, I'd been worried that my mother would attack me—maybe kill me—if I ever voiced the memories that had been bludgeoning me for a week. Instead, she seemed almost glad to support my assertions. But now it was clearly time to tidy up the mess, lock it away, and move on with life.

"He's been just impossible to deal with lately," she said. "Now can you see what I've had to deal with, all this time? Honestly, that man . . ."

As surprised as I was that she agreed with me, I was more surprised as I realized why she was so willing to agree. The reason was that what had happened to me didn't matter. It simply didn't matter. Life would go on exactly as it had before I remembered. My father was a legend, God's chosen servant, and all of us had to help manage the annoying quirks that accompanied his mighty calling. Nothing could get in the way of that.

"He likes that yellow cake I used to make," said my mother. "With the seven-minute icing, you know."

This took a minute for me to process. I'd spent the past days besieged by intrusive flashes of such awful memories that I thought I'd lose my mind. I felt as emotionally battered as if I'd just crawled out of an alley where I'd been raped and tortured. My mother's reaction was to suggest that I could make the rapist a nice birthday cake. A yellow one. With seven-minute icing. Which is difficult to make under *any* circumstances. I felt like a five-year-old again, realizing in every cell the desolate reality that there never had been and never would be any shelter from my father's terrible God.

Then it occurred to me that millions of women have probably been expected to cook and serve tasty treats to men who have raped them. Maybe it really was no big deal. After all, my father was a hero to his country and his Church, a courageous spiritual giant who had channeled all the tragedies of his own life into the service of God. Considering everything he'd done right, maybe what he'd done wrong—what he'd done to me—really *was* insignificant. Nevertheless, as my mother and I agreed on a time for me to bring my father's birthday cake, I felt as though a ton of gravel had been dumped on my head. I had never known such utter despair.

• • •

Three days later, numb as a block of salt, I drove my children to the swimming-pool-blue house. My mother didn't mention anything about our phone conversation. We sang "Happy Birthday" to my father and cut the cake, and I carried a plate to him just as I had hundreds of times throughout my childhood. Until then, I was fine. I just kept my eyes turned away from him and thought about faraway things. In fact, it occurred to me that I was behaving toward my father exactly as he had behaved toward me for as long as I could remember. But when I served his cake I could see his hands, and (much worse) I could *smell* him. He had the smell of slightly musty clothes, nothing offensive in and of itself. But the display of images that forced themselves into my mind when I inhaled that scent nearly made me retch.

I abruptly rounded up my children, carried the two little ones to the car, strapped all three into their car seats, apologized as best I could, and screeched out of the driveway going much, much too fast. I drove home with the radio turned up high, hoping my kids couldn't hear me crying. I really didn't know that I would never go back.

CHAPTER 21

Silence

These days, I love silence. Crave it, in fact. I go out of my way to hear it every day, using all sorts of strategies I learned during my spiritual camel phase (including the meditation technique taught to me by my favorite anesthesiologist). For the first few minutes, my brain clatters and clangs like a stovetop of agitated, boiling pots and pans. But then I begin to hear the great silence around me, the stillness that underlies all sound. It seems to awaken a version of the same silence that lives within me. The two pools of quiet reach out for each other like magnets, like water droplets on a windshield. When they meet, the cacophony of my mind slows, calms, and on a good day, for a moment, stops.

This isn't a dramatic event. No angels appear, no bushes burst into flame. I don't even get a quick visual of my old pal the White Light. It's better than that. In the silence, I feel a gentle, infinite peace, as sweet as the feeling the Light brought with it, and always available. It trickles into me like cool water down a parched throat, like love into a lonely heart, and I don't really care whether it comes from a higher power or from the working of my meditation-primed brain. Whatever its source, connecting with it makes life feel like a gorgeous unfolding miracle instead of a doomed Sisyphean struggle.

It's strange to look back now at a time when silence was my worst enemy—though of course, that was a different sort of silence. Silence comes in two varieties: one that nourishes and comforts; another that chokes, smothers, and isolates. Solitary confinement is the worst kind of imprisonment we can inflict on fellow humans, and if you are forced to keep silent about some dark secret, you live in solitary confinement. Without the bridge of communication connecting you to other human beings, you can't share your burdens, can't receive comfort, can't con-firm that you still belong. Silence is the abyss that separates you from hope. The silence I kept in the weeks after my flashbacks began was this second kind, as malignant as cancer. I'd enforced my own silence to avoid interfering with other people's connection to God. Now I know that it had exactly the opposite effect.

· · ·

My mother called me the morning after my father's aborted birthday party, and from the moment I heard her voice, I knew our recent mother-daughter lovefest was over. The night before, I'd furtively slipped her a book on sexual abuse that included a section on sons molested by their mothers. I thought it might help her understand my father, who, judging by what I knew of his history and personal quirks, was a walking textbook of unhealed incest wounds. My mother, always an avid reader, polished off this particular book within a day.

"It's all nonsense," she told me on the phone, without even saying hello. I could see her in my mind's eye, scowling at the offending volume. "If you believe this woman" (she meant the author) "we should *all* be in therapy. I mean, I was molested as a child, and it never bothered me a bit."

"You were?" I said. "It didn't?" I might have guessed; this history was typical of women who end up married to abusers.

"Yes, more than once," she said irritably. "When I was six, and then a few years later—he was a teacher—and it had no effect on me at all."

"But, Mom," I said. "I mean, Mother, it probably did. I mean, you were depressed for so many years. Don't you think you should maybe see a therapist or—"

"Ridiculous!" my mother fumed, still fussing at the self-help book. "I don't believe a word of it, and you shouldn't either."

"Well," I said, "but—"

"And your father would never do any such thing," my mother continued.

I felt dizzy again. "But you said—"

"I said nothing of the kind. You've always made up stories like that. Ever since you were a baby."

The world was upside down. Oh my God, I thought. She must be right, she's my mother. I must have made it all up—even the conversation where she supported me—but the crazy thing was, I could still remember all of it. Could I possibly be so sick, so fundamentally evil, to invent fantasies of abuse by my own father and then imagine that my mother believed me? I wanted to kill myself, but I didn't think I'd have to, because I was pretty sure my skull was about to implode under the weight of so much shame. But then I heard other voices, the voices of my brothers and sisters gossiping after our parents were asleep, when I was in grade school and my siblings were teenagers.

"I don't think she's . . . normal."

"I don't think he is, either. They're both crazy."

"No kidding. Look at this house."

"What is *wrong* with them?"

I truly think that those memories—the strong, clear, never-forgotten memories of my brothers and sisters—saved me from dying when my mother retracted her support. The child in me still had allies, and because of that, because of Valhalla, I could stay connected to the core of me, the part that knew everything.

When my mother spoke again, her voice had lost its angry edge; now she sounded placating. "They just announced that your father won the Exemplary Manhood Award," she said. "They're having a ceremony next week. He's just fit to be tied, he's so nervous. Will you come?"

I couldn't even follow her train of thought, let alone climb aboard. "Um, Mom, I'm sorry, but I'm not doing very well. I think I need to see a therapist or something."

There was a long silence. A bad silence. The kind of silence that had terrified me as a child, a silence with long, sharp teeth. Finally my mother said, stiffly, "You're not going to tell some therapist . . . what you told me. Are you?"

This was very confusing, because now she *did* seem to remember that we'd had a conversation. I leaned my head against the wall. "I have to do something," I said. "I can't sleep. I can't eat. I can't take care of my kids. The books say therapy helps."

"Hmph!" my mother snorted, dismissing the books. "This is not just about you, you know. You've always been this way, so self-centered. There are bigger things at stake here."

I nodded. Of course. What was I thinking? I can't see a therapist. Other people can. People whose fathers aren't pillars of major world religions. But not me. For me, there's no way out of solitary confinement.

"Think how many people's testimonies of the Gospel depend on your father."

Yes, yes, she was right again. A "testimony of the Gospel," the belief that the Mormon Church is the one true religion, matters more to Latter-day Saints than life, liberty, and the pursuit of happiness put together. What had I been thinking, to consider a course of action that might potentially damage other Saints' testimonies?

"Okay," I said. I wasn't sobbing, but tears had begun flowing from my eyes in a continuous stream. "But if I only told a therapist—"

"What about the *therapist's* testimony?" said my mother.

"I'll go to a non-Mormon," I said. "Someone who's never heard of him."

"There is no one who has never heard of your father." My mother spoke with such absolute assurance that I realized it was hopeless to disagree.

"Whatever, Mom," I murmured.

"And I don't like it when you call me that," she added. "I hate the word *Mom*."

I almost said, "So do I," but stopped myself in time, shocked at my own filial impropriety.

I later learned that immediately after this conversation, my mother began her telephone campaign, calling everyone she knew to warn them that I'd gone nuts and was spouting lies like some sort of berserk Greek tragedian. This spread the word about my allegations far faster than I could have, even if I'd wanted to—which I didn't. At the time, I was determined to behave exactly as my mother wanted me to: deal with my problems privately, get on with my life, and keep my mouth shut. That really was my plan. Its only flaw was that it made being me completely unbearable.

. . .

Of course, I wasn't utterly alone; I talked to John endlessly, and though his support kept me from acting on frequent suicidal impulses, he couldn't fix me. He was having enough trouble dealing with his own feelings, his sadness, horror, and rage, while trying to respect my urgent request to keep quiet. I began to long for someone else to talk to, someone who knew how to handle the enormous mess in my mind.

After a few wretched weeks, I decided to confide in a close friend from Boston (I'll call her Laura) who was a psychotherapist as well as a devout Mormon. I knew I could count on Laura to keep my secret and desperately hoped she might be able to help me feel a little less like blowing my head off. You should have seen the circus act my hands put on when, after swearing Laura to secrecy, I began to describe my memories over the phone. I had to hold the receiver between my shoulder and my ear, watching in amazement as white bands appeared around both of my wrists and my jerking, twitching fingers turned deep purple. It distracted me but not enough to stop me from dreading my friend's response. I was desperately afraid she wouldn't believe me, desperately afraid that she would, desperately afraid of what she'd think of me, either way. I was a little taken aback when her first response wasn't about me at all.

"This could be a serious problem for the Church," Laura said.

"The Church?" I said, sounding young and stupid.

"Yeah, there are a lot of testimonies at stake. Ordinarily I'd advise someone in your situation to talk about it, but you really can't. You understand that, don't you?"

"Um . . . yes?"

"I mean it, Martha," Laura said. "You can't tell anyone anything. At all. Okay?"

"Okay," I said, trying not to let her hear that I'd begun to cry. Again.

"Maybe this is your mission," said Laura in a soothing voice. "To protect the Church. To honor the secret."

"Okay," I said again. I don't remember the rest of the conversation. All I remember is the silence closing in around me, closing out hope.

A few days later I tried one more time, with one more friend. Deborah was another pedigreed Daughter of the Utah Pioneers, with an aristocratic Mormon heritage at least as impressive as mine. She listened to my shaky-voiced story and then heaved a deep sigh.

"Martha," she said. "Just let it go."

"I'm trying," I said. I wanted to explain to her that this was like telling someone who's being mauled to death by a bear to let the animal go, while it was still worrying what was left of her leg. I didn't have my situation; it had me. There was nothing I wanted more than to let go of it, but I didn't know how. I eventually figured it out, but the method that worked for me proved to be exactly the opposite of what Deborah intended. She meant that I should never tell the story, but telling the story is the only way to let go of trauma. Letting it go is precisely what I am doing right now, in the hope that it will help others in similar situations find the courage to tell their own stories, but I sincerely doubt that Deborah will approve.

·   ·   ·

My interaction with friends and loved ones—with anyone, for that matter—trailed off to nothing rather quickly after that. I simply couldn't make myself chat politely about the weather, PTA meetings, or my PhD program, with my mental tempest howling in my ears. It was like witnessing the murder of a child, then having to pretend I hadn't seen it.

One day, as I was trying to dodge my demons long enough to grade papers, the doorbell rang. The visitor was the woman I'm calling Rosemary Douglas, who worked in our ward's women's organization, known as the Relief Society. The Relief Society is a remarkable organization, providing a female safety net for Mormon families at times of joy and crisis, birth and death. Latter-day Saint "sisters" care for each other with amazing efficiency, and Rosemary was one of its most pragmatic, goodhearted members. She was also the woman in my recurring nightmare who drove up in the midst of a landslide to tell me I should stand in the open. Because of the dream, which I'd begun having months before I'd ever spoken to Rosemary, I always felt strangely self-conscious around her. When I saw her standing on my porch, the images and impressions from my recurring dream popped to the front of my mind so vividly that I blushed like a boiled lobster.

"Hello, Martha," Rosemary said, "I've just come from visiting your neighbor." She named another woman in the ward, a young mother about my age, who I knew had been having health problems.

"I'm worried about her," Rosemary said, "and I think you might be able to help. May I . . . ?" She raised her eyebrows and nodded toward my living room, which in Mormon country is equivalent to ramrodding the door.

"Uh . . . oh . . . yes, of course," I stammered. "Come in." I offered Rosemary a glass of water, which she politely refused, and we sat down at my dining-room table.

"I do believe there is something physically wrong with the poor girl," she said, getting right to the point about my neighbor, "but the doctors can't really explain her symptoms, and I think she also has some psychological wounds. Deep ones."

This interested me. At the time, deep psychological wounds were the *only* things that interested me.

"The bishop asked me to help find out if her family has a history of some rare disease," Rosemary said. "But she was raised in foster care from the time she was six or so, and she says she doesn't remember her birth family at all."

It was all I could do not to jump up and run from the table. Why did this topic, this stuff about forgetting one's childhood, keep forcing itself into my attention?

"So I did some research," Rosemary went on, "and I found out that her birth father is in prison, because of what he did to her. There was abuse. Sexual abuse."

Well, of course there was.

"The strange thing is that she tells me the police reports must be wrong, because she doesn't remember anything," said Rosemary. "But I think there might be a link. I know you're a psychologist—"

"I'm a sociologist," I said. "Going to be."

"Yes, but I thought you might know someone we can consult with. Someone who specializes in this kind of problem. I'm no expert, but I know she can't deal with this on her own. No one could."

I could tell I was blushing more furiously than ever. I felt strange, slightly out of control, confused by the nightmare I kept remembering. "Stand in the open!" Rosemary always shouted in the dream. "You'll be safer there!" My throat closed, my eyes stung, and I had to chomp hard on my lower lip to keep from breaking down. I did my best not to let Rosemary notice, but she was far too observant to be fooled. Her next words followed a long pause, and she spoke them very slowly, as though she were choosing them with great care.

"Martha . . . I don't believe God would ever ask anyone to endure that sort of thing without talking about it. No one. No matter what."

Her voice went through me like an arrow, through all the pain and confusion and fear to something at my very center. My body filled up with a kind of resonance, like one of the huge gongs I'd seen in Shinto shrines that make the air throb when they ring. It shattered my reserve, and as usual, I started crying. Rosemary just sat there, not a shred of tension or resistance in her presence.

"Was it your father?" she asked, quietly.

I covered my face with my hands to keep myself from falling apart, but it was like trying to protect a sand castle from high tide. "I didn't tell you!" I gasped, when I could speak. "Where did you hear that?"

She shrugged and tapped her chest. I felt that sense of resonance again, crumbling all the barriers in my mind.

"You can't tell anyone!" I whispered. "And I can't tell anyone! Ever! I can't!"

"Martha, listen to me." Rosemary's voice was no louder, but it had taken on a peculiar intensity. I remember thinking that I should pay close attention. I was right. The next three words Rosemary Douglas spoke changed my life forever. The moment she said them, I knew that this was the stable patch of earth in the landslide, the single great spiritual truth upon which I could build my life now that all other foundations had proven frail and uncertain. The words weren't *God loves you,* or *Jesus is Lord,* or *Keep the faith.*

Rosemary put her hand on mine, looked me right in my soggy eyes, and said, "You are free."

All my life, I'd read and reread a thousand religious epigraphs to the effect that "You shall know the truth, and the truth shall make you free." I'd always been told that this had to do with joining the true religion, learning the true description of the Holy Trinity, memorizing the true Commandments. Now, with that gonglike tone thrumming through me, it all seemed so much simpler. The truth I needed to be free was simply the reality of my own life: This is what I think. This is what I feel. This is what happened to me. To know these small truths was to know myself; to speak them was to connect with my real self, other human beings, and God.

•   •   •

That was the moment when I noticed, very vividly, that my spiritual search had changed. Later I would recall the text where I'd read about the camel, the phase of a spiritual quest that eventually gives way to the lion. The quotation goes like this:

> When we have discovered the heart's capacity to face any situation, the joys and sorrows of existence as they are, we awaken to freedom. Then the golden lion speaks with a roar. Out of the mouth of the lion comes the undaunted voice of truth, the liberation of the unbounded heart.

From the moment I had my first flashback, I'd left the persona of the camelish acolyte whose highest good is to subordinate all personal initiative to an established religious tradition. Knowing my own truth made me responsible for choosing a course of action based on that truth, even if it meant breaking with traditions and institutions. I had become a lion—a small sickly cub, to be sure, but a lion nonetheless.

I didn't say all this to Rosemary Douglas, of course. I just kept decompensating into a pile of undifferentiated, tear-stained plasma. And this remarkable woman, who came to me compliments of the very religion that supposedly needed me to hide the truth, sat there blessing me with a silence different from anything I'd ever heard. It had nothing to do with hiding dirty laundry, protecting reputations, avoiding retribution. It was the quiet of openness rather than secrecy, of reunion rather than isolation, of calm rather than fear. It was the hush of a mother rocking her child to sleep, rather than forcing that child to keep the family secrets. This unfamiliar quiet radiated from Rosemary, shimmered outward until I noticed that it had blended with a greater stillness all around us, a huge, bright, vibrant Silence that was to my ears what the Light had been to my eyes.

See, kid? it said, in that voice without words. *I told you I'd be right here.*

CHAPTER 22

Father Abraham

S o, between your childhood and the war," I tell my father, "it doesn't take old man Sigmund to understand why you did what you did. Frankly, I'm amazed you didn't end up in an insane asylum." I think about this for a second. "Although our house may have qualified."

I grin, but my father is not amused. He looks longingly toward the hotel room door, apparently realizing I'm not about to let him leave. I'm stabbed by the pity I feel for zoo animals locked in cages that are too small for them. I wonder if he ever felt the same way looking at me, when I was five and six and seven. *Abraham built an altar there, and laid the wood in order, and bound Isaac his son, and laid him upon the altar on the wood.*

"So I think I understand *why* you did it," I tell him. "It's what you might expect from anyone with your psychological history." I lean forward and put my elbows on my knees, studying my father's face without any attempt at subtlety. "The part I don't understand isn't the why. It's the *what*. What exactly were you doing?"

My father sits there with the sullen look of a POW who is resigned to his imprisonment but has no intention of talking to his captors.

"Okay, let's start at the beginning. I remember your saying it was an Abrahamic sacrifice. I've always remembered that."

My father jerks backward about an inch. I've touched a nerve. He's always had a special reverence for Father Abraham, seems to identify with him strongly. A famous sociologist whom I met at Harvard once called my father the Abraham of the desert. Like Abraham, he knew himself to be pivotal in bringing God's words and intentions to a whole faith—Judeo-Christianity, in Abraham's case, and Mormonism (equally important, though too fresh to seem so) in my father's. I've actually seen his eyes turn misty when he's given speeches about the ancient prophet. This would not be out of character for most Mormon speakers, who get weepy talking about subjects like researching their genealogy or stock-piling ammunition for the Apocalypse, when atomic weapons will be loosed, civilization as we know it will be destroyed, and non-Mormons will head to Utah in covetous droves, lusting for the stored wheat and homemade preserves of the faithful. But my father is typically not a weeper. He identifies with Abraham. It's a subject that goes deeper into his emotional core than almost any other.

"But I'm not at all clear how the Egyptian stuff ties in," I continue. "It was so bizarre. Do you remember that?"

I stop for a moment, hopeful that the details will knock him into con-fessional territory, but he only mutters, "You can't prove it. You can't prove a thing."

"I know, I'm just curious. Were you reenacting the scene in the Joseph Smith papyri? When I first remembered, it made no sense to me. I didn't know anything about the papyri. Now I think I get it, but I'd love to hear your version."

The peculiar details of my memories had at first made me doubt myself—they were so *weird*—but in the end, reinforced my conviction that I hadn't unconsciously made something up. I simply didn't know enough, either as a child or as an adult experiencing intrusive memories, to understand why references to Egypt would be part of my father's delusions. The flashes of memory included hearing him mention Egypt repeatedly, and this aspect of my memories baffled me at first. However, it also explained my lifelong strange reaction to all things Egyptian.

As a child and teenager, I was fascinated by everything in the library except for the landfill-sized pile of kiddie books on ancient Egypt. And, of course, there were (yet again) my nightmares. As a small child, I had one in which I was trapped in the two-dimensional world of an ancient papyrus drawing, running through level after level of some mazelike dia-gram as the corpse of a dead man scuttled along behind me, right on my heels. I used to wake up sobbing, begging my mother to let me move out of the downstairs room I shared with my little sister, up to the rooms where my older siblings slept. Once I did that, the trapped-in-papyrus nightmare stopped completely.

In another dream, which tortured me throughout my adolescence, I would think I'd woken up, then hear slow, heavy footsteps creaking on the floorboards outside my room. Just as I decided it was nothing, the doorway would fill, top to bottom and side to side, with the probing head of a huge crocodile, atop a tawny body that seemed to belong to a dog. The stench of stagnant water and death shriveled the air around it as the monster walked heavily, inexorably toward me, and there was nowhere I could run. Then I'd wake up.

I stopped having that dream when I moved away from my parents' house, and didn't think about it until years later, when my daughter Katie was four and developed the typical child's interest in ancient Egypt. I bought a children's book on the subject, ignoring my vague unease, and sat down that evening to read it to Katie. I wasn't surprised by the drawings of mazes that used to haunt my dreams—reproductions of such drawings show up all over the place, and I was as used to seeing them as anyone else. But then I turned a certain page and got a shock that hit me like a fist. There was my nemesis from what I used to call my alligator dreams, a monster with the head of a crocodile, the body of a lion, and the feet of a hippopotamus. The hippo feet didn't make it into my dreams, but the odd combination of reptilian head and golden mammalian body were unmistakable. I stopped reading aloud and scanned the text, heart pounding almost audibly.

The monster's name was Amut the Destroyer, and its job was to devour the souls of people who did not qualify for redemption in the afterlife. But I hadn't known that as a child. Had I? I was so stunned—and so puzzled by my own reaction—that I put Katie to bed without another word. I never could read clear through that book. It reminded me too much of . . . I had no idea what. I wouldn't understand my feelings for years.

"Do you remember my alligator dreams?" I ask my father now. "The nightmares I had every week or two?"

He gives a POW grunt.

"Do you remember what you told Mom about those dreams?"

No answer.

"You told her I was being 'pursued by an evil spirit.' You may not remember, but I do. And to me, that seems odd. I mean, whatever happened to 'It's nothing, child, go back to bed'? It seems like a hell of a way to put a kid to sleep."

My father suddenly gets a surge of energy. He shifts in his chair, raises his eyes, and lets them zip from left to right in the air above my head. "Well," he says, forcefully, "we were poor!"

"Huh? What on earth does *that* have to do with it?"

"We were poor! We had nothing! All those kids . . ."

My psychological training tells me that this comment is probably metaphorical, an effort to tell me (and explain to himself) that he had nothing to give his children in terms of emotional support. But there is a sense in which he's correct literally, as well as figuratively. I believe that whatever my father did to me was in large part triggered by poverty, specifically by my family's economic dependency on the Mormon Church.

"I know we were poor," I tell him. "And I know you must have felt you had to protect the Church. I can't imagine the pressure you must have been under."

I've thought about it a thousand times, the absolute dead-end my father had faced when I was five, the year I suspect he got a fateful assignment from the brethren in Salt Lake City. He was a fifty-two-year-old Mormon apologist—a profession that didn't even exist outside of Utah—with virtually no possibility of getting a job outside of Mormon-run BYU. With eight children to feed (eight!), what options were open to him? He could either lose his job, his livelihood, his social standing, his bully pulpit, by publicly revealing information that would undermine the very foundations of Mormonism, or he could lie flat out. In a way, I admire him for choosing the only other alternative: he went crazy.

"We had nothing," my father reiterates, with evident pride. Most Mormons see financial wealth as a sign of God's favor, but my father has always been the outspoken exception, the atavistic champion of the United Order. His view of poverty as both a virtue and an excuse smacks more of hard-core Marxism than Latter-day Saint conservatism.

"Okay, but *what were you doing?*" I persist, with the stubbornness I learned in my interviewing methodology classes at Harvard. "Now that I know about the Joseph Smith papyri, I get the connection between Abraham and the Egyptian documents. But I'm not sure how that got you acting it out—did you combine the sacrifice of Isaac with the Book of the Dead?"

He's fidgeting in his chair as though it's covered with burrs. I think of the twelve-step saying "My mind is a dangerous neighborhood. I try not to go there alone." I've apparently pushed my father into a very unsavory part of his brain. The whole issue of the Joseph Smith papyri seems to create unbearable anxiety for him, and I can certainly see why. Anyone who knows Mormon history would understand.

Now, it's true that the Church has done a good job of making sure that this particular part of Mormon history remains obscure even to most Latter-day Saints. Outside the Church (and inside it, for that matter) almost no one has ever heard the strange story of the Joseph Smith papyri. Perhaps, if the lost papyri hadn't reemerged one fateful day in the early 1960s, right around the time I was born, my father wouldn't have been pushed over the brink. But the Mormon powers that be couldn't keep the issue completely out of public awareness, and they needed someone to explain, to spin, the parts of the tale that couldn't be suppressed. Someone reputable and educated. Someone brilliant yet absolutely committed to the faith. Someone like my father.

In the end, my reluctant quest to understand the worst part of my childhood became an expedition into some of the most startling aspects of Mormonism. It took me many months, working from the patchy memories of a devastated child, to understand how my father's role as an apologist for the Mormon Church figured into the things he did to me. I've long hoped that he would be able to verify or correct my theories.

Right now that doesn't seem at all likely.

My father is a caricature of uneasiness. He's muttering constantly, his hands plucking at slubs in the fabric of his chair, his shoulders twitching, his head jerking a half inch to the right, then sliding back, then jerking right again. It takes a lot of work to suppress both intellect and emotion when someone just won't drop a difficult subject, but it's work my father is clearly willing to do. He's not going to explain his actions to me. But because I find them unusual and interesting—so much so that learning them made me feel like a detective in an improbable pulp novel—I will, to the best of my ability, explain them to you.

CHAPTER 23

The Mummy

In the spring of 1966, I was three and a half years old. My interests focused on mud, crayons, and learning to climb the large fir (my siblings and I called it the bear tree) that grew next to my parents' turquoise-colored house. I had no idea that three thousand miles away, in New York City's Metropolitan Museum of Art, a professor of Arabic studies was unearthing documents that would catalyze a quiet but dramatic response in the Mormon world and eventually detonate a nuclear bomb in my life.

I would know nothing about the professor or his discovery until nearly three decades later, when I learned about them in bits and pieces, astonished to find out how neatly this aspect of Mormon history dovetailed with my strange memories. What follows is my best estimate of the story behind my story, the social context of my personal nightmare. It is a tale of charismatic religion, diligent scholarship, and just plain craziness that took much longer to learn than it will to tell and is much stranger than anything I could have made up.

• • •

Nineteen sixty-six was the year that Dr. Aziz Atiya, a Distinguished Professor of History at the University of Utah, traveled to New York City to gather material for an academic book he was writing. While passing through a storehouse of documents at the Metropolitan Museum, he noticed some images that seemed familiar. He asked to have a closer look at a few of the Egyptian papyri that had spent years locked away for safekeeping. Dr. Atiya was curious about these particular documents because, though not a member of the Mormon Church, he knew a great deal about the Latter-day Saints, their culture, their beliefs, and (most pertinent to this story) their scriptures.

There are four "standard works" in the Mormon scriptural canon. All are read, studied, and cross-referenced by diligent Saints. Not only are truly devout Saints expected to conduct daily "scripture study" alone and with their families, but they attend weekly Sunday school lessons with rotating lessons that examine the whole canon in detail, month after month, year after year. The oldest is the King James Bible. However, Joseph Smith taught his followers that it contained serious errors—for example, he declared that the sensuous Song of Solomon ("By night on my bed I sought him whom my soul loveth"; "Thy two breasts are like two young roes that are twins") was not inspired scripture but a lurid, godless, borderline pornographic invention of the human mind.

The second book—second in chronology, that is, but first in significance—is the famous Book of Mormon, which Latter-day Saints believe was originally written on golden plates, in a language called "reformed Egyptian," by pre-Columbian Americans. Smith claimed that in 1823, he was led to the plates by an angel named Moroni (a gold statue of whom graces the top of the spire of the famous Salt Lake City temple). According to Smith, the plates had been placed in a stone box and buried in New York State by the last surviving member of a light-skinned Christian people called the Nephites, who immigrated to the Americas from Jerusalem some six hundred years before the birth of Jesus. Smith said he used his natural gifts as a "seer" (along with a special pair of spectacles, called the Urim and Thummum, that had been buried with the golden plates) to translate the Nephite records and create Mormonism's scriptural cornerstone, which he published in 1830. Sadly, he was required to return the golden plates to the angel, so his translation can never be verified against the original.

The Book of Mormon is the real foundation of the Latter-day Saint religion. Even before its publication, Smith's family, friends, and acquaintances began reading it and gaining a "testimony" of its inspired nature. Mormons consider it more pure than the Bible, more convincing and informative. It is the written validation of Joseph Smith's status as the most important human being ever to live, besides Jesus. (In fact, Smith himself commented that even Jesus hadn't managed to create and maintain a religion as large and impressive as his.) The Book of Mormon was the principal tool the prophet used to draw converts and keep them converted. By 1831, more than a thousand people had become convinced of its truthfulness and banded together with Smith as their leader. Nine years later, membership had swelled to more than fifteen thousand. (By 1872, when Mark Twain published his autobiographical *Roughing It,* in which he likened the Book of Mormon to "chloroform in print," membership had swollen to one hundred thousand. Nineteen years later, it doubled again. Today there are an estimated 11 million members.) To this day, the Book of Mormon enjoys premiere status among Latter-day Saints. All are encouraged—commanded, really—to read, reread, ponder, and discuss it throughout their lives.

Most people outside the Latter-day Saint community have never heard of the third and fourth books that complete the Mormon canon, but like the Bible and the Book of Mormon, they are studied diligently by conscientious Mormons (the four books are often published in one set, so that the faithful can access them all with equal immediacy). One volume, the Doctrine and Covenants, is made up of revelations Joseph Smith received and recorded during the time he was establishing his church. The chapters range from inspirational essays Smith received metaphysically during times of stress or doubt, to fussy-sounding rebukes God sent (again, through Joseph) to Emma, the prophet's wife, telling her to stop pestering her husband about his habit of marrying other women. Last but not least is a book called the Pearl of Great Price. It is the shortest of the Mormon scriptures, but in some ways, I think, the most interesting. For one thing, it has pictures. Egyptian pictures, copied directly from real, ancient papyri. Pictures that would be recognized by Dr. Atiya as he strolled through the Metropolitan Museum more than a hundred years after the Pearl of Great Price was published.

But I'm getting ahead of myself. To understand how the Egyptian images got into Mormon scripture in the first place, we must go to yet another place and time: the small city of Kirtland, Ohio, in the year 1835.

That was an eventful year for the prophet Joseph Smith and his followers, including my great-great grandfather, the formerly Jewish dentist. Mormons were not particularly popular among nonmembers; their clannishness, evangelical fervor, and unusual doctrines upset less Saintly folk to the point of perpetual harassment and occasional violence. In fact, the Mormons had encountered such hostility from "Gentiles" (the Saints' term for nonmembers, which must have been a bit confusing for Great-Great Grandpa) that they'd already had to relocate twice, first from New York State to Missouri, and then to Ohio. After the second move, Brother Joseph received orders from God that he should field an army to reclaim the Mormon territory in Missouri, but the forces he marshaled were devastated by a cholera epidemic, which (God told Joseph) was punishment for the Saints' less-than-total obedience to the faith. Most Church members humbly accepted this censure, but others seemed discontented.

To make matters worse, God had also recently commanded Joseph Smith to start taking multiple wives. No actual numbers appear to have been specified. Historians quibble over how many women he married, but the number was probably somewhere in the forties—more than a grundle, less than a horde. Even more inconveniently, some of the women Smith was commanded to wed were already married to other men, including friends and followers of the prophet. Despite the delicacy of this situation, Smith was diligent in obeying his new orders. He kept matters as private as he could, publicly denying his multiple marriages, but by July of 1835 rumors had begun to leak out. The rank and file of Latter-day Saints had begun, in the popular Mormon idiom, to "murmur against the prophet." They were tired of being transplanted, losing their possessions, building a large house for Joseph and his first wife while he took their own wives as his "spiritual" brides. Some began to suspect that the Book of Mormon might not even be a translation of a real document and that Joseph Smith might not be a modern Moses after all but rather a philandering opportunist. Things were looking a mite dicey for the prophet.

• • •

I know what you're probably thinking right now, as you read this account. You're thinking, "I'll bet this situation was enlivened by the arrival of a traveling Irishman and his cartload of ancient Egyptian mummies!"

Of course, you are correct.

Michael H. Chandler, the Irishman in question, made his living by dragging around four honest-to-goodness mummies, charging nineteenth-century Americans a small fee to peer and poke at them. Chandler's arrival in Kirtland on July 3, 1835, caused a pleasant commotion, partly because of pure freak-show entertainment value and partly because the Latter-day Saints, with their belief in "reformed Egyptian" documents and pre-Columbian Jewish immigration, were even more interested in ancient Middle Eastern artifacts than your typical American citizens.

The Mormons also took special note of several papyrus documents that had been buried with the mummies and were part of Chandler's display. The papyri were written in Egyptian hieroglyphics, which meant that no one on earth could read them; the ancient culture had died centuries before, leaving not a soul alive who could speak its language or read its hieroglyphic symbols—except, thought some of the Mormon mummy viewers, for one man. Joseph Smith Jr. had proclaimed himself a "seer," and seers were defined in the Book of Mormon as people who could translate "all ancient writings." It seemed especially likely to the Saints that their prophet would be able to read Egyptian, since it was similar to the language used by the inscribers of the famous golden plates delivered by the angel Moroni.

Some of the Latter-day Saints in Kirtland convinced Michael Chandler to let them borrow the papyri, so that Brother Joseph could take a stab at interpreting them. The prophet immediately confirmed that he could understand and translate the documents, though he said it would take some time to do it right. The Saints were so excited by this that they scrounged up over two thousand dollars—a serious sum, in those days—and bought Chandler's entire exhibit. As gawkers continued to visit the mummies, Smith set to work on the papyri.

"I commenced the translation of some of the characters and hieroglyphics," the prophet wrote, "and much to our joy found that one of the rolls contained the writings of Abraham, another the writings of Joseph of Egypt, etc." In other words, the Mormon Church now owned the original, physical manuscripts upon which the Pentateuch (the first five books of the Old Testament, the Torah) had been written. Over the year, Joseph Smith managed to translate the sections he said were written by Moses and Abraham, and he published his translation of the Book of

Abraham in 1842. The resulting works were similar to the stories found in Genesis, but more detailed, and different in some key particulars. Joseph Smith's translations of the papyri, along with more of the prophet's divine revelations, became the Pearl of Great Price, the final volume of Mormonism's standard works.

From the beginning of his religious career, Joseph Smith had gained credibility by celebrating his magical ability to translate ancient documents. The fortuitous acquisition of the papyri, Smith's new translation project, helped inject his followers with a fresh dose of enthusiasm and belief in their leader's prophetic powers. They needed all the morale they could get, since they were becoming less and less popular with non-Mormon settlers of the western frontier. Hostility from prickly neighbors, angry mobs, and anti-Mormon politicians continued to make life difficult and dangerous for the Saints, and the continued flow of validation from Joseph Smith's historic documents no doubt salved many of their psychological wounds.

The more Smith translated, the more the ancient prophets backed up all his Latter-day claims. For example, some Mormon dissenters objected to Joseph's ordaining himself and others as "high priests," until it turned out that Abraham had held the same office, given by God in the same way Smith claimed he had received it. Abraham, like Joseph, preached that men could progress in heavenly rank until they became gods—a doctrine that had stuck in the craws of some nineteenth-century Mormons. Most important of all, Smith's translation of the Book of Abraham revealed that the ancient prophet had been commanded to take multiple wives and to lie about it in public. In the Pearl of Great Price account, Abraham is told, by no less an authority than God himself, to tell the Egyptians that his wife Sarah is actually his sister. The new scriptures—published biweekly in a Mormon newsletter, referred to repeatedly in Joseph Smith's speeches and sermons—helped calm tensions and bolster the faith of the Saints during a period of smoldering unrest within the Mormon community and outright aggression from secular society.

On June 27, 1844, Joseph Smith and his brother Hyrum were assassinated by an angry anti-Mormon mob in Carthage, Illinois. Several years after Joseph Smith's assassination, the Mormon papyri disappeared.

Church-approved Mormon history books had it that the documents, which Smith's widow Emma had sold in 1856 to a Chicago museum, had been lost in the Chicago Fire of 1871. No one could prove otherwise— that is, until Dr. Atiya took a second look at the documents that had caught his eye in the Metropolitan Museum's storage area. These papyri had been glued to pieces of backing paper in an attempt to preserve them, and some of the partly disintegrated drawings had been filled in with images that looked decidedly un-Egyptian. Atiya recognized these patched-up drawings as the illustrations in the Pearl of Great Price. Furthermore, the reverse side of the pages contained writings and pictures (for example, an architectural sketch of the Mormon temple in Kirtland, Ohio) that indicated these were the very same papyri owned by Joseph Smith.

This discovery thrilled the Latter-day Saint community. Friends of mine who lived in New York at the time remember seeing the second-in-command of the Church clutching the newly rediscovered Joseph Smith papyri to his breast as though they were the Baby Jesus himself. The reemergence of the documents created the perfect opportunity to convert all the world to Mormonism by proving, once and for all, that Joseph Smith was a true prophet.

An academic development that had begun even before Smith discovered the papyri had now advanced to the point that it would make this confirmation even easier. In 1822, a scholar named Jean François Champollion and others had translated the famous Rosetta stone, a slab of basalt, discovered in 1799, that had the same text written in three different languages: Egyptian hieroglyphics, Demotic, and Greek. Though it was only a fragment, and it would take several decades to analyze, scholars gradually succeeded in "cracking the code" of ancient Egyptian and learning to read its hieroglyphics. This meant that modern Egyptologists, unlike the few people who studied the little-understood language in the nineteenth century, could translate the Joseph Smith papyri, verify his interpretation, and confirm that the Mormon founder really was a "seer."

Well, things didn't work out quite that neatly. Non-Mormon scholars immediately recognized the Joseph Smith papyri as copies of two Egyptian funerary documents, the Book of the Dead and the Book of Breathings. They were basically directions to help deceased Egyptians negotiate the tricky netherworld tests they expected to encounter on their way to eternal life. In ancient times, every well-to-do Egyptian saved up to have scribes copy down these instructions, inserting each customer's name in the correct places to personalize them, like postmortem travel documents. The versions supposedly translated by Joseph Smith postdated the biblical Abraham by some fifteen hundred years and bore about as much similarity to Joseph Smith's "translation" as they did to *The Cat in the Hat*.

One part of the Book of Abraham would have a particularly direct impact on my childhood. It was a drawing of a scene frequently depicted in Egyptian funerary documents of this type, which depicted the mythological jackal-headed god Anubis bringing life back to the reassembled body of Osiris, god of the underworld. In the case of Joseph Smith's particular papyrus, the drawing had partially disintegrated. Before including this illustration in Mormon scripture, Joseph (or someone else who was allowed to handle the papyri) had fixed the papyrus to another sheet of paper and filled in the blank spots. In the doctored drawing, which is considered an inspired part of Mormon scripture, Anubis has a weirdly round human head and holds a knife over the body of Osiris. Joseph Smith claimed that the picture shows the prophet Abraham being sacrificed on an altar by an Egyptian priest. Unfortunately for Mormon scripture's reputation in the scholarly world, modern Egyptologists have never found Smith's explanation convincing. Actually, that's something of an understatement: Dr. Arthur Mace, the Metropolitan Museum's assistant curator in the Department of Egyptian Art, offered a typical scholarly comment when he called Smith's account "a farrago of nonsense from beginning to end."

Undoubtedly, Mormon authorities were not happy with this situation. There had been quite a lot of publicity in the Latter-day Saint community about the rediscovery of the papyri, and many Saints were anxiously awaiting the world-changing proof that Joseph Smith was a true prophet. I grew up hearing stories from Saints (my father's acolytes) who were particularly interested in the discovery of the Joseph Smith papyri. They seemed to fall into two categories: the ones who believed, wholly and ingenuously, in their founding prophet's accounts, and those who were a little cagey about the whole affair, perhaps because of some underlying cynicism that made them suspect that Joseph Smith had fudged a little—or a lot—but that this was okay by them. Based on my unscientific but careful observation (adults never realize how closely the rug rats are watching), the higher a person's rank in the Church, the more likely he was to occupy the second category.

This paradoxical faith, which made people cop to the idea that Joseph Smith had lied but vow to protect him as God's true prophet nonetheless, would explain the Latter-day Saint organization's first official response to modern Egyptologists' reports about the papyri: silence. The papyri were kept under lock and key, shown only to those who could be absolutely trusted to support Joseph Smith. But even so, the Church needed help dispelling questions, doubt, and criticism. They needed a learned explicator—or, failing that, a learned obfuscator.

Enter, stage left, my father. Already in his fifties, he had never studied Egyptian, but he did speak several classical languages and had already established himself as a vehement defender of the Mormon faith. His career path was set when an historian named Fawn Brodie published a thorough, critically acclaimed biography of Joseph Smith, titled *No Man Knows My History*. Brodie described Smith as a charismatic narcissist, both compelling and exploitative, adored by some, despised by others. Her book sent a small but uncomfortable ripple through Mormon country, and my father wrote a pamphlet-sized rebuttal he called "No, Ma'am, That's Not History." The Latter-day Saint community breathed easier, Fawn Brodie's book was summarily dismissed, and my father was on the road to religious celebrity. So, during the months after the rediscovery of the Joseph Smith papyri became public, my father was hustled off to study Egyptian with experts at the University of Chicago. I suspect that he—and the Church officials—thought he might be his religion's final line of defense in regard to this rather esoteric, but nevertheless nasty, little problem.

I wonder what my father must have thought as his able mind soaked up Egyptian and he began to read Joseph Smith's famous papyri. According to Egyptologists I consulted during my research, no informed scholar could possibly believe that the papyri matched Joseph Smith's interpretation. Moreover, to put it in official, technical language, the Book of Abraham is kind of kooky. For instance, here's a snippet of text. After stating that God lives in a residence near the planet Kolob, the scripture goes on to describe a picture of an ox (Fig. 5) as follows:

Fig. 5 is called in Egyptian Enish-go-on-dosh; this is one of the governing planets also, and is said by the Egyptians to be the Sun, and to borrow its light from Kolob through the medium of Kae-e-vanrash, which is the grand Key, or, in other words, the governing power, which governs fifteen other fixed planets or stars, as also Floeese or the Moon, the Earth, and the Sun in their annual revolutions.

I've always been perplexed that when my son with Down syndrome speaks gibberish, people assume it's because he's mentally retarded, but when Mormon leaders do the same thing Latter-day Saints assume it's because the power and depth of their insights boggles ordinary understanding. At some level, it must have occurred to my father that the supposedly Egyptian material in the Pearl of Great Price read like the graffiti from a psych-ward restroom. Yet I'm sure he felt that he *had to* defend Mormonism, that he *must* find some legitimate-sounding argument to keep Joseph Smith from being successfully discredited. There was so much at stake, not only the prophet's status as a seer but many of the Church's core doctrines as well: the "plan of salvation"; the belief in man's ability to achieve godhood; the justification for the Church's early practice of polygamy; and the policy, maintained until 1978, of denying the priesthood to those of African descent.

My father tried several approaches for explaining how Joseph Smith's "translation" could in some way have resulted from examination of the papyri. For example, he considered the idea that Smith used the papyri as a "super-cryptogram," a code that was only the jumping-off point for a much more elaborate and Mormon-friendly interpretation of the texts. He also spent years simply trying to link anything Egyptian with the Mormon Book of Abraham. He published hundreds of pages justifying stories from the Pearl of Great Price in which Abraham traveled to Egypt, lied about his multiple marriages, and survived a ritual in which he was tied on an altar and nearly stabbed to death (an echo of the aborted sacrifice of his own son, Isaac). In the end, my father seems to have settled for attacking modern Egyptologists, claiming that nobody really understands Egyptian and that therefore the present-day translations of the Joseph Smith papyri by modern scholars are worthless.

Almost all my father's arguments were presented in Mormon magazines and papers; after the brief surge of publicity that surrounded the rediscovery of the papyri, the secular world (assisted by an impressive lack of information from the Church) pretty much lost interest in the whole topic. Many of the faithful read the series of articles my father wrote about the papyri in a Church-published magazine called *The Improvement Era,* but the comment I heard most often from those who admired his scholarship was that they had no idea what he was talking about; his writing was long on impressive scholarly declarations but very, very short on clarity. In a way, the articles were a brilliant success: today, only a tiny fraction of Latter-day Saints even know how the Pearl of Great Price came to be or how its validity was challenged by modern Egyptology, and the majority have never heard of the Joseph Smith papyri. In any case, the faith of most Latter-day Saints isn't based on the belief that their founding prophet could translate Egyptian but on deeply held values and passionate allegiance to things like honesty, kindness, the nuclear family, and top-quality home-baked desserts. Nonetheless, preserving the innocent faith of the majority requires silencing the few nitpickers who worry about testing Joseph Smith's claims, and this ultimately meant the sacrifice of my father's time, his mind, his career, the last half of his life. To the Mormon authorities, I'm sure this fell under the category of acceptable losses. I may be the one person on earth who sees it only as a waste.

Such a terrible, terrible waste.

CHAPTER 24

The Man in Tweed

I knew virtually nothing about the origins of the Pearl of Great Price when I started having flashbacks. Growing up, I'd heard my father talk a great deal about Egypt, Mormon scripture, and especially Joseph Smith. But no one had ever simply told me the story of the scripture (the Church seems committed to preventing frank discussion of the issue, brushing over it in manuals for seminary and adult Sunday school students and leaving it out of historical accounts), and I'd never really understood why my father's work was so important. All I knew was that the faith of many Latter-day Saints had been strengthened because of what my father did for a living and that it was my duty to uphold his image and reputation.

I still felt this way after I remembered what had happened to me during my childhood, and because of this, dwelling among the Saints—once such a comforting and comfortable part of my spiritual search—came to be about as soothing as plowing a minefield. Every time some well-meaning Mormon asked me to give regards to my father, I felt such a storm of conflicting emotions I practically fell down. On one hand, I was virtually frothing at the mouth with the outrage that followed hard on the heels of every flashback. On the other hand, the Mormons around me were such good people, and much of their goodness was grounded in their religion, and their religion was stronger because of my father.

Rosemary Douglas, for example, treated me with the kind of pragmatic compassion that made the term *Latter-day Saint* sound completely appropriate. She told no one my secret but checked in on me almost every day, inquiring after my welfare and offering steadfast emotional support. One day we were standing in my front yard talking when an-

other ward member stopped to say hello and tell me how much my father's work meant to him. I smiled and said thanks.

Once he was out of earshot, Rosemary whispered, "How can you do
that?"

I shrugged. "Habit," I said. But the real answer was something closer
to noblesse oblige, the burden of protectiveness an aristocrat feels for
those not born into nobility. It came easily enough—I'd been doing it all
my life—but it stoked the hidden fires of my anger and despair almost
beyond endurance. Survivors of trauma recover by telling their stories to
people and groups outside the dangerous system—in the case of child
abuse, the family—that inflicted the damage. My entire community, with
the exception of John and Rosemary, seemed to be part of one huge dysfunctional family, heavily invested in protecting my father.

•   •   •

After a few weeks of trying to cope with my situation on my own, I
began seeing a therapist. True to the promise I'd given my mother, I managed to find a non-Mormon. The social worker who became my counselor (I'll call her Mona) was a friend of a friend who lived in a largely
non–Latter-day Saint mountain village an hour's drive from Provo. My
chief criteria for choosing her were that she didn't know my father from
Bonzo the Chimp and that she seemed to have no problem believing my
memories were accurate. I let these qualifications override my reservations about her therapeutic technique, which included not only taking
but placing phone calls during sessions, assigning me to do research for a
screenplay she was writing, and calling me at night or on weekends to say
she was lonely and just needed to talk.

"I'm having kind of a rough time," I told Mona one day.

"What?"

"I said I'm having a rough time." I raised my voice to project past
Mona's enormous, fluffy Alaskan husky, who liked to sit on my lap during
sessions.

"Hang on a second," said Mona, dialing her phone. "I have to call these
idiots at Paramount—" She gave her name to someone on the other end
of the line, then fell silent as she was put on hold.

"I'm really depressed," I ventured, trying not to get fur in my mouth.

"I don't know what to do about my family. I can't make myself call my parents."

"You'll be fine," said Mona. "You'll be over this in six months, at the very—What? Hello?" She listened for a few moments, then reared back in her chair. "Listen, buddy, I was abused my whole childhood, I'm not taking it from you. *What?* All right, then! Fine! Go to hell, you bastard!" She slammed the phone back in its cradle. Then she took a deep breath and turned back toward me.

"Now, where were we?"

I stroked the dog, which leaned ecstatically against my chest, making it difficult to breathe. "I feel like I'm going to die," I said. "I cry all the time. I'm scared of everything."

"Don't worry about it," said Mona. "You're much better already."

"I don't feel better," I said.

"That's a good sign," said Mona. "Just a minute, I have to make one more call."

When the hour was up, I wrote Mona a check. It was supposed to be $150, but the number I actually wrote on the check was $15. There really is such a thing as a Freudian slip.

•   •   •

When I wasn't in therapy, I tried to continue living my life as if nothing had happened. I had plenty to keep me busy. My children were still very young (neither Adam nor Lizzy could walk, talk, or use the potty), I was still teaching at BYU, and I was working on my PhD dissertation under the stern though distant eyes of my Harvard advisers. My hardest labor, however, happened in my head and heart as I made the transition in my spiritual quest from camel to lion.

This phase of inner change involves one of the most dramatic paradigm shifts in the human psychological repertoire: the move from what psychologists call an "exogenous locus of control" to an "endogenous locus of control." It means the process of dropping one's dependency on external structures and establishing a sort of moral guidance system that comes from within.

I'd spent the better part of three years trusting external structures and organizations, keeping every rule of every spiritual discipline I could imagine, quieting my own resistance, aiming for total obedience and humility. But continuing to do this would mean protecting the Mormon Church by keeping a dark secret, which would isolate me in a life of smothered rage and hopelessness. It felt wrong. I was in what felt like a no-win situation: my internal moral system was directly at odds with my family, my community, my ancestral religion.

Something a bit like this had happened to me once before, when I'd rejected the advice of every obstetrician and adviser at Harvard by deciding not to end the six-month pregnancy that later produced Adam. That time, however, I'd known in the back of my mind that millions of Mormons, including my natal family, would agree with my decision. This time was much harder. This time, the child I wanted to defend was my own five-year-old self, someone who no longer existed except in my memory, and the people I would offend were my flesh and blood, my ward family, my brothers and sisters and my Brothers and Sisters.

The Chinese have a phrase to describe the confusion that accompanies the change of dynasties: "when earth turns over heaven." I kept remembering this phrase as I slogged through my days, watching everything I'd thought solid and reliable fall into the sky, while unexpected new beliefs appeared in parts of my mind and heart I had thought were empty space. I diapered my babies, taught my classes, wrote my dissertation with dull mechanical effort, robotic on the outside, tumultuous within.

Things might have gone on this way until I spontaneously burst into flame, if a complete stranger hadn't broken social convention before I did.

•   •   •

That afternoon found me standing in the frozen-foods aisle at the grocery store, trying to decide which brand of vegetables to buy, microwave, and forget to eat. A thirty-ish man with a short beard and a tweed jacket pushed his cart past me, and from the corner of my eye I saw him do a double-take. I was used to this and figured (correctly, as it turned out) that the man in tweed had recognized me as my father's daughter. He reached the end of the aisle, then abruptly turned his cart and pushed it back toward me. I prepared myself to offer the usual smiles and thanks on behalf of my famous parent.

But Tweedy had a surprise for me. After politely asking my name, he drew the kind of deep breath you take just before you jump off the high dive and said, "Your father is a liar."

He glared directly into my eyes for a half second, looking scared but resolute, then dropped his gaze and rushed off, cart rattling in front of him.

I just stood there, like a frozen vegetable, for two or three seconds. Then I left my own cart behind and ran after Tweedy.

"Stop!" I called. "Please stop!"

He glanced back at me warily, then slowed down a little, apparently seeing in my face and posture that I wasn't angry. He turned to face me as I reached his spot on the aisle.

"Why did you say that?" I asked. "Why is my father a liar?" The question sounded so strange and confrontational that I gave the man a huge smile, to compensate. He studied my face, his brow creased in confusion.

"I mean, I'm not saying he isn't," I babbled. "I mean, he is—I mean I believe he is. I mean, I don't know what I mean. What did *you* mean?"

The sublime inarticulateness of this speech finally put Tweedy at complete ease; I was obviously no threat. He smiled back at me and told me his name.

"I used to have a job for your dad's publisher," he said. "I was one of the flunkies who checked his footnotes."

I nodded. My father's footnotes were part of his legend. He had hundreds in every book. Practically every sentence he wrote referenced some impressive primary source. I'd always assumed it was part of having an Allusion Manager for a brain.

Tweedy paused for a few seconds. I said nothing, just looked at him eagerly, like a sea lion waiting for a trainer to toss more shrimp.

"He makes them up," Tweedy finally said. He didn't sound angry or accusatory, just tired. "His footnotes. He makes them all up."

I took a moment to process this, then said, "All of them?" I'd never checked any of my father's footnotes. It had never occurred to me.

"No, not absolutely all," Tweedy amended in that weary voice. "But I'd say, conservatively, 90 percent of them."

"Seriously?"

Tweedy peered at me curiously. "You're not surprised, are you?"

"I'm . . . no, not really." Actually, I didn't know how to react. I felt noticeably, physically stronger, as though someone had pumped more oxygen into the thin Utah air.

"I helped cover it up, you know," Tweedy said. His voice reminded me of the ancient mariner, the former wrongdoer compelled to recount his sins to strangers in search of absolution. "At first I was shocked. I went to the guy in charge of our team and showed him a couple of the sources your dad said he was quoting. Sometimes what he said was exactly the opposite of what the author meant. Sometimes a quotation he'd foot-noted just wasn't there. My team leader told me your dad's gift was that he could see anything on any page that needed to be there."

I don't think that in all my life, I'd ever been as interested in any story as I was in Tweedy's. "What did you do?" I said.

He shook his head sadly. "I just . . . pretended. We all did, every-one on the team."

"But . . . why?" I said, though I suspected I could make a pretty fair guess.

"I needed the job. I wanted to finish school. I'd already been working toward a PhD for four years. If I'd gotten kicked out with bad references, no other school would take me."

"You think BYU would have blackballed you?"

"Not just BYU. The Church. And no, I don't *think* so, I *know* so. I'd have been lucky to get a job sweeping floors." Tweedy sighed. "The Church gets pretty much anything it wants, and it wants your father protected."

I felt sick to my stomach. "You don't think that's a little paranoid?"

The man looked at me for a long moment, one eyebrow cocked. "You're the daughter who went away, right? You left Utah for college?"

"I . . . well, yeah." I'll never get used to the fact that strangers in a grocery store know my life history.

"That's why you don't understand," Tweedy nodded. "In this state, you don't just go around spouting stuff that may be a problem for the Church. Like, some of the other fact-checkers on my team got a little mouthy after we finished the project. They're not doing well. Can't get jobs. Incredible pressure from their families. Hints about excommunication." He sighed, looking more tired than ever. "So I keep my mouth shut."

I felt a chill, and not just from the refrigerated shelves. "Why did you tell me?" I asked.

He had to think for a minute. "I don't know," he said slowly. "I suppose because I'm pissed off. And because I lost part of myself when I decided to start pretending." He gave me his weary smile.

"Well," I said to the man in tweed, "that makes two of us."

CHAPTER 25

Herding Parrots

Do you know what we were living on when I started teaching at BYU?" my father asks me. "Just a little more than two thousand dollars a year. Imagine!"

Again, I feel oddly touched that he's talking to me so directly, as one parent to another. He knows that now I understand how hard it is to keep a brood of children fed and clothed. Of course, I've already heard the stories from my oldest siblings: how they got three outfits for each school year, all purchased at Deseret Industries, the Mormon equivalent of the Salvation Army; how they survived economic crises only because they got donations, some open, some anonymous, from my father's admirers.

"It must have been awful," I tell my father. "I can't imagine how much stress you were under."

He sits back in his chair with a small, affirmative grunt.

"You know what really kills me?" I say. "It kills me how much of you the Church bought for that little lump of money."

Actually, there's good evidence to suggest that when it comes to propaganda, small bribes are better than large ones. In psychological tests, people who are paid one dollar to tell a lie are more likely to believe what they're telling than people paid twenty dollars. Apparently, the paltriness of the bribe creates cognitive dissonance in the one-dollar folks, making them prone to deceive themselves rather than admit they lied for such a negligible reward. During and after the Korean conflict, the Chinese managed to "flip" American POWs by giving them tiny rewards—a cigarette, a piece of candy—for writing pro-Communist essays. Perhaps my father's small salary not only saved the Church money but made him more likely to buy into his own contrived apologia.

He is glaring at me, but in the expression I see sorrow, as well as anger. I can tell he felt as hopeless as any prisoner, back at the beginning of his career, and perhaps even now. Because money alone hadn't forced him into a defense of the Joseph Smith papyri. He had his own faith, his own deep beliefs, of course, but the Church controlled not only his living, but his life—right down to the bedrock of his social conditioning. He might have escaped economic dependency if his religious culture hadn't possessed him to the marrow. I have no trouble believing that when the highest Mormon authorities assigned him to defend the holy scriptures, he felt caught in a trap from which there was no exit. "No exit," my Allusion Manager reminds me, was Sartre's synonym for hell.

A Latter-day Saint hymn runs through my mind as I watch my father's defeated eyes contemplate the knees of his secondhand polyester pants. *True to the faith that our parents have cherished, true to the faith for which martyrs have perished* . . . By the time he could talk, my father was singing along with this, primed, like every other Latter-day Saint child, to put the Church and its leaders far above personal needs or logical thought. Mormonism already owned his psychological allegiance, his mind, his will. In the end, it owned even my favorite thing about my father: his sense of humor.

I came to this conclusion after my encounter with the man in tweed, when I began doing research about Mormonism and its apologists. It was a bizarre privilege to have so many sources of information about my father; I doubt that many survivors of troubled childhoods can find pertinent facts about their parents in dozens of published books and articles, not to mention well-informed strangers.

Tweedy had given me the phone numbers of other fact-checkers who had worked on my father's publications, and when I contacted them I heard unanimous confirmation that a great many of the footnotes in his works were splendiferously fictional, sparsely stippled with the occasional accurate reference. I also began reading about the origins of Mormonism, learning for the first time how the Pearl of Great Price came to be. I found much of what I discovered appalling. Far worse, I found even more of it just plain silly. If my father had sacrificed his mind and my childhood to vital principles like equality, honesty, or peace—the beliefs I'd been raised on in the Mormon Church—perhaps I wouldn't be so struck by the futility of it all. But I found the Mormon beliefs spelled out in the Pearl of Great Price—beliefs my father spent so much of his life defending—as nutty as a Hickory Farms cheese log.

I have to believe that my father found some of Joseph Smith's "translations" funny. No scholar of Egyptian could read Joseph Smith's statements about the language without at least a chuckle or a shake of the head. For example, Smith wrote in a Mormon newsletter in 1835, "Were I an Egyptian, I would exclaim *Jah-oh-eh, Enish-go-on-dosh, Flo-ees-Flo-is-is* [O the earth! the power of attraction, and the moon passing between her and the sun.]" I've been assured by Egyptologists that were he an Egyptian, Smith might as well have exclaimed "Wugga wugga wugga!" or "I like big butts and I cannot lie!" The people near him would have responded the same way, with the ancient Egyptian equivalent of "Huh?" because the string of syllables quoted above means the same thing in Egyptian that it does in English: Nothing. Zilch. Zip.

This is an amazing coincidence, too, because according to the "Egyptian Alphabet and Grammar" Joseph Smith began writing in the 1830s, *zip* was a very important Egyptian word. He translated one hieroglyphic character as *Iota toues-Zip Zi,* meaning "the land of Egypt which was first discovered by a woman while under water, and afterwards settled by her sons, she being a daughter of Ham." This is a lot of content for one small character, but Smith could dig major marrow out of the bare bones of a single hieroglyphic symbol. Here's his translation of a character that actually means "the" or "this":

> Now, this priest had offered upon this altar three virgins at one time, who were the daughters of Onitah, one of the royal descent directly from the loins of Ham. These virgins were offered up because of their virtue; they would not bow down to worship gods of wood or stone, therefore they were killed upon this altar.

Some Mormons consider this to be a vindication of Joseph Smith's translation, since the word *this* does appear in his version. There's a kind of innocent credulity to this position, sort of like the unquestioning acceptance my beagle gives me when I have him take the medicine prescribed by his vet.

The altered (or should I say "altared") drawings in the Joseph Smith papyri, for example, the one that ostensibly shows Abraham being sacrificed on an altar by an Egyptian priest, are also laughably amateurish. Apparently, the visual arts weren't all that well represented in the world of nineteenth-century Latter-day Saints. One of my favorite comments about the papyri concerns a drawing that appeared on one of the papyrus scraps. It came from Joseph Smith's most famous scribe, a man named Oliver Cowdery, who wrote the following swooning praise about a picture of a line drawing on one of the ancient pages:

> The serpent, represented as walking, or formed in a manner to be able to walk, standing in front of and near a female figure, is to me one of the greatest representations I have ever seen upon paper, or a writing substance; and must go so far towards convincing the rational mind of the correctness and divine authority of the holy scriptures . . . as to carry away, with one mighty sweep, the whole atheistical fabric.

This is what the picture looks like

One can only assume that Oliver didn't get out *at all*.

·   ·   ·

Scholars of ancient Egyptian could criticize Smith's translation of the papyri that became the basis for the Pearl of Great Price because they now had the actual papyri for comparison. With the Book of Mormon, Smith claimed that the angel Moroni had repossessed the golden tablets on which it had been originally written, so it was impossible to compare and contrast. In this case, scholars wanting to contest the Church's interpretations could call on secular scholarship to refute its claims. The Mormon apologists, including my father, would then scramble to refute the refuters.

One of my favorite images over which the apologists scrambled is from the Book of Mormon. The text described how the Israelite immigrants, who settled the Americas in about 600 BC, found a wilderness filled with horses, sheep, and goats, and immediately began tending "flocks and herds." The problem, for Mormon apologists, is that none of these animals actually existed in the New World until they began to be introduced from Europe in the fifteenth century. So one well-known defender of the faith (not my father, for once) asserts that the authors of the Book of Mormon simply mistook American mammals for the animals that were familiar to them. The word *flocks,* for example, might refer not to sheep or goats but instead to flocking birds, such as parrots. The animals the authors of the Book of Mormon called "horses," which they used for riding and pulling war chariots, could have been, say, tapirs. (The tapir is a stout, short, extremely shy creature with a prehensile nose, which lives in swamps and only comes out at night.) As depressed as I was when I did my religious research, as unnerved as I was by the death vows I'd taken during my marriage ceremony, I just couldn't get serious about the image of a prehistoric American Jew leaping astride his tapir to go out herding parrots.

To me it hardly even seems worth mentioning that the emperor has no clothes. I hate the fact that my father, who could be a really funny guy, spent so much of his life praising the royal accoutrements. I think I understand why, because I know that my father went through the Mormon temple ceremony—and in his time, the vows were even more graphic than the later version I experienced. I can vividly recall the booming, disembodied voice from the temple loudspeakers, right in the midst of the go-ahead-and-kill-me pantomime, explicitly forbidding "loud laughter" or "evil speaking of the Lord's anointed" and stating emphatically that "God will not be mocked."

Still . . . tapirs?

•   •   •

"Didn't you ever think it was just ridiculous?" I ask my father now. "Everything the Church wanted you to say?"

He doesn't take offense, as I expect him to. He just draws in a long breath and then sighs, and though he's still looking down at his knees, his eyebrows go up in an expression of dejected helplessness. Suddenly, I see two men sitting across from me: the one who was made a champion of a beleaguered religion and the one who knows how to laugh—who would love to have laughed at the whole silly charade, if only he hadn't felt that his life and the lives of his family depended on his willingness to keep a straight face.

I remember the laughter I felt during my moments with the White Light, the hilarious, joyful, bubbling jollity. It seems to me at this moment that laughing is a serious thing, that it connects us with truth and love and God. The Light couldn't have cared less about being mocked or about how loudly people laugh; that would be like the air blaming the leaves for sparkling in the wind.

"I wished you'd laughed at it all, Dad," I tell my father, though it's water long gone under the bridge. "It was so ridiculous, all of it. I really, really wish you'd just laughed."

CHAPTER 26

Anger

I tell my life-coaching clients that anger is the immune system of the psyche, necessary despite its dangerous, volatile energy, because it is the only healthy response to injustice. If not for anger, American plantation owners would have been able to preserve the myth of the "happy slave." If not for anger, Hitler would have enjoyed a long and prosperous rule over Europe. If not for anger, people everywhere would act a lot more like the typical citizen of Provo, Utah.

I'm sorry. Does that sound a little . . . angry? Well, yes, I suppose it does. Because even though I spent much of my life trying to be the nicest possible member of the nicer gender in the nicest community I know, I do have my limits. And during the winter of my twenty-ninth year, I finally hit them.

One of my favorite cartoons, by Bruce Eric Kaplan, shows two beef cows in conversation, one of them saying to the other, "I suppose if I'm really honest with myself, I'm not totally fine with being slaughtered." The more I learned about Mormonism that tempestuous year, the more I came to believe that to be loyal to my family and religion, I would have to slaughter either my mind or my soul. And I wasn't totally fine with it. I was so not totally fine with it that waves of anger often kept me awake all night. At other times, there were no waves; it was more like drowning at the bottom of an anger ocean, crushed beneath a million tons of anger-pressure per square inch.

One day I noticed that an old wooden bench in our backyard had become so desiccated and splintery it might be a health hazard. I kicked it a few times until one of the boards broke. It felt good. My stored anger seemed to pour itself into the muscles of my leg, exiting through my foot when it struck the bench. This initiated the most politically incorrect phase of my recovery from trauma, because after kicking the bench a few more times, I went to the hardware store, bought myself an ax, and named it Lizzie Borden. Whenever I felt overwhelmed with anger, I'd park the kids in front of a Disney video, go out into our snowy yard, and hack our former bench into smallish pieces that would fit in our fireplace.

When the bench was gone, I moved on to our weeping cherry tree, which had passed away from old age and needed to be removed. In the middle of icy, sleepless winter nights, when John, my children, and (I hoped) all the neighbors were asleep, I'd climb the tree, wedge myself into a secure spot near the trunk, and chop away at the hoar-frosted branches until I was so warm I'd have to take off my coat. My sweaty clothes steamed in the blue light of the streetlamps, making me look, as well as feel, like an enraged cartoon version of a young, cherry-tree-chopping George Washington. When my adrenaline surge was over, I'd climb down from the tree and pick up what I'd chopped, adding a few more logs to the supply of firewood by our back door.

During all of this, my Allusion Manager kept repeating a quote from Barbara Deming, the famous nonviolence theoretician: "Our task is to turn the anger that is affliction into the anger that is determination to bring about change." Even if all I could feel was the wild lust to smash things, I was determined to direct that energy into clearing away things that needed to go and creating some useful order in their place. That whole winter, whenever we built a fire, I'd gaze at the burning wood and see the physical manifestation of my anger gradually going up in smoke. We used my anger to warm up stiff winter boots before we put them on our feet. We read books to the kids by its light. We toasted marshmallows in its circle of fierce, contained heat. With every chopping session, every cozy fire in our hearth, a little more of the anger in my mind and body rose up the chimney, grew wispy in the dry Utah air, and finally disappeared.

Physically, I was healthier than I'd been for years. I regained weight, energy, and muscle tone (especially in those ax-swinging muscles around the shoulder blades) and began to suspect that holding back my rage had long consumed the lion's share of my physical strength, leaving very little to spend on actual living. Now I was getting all that energy back, and although the intensity of my anger often alarmed me, allowing it to exist made everything else feel lighter, easier, less exhausting.

Unfortunately, while my demolition projects off-loaded some of my childhood rage, I kept making grown-up discoveries that replenished my anger supplies. The problem was, I read too much. Mormons are discouraged from reading any materials about the Church that are not produced through official channels and approved by a panel called the Correlation Committee, notorious among Mormon authors (including my father) for its strict censorship. These are the folks who create the standardized teaching manuals for the whole worldwide Church, who carefully edit out even tangential references to the "alternative voices" that teach things like evolutionary biology, modernist moral reasoning, and the wearing of nonstandard underwear—anything, in other words, that might shed the slightest shadow of doubt in the minds of the faithful.

When I began reading about the history and doctrine of the Latter-day Saints, I saw why the committee is so active and so vigilant. I doubt that any Mormon gal could proceed far on this course of study without becoming at least mildly disgruntled. If she kept learning for a couple of months, disgruntlement might rev up to peevishness, and if the gal in question had been raised on faith-promoting Latter-day Saint legends that carefully omit much of the truth (the details of Joseph Smith's marital history, for example, or the story of the 1857 Mountain Meadows massacre, in which a village of Utah Mormons offered safe passage to a group of pioneers from Arkansas, then shot them at point-blank range and took possession of their property), she might get downright pissed. And this is what happened to me.

The more I wrestled with my neuroses, the more I wanted to understand how my religion had created the context for my father's behavior. One of the first things I learned is that Mormonism has a long-standing, proud tradition of lying about sexual behavior. It began with Joseph Smith's very colorful, very carefully concealed sex life. When Smith first heard God calling him to marry multiple women, he apparently didn't tell his acolytes that any other man had the same assignment. Gradually, as rumors spread, God began sending revelations that allowed Joseph's closest cronies to practice polygamy. In the end, by what I can only assume is blessed coincidence, the prophet announced that having several wives per husband was "the True and Eternal Order of Marriage" for all righteous people. "If any man espouse a virgin, and desire to espouse another" says Mormon scripture, "then he is justified; he cannot commit adultery for they are given unto him . . ."

As someone who had once been just such a donated virgin, I found such statements downright vexing—especially because the divinity of plural marriage is still official Mormon doctrine. Although the Church officially renounced polygamy in 1890, citing pressure to conform to "the laws of the land," its leaders couldn't very well agree that Joseph Smith and the Church presidents who followed him (who were also believed to have become prophets, as part of their role in the Church) had been wrong in declaring plural marriage the "everlasting covenant" of divine marriage. So the Church's twenty-first-century position (not widely known among younger Mormons, let alone nonmembers) is that God has temporarily disallowed "plural marriage" in order to spare the Saints legal and political problems, but that at some point—it could happen any moment now—the current, living Mormon prophet (that is, the sitting president of the Saints) to whom the twelve apostles report—will give the word, and Latter-day Saint men will once more be called upon to marry multiple wives.

Many Mormons struggle with unrighteous, rebellious impulses when it comes to accepting this doctrine, and by "many Mormons," I mean women. A group of my students once conducted a survey at BYU to find out how their fellow students felt about the imminent switch back to polygamy, that Damocles' sword of Mormon doctrine. The male subjects finished the survey in a few minutes, saying that though it would be difficult, they'd bite the bullet and marry whole bunches of women, especially (I'll admit that this is my own assumption) really hot ones. The female students who took the survey agonized for hours, often bursting into tears before they finished it. They expressed—surprise, surprise—a lower level of satisfaction with the doctrine of polygamy than their male classmates.

Historically, Mormon women who got fussy or resistant toward polygamy were seen as thorns in the sides of their husbands, their anger an attack on God's order. Even Joseph Smith himself was forced to communicate several revelations from God to his first wife, Emma, commanding her to stop bothering him with questions about his multiple marriages, including some to girls as young as fourteen. "And I command my handmaid, Emma Smith, to abide and cleave unto my servant Joseph, and to none else," says God in one of the prophet's revelations, "but if she will not abide in this commandment she shall be destroyed, saith the Lord, for I am the Lord thy God, and will destroy her if she abide not in my law."

Although the historical record shows that for most of her life, Emma was a vociferous critic of plural marriage, for a while she seems to have been convinced by Joseph's visions, at one point making an impassioned speech that urged the women of Mormonism to speak out against the "scandalous falsehoods" that suggested that her husband was practicing polygamy. At least three of the women in the room where Emma made her remarks were already married to Joseph, but none of them thought to mention it just then. Emma never did get used to polygamy or to swallowing her anger. Oral history has it that she once went after another of Joseph's wives with a broomstick and later pushed the same woman down a flight of stairs, causing her to miscarry a pregnancy and walk with a limp ever after.

There are several splinter groups, known as Mormon fundamentalists, who practice polygamy to this day. One of my friends, whose uncle lives in lavish polygamy, describes his wives as having "self-esteem that makes garden slugs look like celebrities by comparison." My own acquaintanceship with modern polygamists bears out this claim, as do published accounts of life in the Principle, which is what Mormons used to call plural marriage. The overall tenor of life in most polygamous households seems to be a near deification of the male head of household and a suppression of any rebellious thoughts (or "murmurings" as they are known in Utah) from the rest of the family, especially the "sister-wives."

It's virtually impossible to describe how thoroughly Mormon culture still maintains the standard of submissive, obedient women, and powerful, infallible male leaders. This seems to me to be particularly true when you're talking about anything related to sex. Men are to be pleased and protected, both in fundamentalist Mormon homes and in blue-blood pioneer families, and women are to do what they're told. This includes excusing or ignoring sexual shenanigans on the part of the patriarch and siding with the male authority figure in any "he said, she said" conflicts.

It was strange for me to stumble across evidence of this in the journal of my great-great-grandfather, Jewish dentist extraordinaire, a laconic writer who usually penned just a couple of terse sentences a day but waxed verbose when describing a disagreement between Joseph Smith and the wife of Joseph's close friend William Law. Here's the story just as I read it, in my great-great-grandpa's own quirky spelling and punctuation:

> [April] 24 [1844] called at Br J. S. . . . Told about Mr Wm Law—wisht to be Married to his wife for Eternity. Mr. Smith Said would Inquire of the Lord. Answerd no because Law was an Adulterous person. Mrs Law wandet to know why she could not be Married to Mr Law Mr S said would not wound her feelings by telling her. Some Days after Mr Smith going towards his Office Mrs Law stood in the door beckoned to him more the once did not know whether she beckoned to him went across to Inquire Yes please to walk in no one but herself in the house, she drawing her Arms around him if you won't seal me to my husband Seal myself unto you, he said stand away & pushing her Gently aside giving her a denial& going out. When Mr Law came home he inquiret who had been in his Absence, she said no one but Br Joseph, he then demandet what passed Mrs L then told Joseph wandet her to Married to him.

Other accounts record that around this time, William Law, Joseph Smith's "second counselor" and close friend, confronted the prophet and accused him of making "the most indecent and wicked proposals" to Law's wife. Smith responded by having Law excommunicated. Law then bought a printing press and began publishing a newspaper that recorded Joseph Smith's "abominations and whoredoms." Smith ordered two hundred of his soldiers to break into Law's newspaper office and destroy the printing press, along with all the other property on hand. William Law, fearing for his life, left the Mormon settlement not long after.

My point in recounting this is that to me, it's not abstract Mormon history; it's an example of the social dynamics in my community, my family. My great-great-grandfather was one of the people to whom Joseph told his cover story ("Just in case Jane Law says I made a pass at her, I want you to know ahead of time that she's a lying slut"). Great-Great Grandpa may have helped smash the printing press so that Joseph's sexual behavior could no longer be publicized. This leads me to believe that my family specifically, along with Mormons generally, has a tradition of winking at sexual "abominations" committed by men in the leadership structure, helping cover up any remaining gossip and condemning the women involved as untrustworthy and devious.

I was taught from early childhood that Joseph Smith and his fellow polygamist men were brave victims of the only pure, divinely ordered system of family life, who had no choice but to marry and marry and marry and who were sorely persecuted as a result. Sunday school and Primary teachers urged me to pity the polygamous Mormon husbands, because it was so hard for them to juggle many sexual relationships, settle jealous squabbles between selfish women, and heroically bear the slander of unenlightened people who accused them of simply wanting to have lots of sex with lots of broads. The word *persecution* comes up over and over again in Mormon discourse, especially discussions of the early male Saints. The image of the slandered patriarch, accused of sexual misconduct by malicious villains, is one of the central archetypes in Mormonism.

What we born-and-bred Latter-day Saints never hear in our Sunday lessons, never read in our Correlation Committee–approved texts, is any hint that the "persecution" of the early Saints was sparked by their own behavior. As a child, I heard countless times that nineteenth-century Mormons were driven from the land they had settled but not that they pillaged non-Mormon towns and burned down the homes of nonmembers. I knew that Joseph Smith had been tarred and feathered by a mob but not that they were there because he'd had sex with the fifteen-year-old daughter of a man who had rented a room to Joseph and Emma. I knew Joseph was condemned by many non-Mormon politicians but not that, in addition to having himself crowned king, he fully expected to become president of the United States and had selected a special council of Mormons meant to replace the legislative and judicial branches of the U.S. government. I never heard Joseph's modest claim that "if [non-Mormons] come on us to molest us, we will establish our religion by the sword. We will trample down our enemies and make it one gore of blood from the Rocky Mountains to the Atlantic Ocean."

In short, until my late-night reading of Mormon history, I never heard anything that explained why anyone might have been justifiably angry at the Mormon organization or its leaders. The history of my people was taught to me, and to all my childhood peers, as a tale of pure victimization. The Latter-day Saints had always been a placid, sexually boring people, inexplicably tormented by liars both within and outside the Church, who were, for some unknown reason, fixated on their mating behavior. Joseph Smith was a cross between Gandhi and Gandalf, persecuted because he had "done more, save Jesus only, for the salvation of men in this world, than any other man that ever lived in it."

.   .   .

The problem with this sort of claim, the reason modern Latter-day Saints are admonished to read only carefully edited history, is that the psychological immune system cannot be wholly suppressed. Even the most carefully educated female Mormons have been known to feel surges of anger when learning about the principle of plural marriage. Anger may pop up in the mind of the unguarded Latter-day Saint who unexpectedly hears about a Mormon prophet ordering an unwilling teenaged girl to marry her stepfather. Latter-day Saint "sisters" may feel the uneasy tug of anger as they sit in their segregated meetings, reading the diaries of women who struggled against (but overcame!) their unhappiness at hearing their husbands' boots drop to the floor in the bedroom of the next-door wife.

The more I read, the more I realized that the embers of my own anger had been smoldering for a long time. My discontent was a reaction to many factors and experiences—not just childhood abuse but the whole social view of women, men, and sexuality that has pervaded Mormonism since its beginning. I realized that the only way I'd kept from feeling angry as a child and adolescent was to believe that my natural reactions to these issues were hopelessly defective, innately wrong.

As if my historical studies weren't enough to chap my hide, the Women's Research Institute at BYU bravely chose to fund current research on the way modern Mormon leaders, from the illustrious General Authorities in Salt Lake to the local ward bishops, deal with women who come forward with reports of being sexually abused. I was asked to help with the research; I declined, on the (unstated) grounds that I might bring some unintended, subtle bias to interviews with victims. However, I did assist with the analysis of the study's results and the writing of the subsequent article, which was published in a peer-reviewed social work journal. What researchers found in modern Mormonism was similar to the attitudes expressed in my great-great-grandfather's journal: Women who sought advice or help after being sexually abused were most often told to be silent, keep their secrets, and ask themselves whether they were really sure it wasn't their fault—or their imagination. They experienced what psychologists call sanctuary trauma, the result of their running for protection to the very places and people who reaffirmed the message of the original abuse. Reading interview after interview with Mormon women who had been molested in various ways, then retraumatized by the reaction of Church leaders, I often felt overwhelmed by despair. There were many times when the only thing that allowed me to continue living was my rage, "the anger that is affliction," and the hope that I could somehow turn it into "the anger that is determination to bring about change." In the dead of night, doing my furious dead president imitation in our dead cherry tree, I slowly let my anger bring me back to life.

Chopping away, I speculated about how widely gossip about my accusations had already spread through the Latter-day Saint community, a community singularly skilled at sweeping allegations of sexual abuse under various homespun carpets. I imagined that certain people now looked at me strangely, spoke to me in guarded, hesitant tones. I suspected that even though the Mormon powers that be might not actually threaten my life, they would probably try to ruin it. Yes, these suspicions were outlandish. Yes, they were paranoid. And yes, they were completely accurate.

CHAPTER 27

Paranoia

I had just finished teaching a class on the sociology of gender. For a BYU instructor, this was a delicate subject (I might as well have taught a course called Grandma, Euthanasia, and You), but given the volatility of the material I thought that the day's lecture had gone pretty well. One of the students had asked about a speech on the role of women titled "To the Mothers in Zion," given by the reigning prophet and president of the Church in the 1980s. Such speeches were considered very important, because ever since Joseph Smith was replaced by Brigham Young, the president of the Mormon Church is said to have "the mantle of prophecy," and to be "the mouthpiece of God" to the entire human race. By sheer good luck, I'd had a copy of the address in my briefcase. I shared a couple of sentences with the class: "Wives, come home from the typewriter, the laundry, the nursing, come home from the factory, the cafe. No career approaches in importance that of wife, homemaker, mother—cooking meals, washing dishes, making beds for one's precious husband and children."

I'd also read the students a poem written by a popular Mormon speaker named Rodney Turner, and delivered before thousands of young Latter-day Saints in the 1970s. It went like this:

> Women are doormats, and have been
> The years those mats applaud.
> They keep their men from going in
> With muddy feet to God.

I refrained from making any comments about this choice little snippet, aside from explaining the first two lines (basically they mean that time applauds women who have always been doormats). I was pleased when the students initiated a spirited discussion on their own, debating whether the poem was high praise for the revered fairer sex or an astonishingly arrogant artifact of male chauvinism.

As I left the classroom, I almost bumped into a casual friend, a professor of clinical psychology who'd let me use some of his research in my dissertation. He looked terrible, his eyes glassy, his face so pale it was almost gray.

"Hey, Allen," I said. "What's up? Are you all right?"

He stopped and stared at me for a few seconds. Then he said, "No. No, I'm really not."

"What happened? What's wrong?"

Allen looked up and down the hallway as though he thought there might be bears hiding in the doorways. The corridor was almost empty; most of the students had already disappeared into their classes for the next hour. Allen leaned toward me and spoke in an almost inaudible murmur.

"Listen," he said, "you can't tell anyone about this, but I could use some advice."

"Okay," I said cautiously.

"A few weeks ago, a new patient came to my office." Allen always counseled a few clients at a time, to keep his clinical skills fresh. "This woman is the daughter of"—he paused, his eyes glancing up and down the hall again—"a man who's . . . financially important to the Church. She says he molested her when she was younger. She's been institutionalized on and off for fifteen years, on heavy drugs. She doesn't like the meds, wanted to find a therapist who would help her get off them. Said none of the psychiatrists she'd talked to were willing to take her on as a client. I thought she was being pretty skittish, but, hey, she deserved to try the therapy she wants, you know? So I agreed to see her. We've had three appointments so far. She's almost off the drugs and feeling a lot better."

"Okay," I said, nodding slowly. I hoped Allen couldn't see my pulse hammering in my throat and temples. Whoever the mystery patient was, she might as well have been me.

"So just now, I was sitting in my office and I got a phone call." Allen swallowed hard, then whispered the caller's name, a name any Mormon would know, one of the General Authorities, the chosen few men who are paid to spend their lives as Latter-day Saint leaders. "He told me that my client belongs back in the institution and that I have to diagnose paranoid schizophrenia instead of posttraumatic stress. He told me to advise inpatient treatment and put her back on the antipsychotics. He said, 'There are plenty of psychologists who have lost their careers over less than this.' That's a quote, Martha."

By this point, I was probably as pale as Allen. I wondered if he'd heard rumors about me, if he was confiding in me partly to warn me what I was up against.

"Now I'm stuck," Allen went on. "I'm just absolutely stuck. How can I put this woman away, drug her into a haze, when I don't think she needs it? How could I live with myself? But Martha, I've got five kids. If I don't do as I'm told, BYU will fire me and say it's for poor performance. I'll never get another teaching job, and they'll make sure I can't start a decent private practice. What's going to happen to my family?"

I forced myself to push aside my own rising fear and think of something to say.

"Allen, I really don't think the Church is that powerful."

He gave a humorless snort of laughter. "Oh, yeah. Tell that to all the non-Mormons who've been run out of business in this state."

I was out of encouraging ideas. The only thing I could think to say was "For what it's worth, I think you did the right thing for the right reasons. That's a big deal, Allen. That's everything, really. You can't let this destroy your integrity."

Allen gave me a small, wretched smile. "Yeah. Thanks." He sighed and began to walk away, then half turned. "Martha, would you do me a favor?" he asked.

"Sure, Allen."

"Would you pray for me?"

My heart felt as though it were literally tearing. "Of course I will."

I watched Allen trudge down the hall, his shoulders slumped like an old man's, and felt a welter of emotions: terror, despair, empathy, sorrow, and of course my new friend, anger. If I'd had my ax handy, I probably would have used it on something, anything, right then and there.

Instead, I took the elevator to my office, sat down in my standard-issue chair, laid my head on my desk, and covered it with my hands. I felt buried alive.

"So, did you hear about Orson Hicks?" (This was not the man's real name.)

I jerked upright and turned around to see another colleague, the bow-tied professor I call Scott, standing in my doorway. He was eating a chocolate doughnut, holding a box filled with more of them in his hand. Along with Prozac—and probably for the same reasons—chocolate doughnuts are consumed in greater quantities in Utah County than anywhere else. Scott walked into my office and waved the box enticingly under my nose.

"Hey!" said a woman's voice from the hall.

"Get back here with those!" This voice was male.

Two more assistant professors—I'll call them Sterling Hunter and Eliza Burke—appeared hot on Scott's heels and confiscated a doughnut apiece. Like Scott (and me) they were relatively new at BYU, born in Utah but educated elsewhere, and fond of chatting with each other in meetings and hallways.

"Who's Orson Hicks?" I said, selecting a doughnut. My appetite had been steadily returning as I processed my mental blocks.

"He's an archaeologist," said Scott. "Up for tenure this year. He got called in."

Sterling and Eliza nodded, but I wasn't sure what Scott was talking about. "Called in?" I said. "What does that mean? Called in where?"

"It means his bishop ordered him to come for a one-on-one scolding," Sterling said. "It's the way the Church jerks your chain—you know, reminds you that they can fire you anytime. It's been happening a lot around here lately. Hadn't you heard?"

I shook my head. I'd been so overwhelmed with my own tasks, from wiping little noses to writing my dissertation to steaming with anger, that I hadn't paid much attention to the news around campus. To be called in by one's bishop, the leader of the local ward congregation, was as serious as a heart attack to a born-and-bred Latter-day Saint.

"So," I said, "what did this Hicks guy do wrong?"

" 'Evil speaking of the Lord's anointed,' " said Scott, quoting one of the cardinal sins mentioned in the Mormon temple ceremony. "He criticized Elder Clement's master's thesis."

"Really?" said Eliza Burke, her eyes widening. Few BYU employees would dare criticize Elder Clement (not his real name), even in private. Clement was one of the apostles, the very highest quorum of leaders in Mormonism.

"Is he as big a dogma freak as they say?" asked Sterling, munching his doughnut.

"Very controlling," Eliza confirmed. "Almost certainly has bed-wetting issues."

Scott grinned. "Have you ever heard him talk about his master's degree? He thinks he's a great intellectual because he wrote this masterful masterpiece of a master's thesis, right here at BYU. He talks about the thing like it's the best piece of scholarship since general relativity. So Orson Hicks went to the archives and read Elder Clement's master's thesis, and he thought it was a piece of crap."

We all nodded. We'd heard Elder Clement speak, so this review of his thesis wasn't exactly a shock.

"Well, that would have been one thing." Scott went on. "But then Orson had to go and *talk* about it. In a room where students could overhear him."

"Uh-oh," said Sterling.

"You got it," Scott said. "One of the students wrote a letter to Elder Clement, and the next thing Orson knew he was having his little chat with the bishop. All very kind. You know: 'Dear, *dear* Brother Hicks, there's no question that we have to discipline a Church member who has spoken evil of the Lord's anointed. We have no alternative but to take action against you unless you say you're sorry.' "

"Did he do it?" Eliza asked.

"Well, sort of," said Scott. "He wrote a letter to the BYU newspaper saying he was sorry that Elder Clement's thesis was such a piece of crap. After the letter was printed, they called him in again. That was yesterday. There are rumors they'll excommunicate him. Or at least hold a court."

"Wait a minute," I said. "They would hold a court over something like that? Now I *was* shocked. Mormon Church courts (officially referred to as Councils of Love) are major tribunals, in which a panel of twelve local men, called the High Council, convenes to try and sentence a Saint who has confessed to or been accused of some infraction. Six men are chosen by lottery to plead the defendant's case, while the other six argue against him. The defendant is rigorously questioned by both sides, the content and quality of the answers duly noted. (Did the accused weep remorseful tears? Did he or she acknowledge the authority of the Church to define moral behavior?) After both sides have been heard, the council votes on a consequence, which may range from nothing at all (if the defendant is found not guilty) to the ultimate penalty: excommunication. Another possible sentence, "disfellowshipment," drastically reduces a person's status without actually cutting him loose. Either excommunication or disfellowshipment would result in a BYU employee like Hicks being ostracized by his community, losing his job, and—as Allen had just told me—probably not finding another.

"They would actually ex someone for hating Elder Clement's master's thesis?" I couldn't believe it. Throughout my life, I'd heard of being "exed" as the ultimate shame, something that only happened to hard-core sinners.

"The Church isn't after Orson because he hated the thesis," Scott explained. "They're after him because he *said* he hated it. It's the eleventh commandment. The most important one, to the brethren. Thou shalt not commit publicity."

The cold lump of fear that had lodged in my stomach during my conversation with Allen was growing heavier and chillier by the minute. As a sociologist, I understood that the Mormon Church was undergoing something common to most rapidly growing organizations: its leaders were having to work harder and harder to manage public image and that meant strictly controlling anyone who might damage the Church's reputation. I felt like a doctor who understands how a virus is going to spread but can't see a way to avoid being infected.

"They called in Jenny Knutsen last week," said Eliza. "They don't like the way she writes about polygamy." Jenny (not her real name) was a passionately devout Mormon historian who wrote both inspirational and academic articles about the Church. "And here's the creepy thing," Eliza went on. "Jenny just moved to a new ward, right? So her bishop barely knew her. But he had a file on his desk about an inch thick, with copies of everything Jenny's ever written, notes on every talk she ever gave in church, even a list of her friends and some of the articles *they'd* published."

I stared at her. "How is that possible? Where did he get that much information?"

"The Strengthening the Membership Committee," said Sterling.

"The what?"

Sterling swallowed the last of his doughnut and reached for another. "It's a squad of investigators who work for the Church. Very hush-hush. A lot of ex-CIA guys. Did you know the CIA recruits Mormons like crazy?"

That much I did know. The Church calls almost all its young men on missions and gives them excellent language training, making these men highly desirable, squeaky-clean candidates for foreign spy assignments. Some of my friends had been approached by CIA recruiters, who sidled up to them in bookstores or restaurants, informed them that they were candidates for spy training, and gave them a complicated scavenger-hunt-style set of instructions for going to the next step of the recruitment process. I knew the brother of a local Amway salesman who became a double agent, working for the KGB until he was prosecuted by the U.S. government. But I'd never heard of anyone coming *out* of the CIA and working for the Church. The Strengthening the Membership Committee was news to me.

"They probably have files on all of us," Scott said matter-of-factly. "They gather information about most BYU professors. Anyone who might influence public opinion. Sometimes they stake out rebels' houses and take down the license plate numbers of anyone who comes to visit them. Then *those* people are suspects. Next thing you know, they're getting hauled in by their own bishops, maybe put on trial."

I put my half-eaten doughnut down on the desk. I was thinking about the television and print interviews I'd given. About Allen and his new patient. How big were our files?

"Hey, here's a good one," said Sterling. "I know an assistant professor over in the English department who got called in a couple of weeks ago so his bishop could order him to stop 'lunching with known dissidents.' That's verbatim."

Eliza and Scott burst out laughing. The best I could do was a weak smile. I didn't have their light-hearted courage. Or maybe they didn't have my problems.

"I wonder when they call out the Danites," said Scott.

I stared at him. "The Danites still exist?"

My friends stopped laughing, probably because I'd gone beyond pale to a fetching shade of green. Mentioning the Danites focused my vague sense of impending doom into simple animal fear. Joseph Smith had personal henchmen (most notably a man named Orrin Porter Rockwell, or the Son of Thunder) who assassinated people who got in the way of Joseph's power or reputation. Brigham Young formalized and anointed these assassins as the Danites, whose mission included espionage, suppression of information, and quietly, permanently disposing of people who threatened the Mormon prophet or the Latter-day Saint organization. Again, not many Mormons know this detail of the Church history, but every now and then, Utah papers record murders with uniquely Mormon flavoring (death by temple-sanctioned methods, for example), and the word that goes out on the Latter-day grapevine is *Danite.*

This was the case, for example, in the murder of one Brenda Lafferty, killed along with her infant daughter by her fundamentalist brothers-in-law, who had broken away from modern Mormonism, decided to revive polygamy, and deplored the outspoken resistance of their brother Alan's wife. Since my sister briefly dated Alan before he married Brenda, the Lafferty murders always made me a titch nervous. Growing up in the midst of ultra-Saints, with a solid foundation of posttraumatic stress disorder from my own childhood, I had a feeling of constant unease about the volatility of the whole central Utah community, which, it seemed to me, was probably sprouting new Danites all the time.

"Naw, they're probably all gone," said Scott, looking at me with puzzled eyes above a comforting grin. "I was just flapping my gums."

Sterling agreed. "Absolutely," he said. "The Church probably hasn't had anyone killed for, oh, weeks and weeks."

"You can still lunch with us anytime," Eliza reassured me. "Without fear."

She was wrong about that. I could—and would—continue hanging out with my "dissident" friends. But I couldn't do it without fear. I wasn't sure exactly what there was to be afraid of. I was just consumed with a vague anxiety that some anonymous representative of the Mormon Church would soon do Something Bad to contain me and my treasonous stories.

Even years later, writing this, I can feel the twinges of that old terror. I've read too much about the Danites, seen too many religious fanatics worship at my father's feet, taken too many death vows to think that Mormonism has no dark side. I don't think most people realize how much the Latter-day Saints' history of quietly perpetrated violence still resonates throughout the community, what a powerful agent of social control it still is. Just after deciding to write this book, I confessed my fears to a non-Mormon friend from New York. She thought it was hilarious that I was scared of the Latter-day Saints. "It's like having a Bambi phobia," she said. "What are they going to do, kill you?" I felt so braced and grounded by this conversation, so free from paranoia, that I called another friend, an ex-Mormon from Utah, and described what I planned to write. "They'll kill you," she said immediately, without a trace of levity.

But despite the catastrophic fantasies that pop up even now, I still feel what I already felt during that conversation in my BYU office: The only thing scarier than telling my secrets would be keeping them. When the "sensitive information" you carry is your own history, going mute to protect the system doesn't keep you from being destroyed; it just means that you destroy yourself. "What profiteth it a man," Jesus said, "if he should gain the whole world, and lose his own soul?" For a long time I felt as though my soul was lost, hidden even from my own understanding, to protect me from the consequences of openness in a culture that demanded my silence. Now that I know what it feels like to be whole, my worst fear is not death, but a return to that soulless existence.

So Eliza was wrong. For months—years—after our conversation, I wouldn't do lunch, or anything else, without fear. Fear stalked me as I rocked on my babies, stood behind me as I taught class, smiled its chilling smile at me every morning when I opened my eyes. I couldn't stop it. But there was one thing I could control: I could choose not to obey it.

The Stream

M y father takes off his hat, allowing me to see that his eyes are angry and afraid. He doesn't know how long I'm going to keep him here, or how he's going to get home. My cousin Diane brought him to the hotel, after dropping into my parents' home and asking if he'd like to go for a drive. He's always seemed very fond of Diane, even though (or perhaps, in some strange way, because) she looks like his mother, the beautiful but famously monstrous paternal grand-mother neither she nor I ever knew. Diane has told me about going to visit my father after he had heart surgery, walking into his hospital room bearing homemade bread and strawberries and seeing his pale face twist into a scream of horror.

"Oh," my father said, panting and hoarse, after Diane rushed to reas-sure him. "I thought you were my mother."

I wonder how he regards Diane right now. I'm sure he feels kid-napped, betrayed, shanghaied in the worst way. Perhaps it reminds him of the monster all over again.

He runs his hands through his hat-mussed white hair, and I have that strange sense of looking in the mirror. That's exactly how I smooth my own hair into place. I didn't copy my father's gesture in childhood; it's something I didn't need to do until I drastically changed my hairstyle during my angry, tempestuous years, around the age of thirty.

It was a feisty time for Mormon dissidents. More than ever before, the Church seemed to have decided to suppress intellectual or political opinions that ran contrary to its teachings or its image. Every day seemed to bring new stories about excessively liberal Saints being "called in" and questioned by the religious authorities. The *Salt Lake Tribune,* the largest newspaper in Utah, began to run stories about Salt Lake City leaders "purging" the Latter-day Saint population, excommunicating people who dared publicly question Mormon views of reality or contradict claims made by Joseph Smith. Someone at the Church headquarters in Salt Lake City leaked a confidential copy of a speech made by one of the apostles, pinpointing intellectuals and feminists as two of the most scurrilous "enemies of the Church in the latter days." I fit squarely into both categories.

Brigham Young University was in a political pickle when it came to "women's issues." Mormon authorities were committed to making sure the school retained its academic accreditation, which meant, among other things, that a certain number of women were appointed to the faculty. The problem was that these women—I should say "we"—were technically not supposed to be employed outside our homes and that we were likely to be schooled in feminist theory. Both the university and its female employees simply lived with the contradiction. However, I noticed that female professors at BYU tended to express defiance by cutting their hair boy-short, something technically permitted under the dress code, but clearly unsettling to the Man. A good Mormon woman has elaborately curled, longish hair until middle age and a permed, upswept coiffure in later life. Either way, the highly sprayed hair moves as a unit, like a padded, shellacked helmet, protecting the brain from injury or information. At the time I was teaching, any female at BYU whose earrings hung lower than her do was probably a feminist, possibly a full-fledged dissident.

My own hair fell straight and loose to my shoulders, until the day I diverted my anger from chopping wood and decided to chop hair instead. I went into a mod-looking beauty salon, found a male stylist, and told him to make my head look like his. The stylist checked my left hand for a wedding ring, then reported my request to the owner of the salon, who asked me to call my husband to ascertain that I had his permission to change my hairstyle. This pissed me off so completely that I contemplated grabbing one of their clippers and shaving my own head. I tried to stay calm, but my manner (flared nostrils, smoking ears) frightened them enough to fulfill my request without husbandly approval. An hour later I went home, shivering at the unfamiliar breeze on the back of my neck, and began to develop the habit of pushing my inch-long hair backward with my fingers, exactly as my father is doing now.

"You know," he says after a moment, "I get everything I pray for."

I'm not sure why he's brought this up. Perhaps it's a subtle threat or boast, but I don't think so. More likely he's praying like crazy to get out of this damned hotel room, and he's trying to reassure himself that it will work.

"I'm so glad," I say, meaning it.

I believe him, because for the past several years, it seems I get every-thing I pray for, too. It has something to do with the way I've learned to pray, which is more about listening than demanding. Every day, if I can still my body and mind enough to hear Silence, I notice that my heart is yearning toward certain things, avoiding others. It's when I voice this deep yearning that my prayers are answered. And nothing else I might ask for really matters.

"More and more," says my father, "the older I get, the more my prayers are answered."

"That's wonderful."

Now I think he may be trying to tell me he's a good man, that I should honor him as much as God does. But I don't believe that having one's prayers answered is a sign of favor; it's just what happens when anyone prays sincerely. My father still believes that God is a white-haired fellow with blue eyes, almost exactly like himself. My God is more amorphous, more of a universal constant, like gravity or magnetism. This constant doesn't pick favorites; it simply flows into any opening we make for it. If Hitler had a kindly moment, a moment when, say, he felt like saving a kit-ten from a flood, I believe that God—barred from Adolf's mind in so many other moments—would have poured into the kindness of that mo-ment and helped the mass murderer reach the kitty. I believe that the line between good and evil doesn't separate human beings into different cate-gories; it runs through every one of us, and every moment is a choice: heal or destroy.

"You know what bothers me?" I ask my father. "Not so much that you did what you did, but that you kept lying about it. Every single day. I mean, you watched me grow up. You knew I was a basket case. You knew what you'd done. And every day, you chose to pretend it never happened. You're still making that choice, right now."

My father's jaw muscles twitch as he works his jaw in anger. Finally, he blurts out, "That John!"

I blink. "John?"

"Yes," says my father emphatically. "He puts this nonsense into your head. He was always so jealous." He raises his hands to his face, palms out, and wiggles his fingers like a rat trying to climb the wall of a terrarium.

"Jealous?" I'm mystified by this conversational twist. "Why would John be jealous? I *married* him."

"He was always that way," my father insists. "This is his doing."

I have the feeling that I'm seeing the tip of an iceberg, a rationale that has been carefully developed in conversations between all my family members ever since I flew the coop. I know that at least some of my siblings have made John the scapegoat for my shocking defection from the family and the faith. In a way, this touches me. Perhaps it means that they still want to love me, still want to believe that my treacherous behavior isn't my own doing. Maybe they want to believe that *my* choices, moment by moment, day by day, are not my own doing but the product of male brainwashing. They want to believe that I am a victim of circumstance, with no choices at all.

This way of thinking, the belief in the unassailable virtue of helplessness, runs very deep in Mormonism, as it does in any culture that tries to instill absolute obedience in its members. In some ways, it would be nice for me to think of myself this way, as a misguided soul whose mind has been taken over by pressure from a jealous husband, or mental delusions, or Stan. Unfortunately, I know this isn't true. While there are many things in life I cannot control, I always have choices. Viktor Frankl said there are two ways to go to the gas chamber: free or not free. Even when the body is an absolute victim, the heart and mind are at liberty to believe their best estimate of the truth.

"John had nothing to do with this," I tell my father. "It surprised him more than it did me."

It's absolutely true that John never tried to "implant" memories in my sorry head and that he was stunned and appalled when I began having flashbacks. On the other hand, once it started happening, he was always

there to tell me that what I was remembering made sense to him, resonated with what he knew about me. And he was the person who helped me learn to pray the way I do now. He was the one who first familiarized me with the phrase *Leaf in the Stream.*

Being a Leaf in the Stream was an idea John learned when he spent his Mormon mission years abroad in Japan. His mission leader was the American-born son of Japanese immigrants, who spoke a style of Japanese most of the natives found hilariously old-fashioned, and often used analogies that would have made no sense to the Latter-day Saint leaders in Salt Lake City. Quite unwittingly, this mission leader blended a strong shot of Asian philosophy into John's Mormonism. The Stream, he said, was the ubiquitous power of God that flowed through every being, sentient and nonsentient. To become a Leaf was to ride the current without struggling, to sense the inclination of a benevolent reality and surrender to it, moment by moment.

This was the way John and I had decided to live after Adam's birth threw our lives and beliefs into chaos. Of all the myriad "spiritual technologies" I tried, this was—and still is—one of the most useful. It became especially compelling after my encounter with the White Light (which was just another name for the Silence and for the Stream), because following the flow of reality always felt like that experience. If I paid attention in any given moment, I found myself *yearning* in one direction or another, toward this action or that one. Sometimes, the Stream carried me into things anyone would call spiritual practice: prayer, meditation, introspection, good works. But at other times, the current of the Stream picked up the pace, splashed me into whitewater. On those days, I might cut off my hair or publicly defy religious authority. Or set up a surprise appointment with my father in a Provo hotel room.

This train of thought reminds me to be a Leaf in the Stream, right here and now. I try to relax, to breathe more deeply, and search with the part of me that is neither my body nor my mind for the sense of God in the current of reality. After a moment, I find it. For just a fraction of a second, I feel this room filled, *flooded,* with the most breathtaking love. Love for me, love for my father. Love that incorporates both our troubled histories, the times when each of us really was a victim, the times when we have unjustly pretended to be victims, the times when we have victimized others. I have always been told by my Mormon teachers that God is the force of judgment, but I feel no judgment whatsoever in this love. Only acceptance.

This is not to say that the Stream has never led me into battle. It just means that even in the heat of combat, it never fed my urge toward malice, my enraged-victim's urge to ruin and destroy. Though I didn't always succeed, I tried diligently to stay tapped in to the Stream throughout the obstreperous phase of my spiritual quest, the phase in which "out of the mouth of the lion comes the undaunted voice of truth, the liberation of the unbounded heart."

Cutting off my hair was a way to declare myself a combatant, a visible signal that I would no longer choose to simply obey the dictates of my religion. Alone at night, during the time I once used to cry or hack up dead wood, I found myself more and more able to figure out what I really believed. Instead of practicing every religious discipline I could read about, I spent hours pulling apart all my beliefs, studying them, weighing their parts, testing them against my newfound sense of truth. It took months and months. I could spend a whole night muddling about one single belief. Did I really think that an elderly gentleman in Salt Lake City was God's "mouthpiece" to the whole world? It would have been very convenient if I did, but the truth was, I didn't. Was I internally compelled to accept that Joseph Smith was the mortal savior of the Latter-day world? Sorry, strike two. Did my heart and soul buy the Third Commandment, "honor thy father and thy mother"? Upon inspection, I found that they really did but that "honor" meant something altogether different to me than it did to my family. An alcoholic father might demand that his children "honor" him by bringing him liquor and making excuses to his boss, but was that really honor? I didn't think so. To me, "honoring" meant serving the person behind the lies, refusing to supply his need for secrecy, rejecting complicity in his self-destruction.

· · ·

"Believe me," I tell my father now, "John didn't put these ideas in my head. No one did. Nobody's making me do this, right now. It comes from me. All my choices come from me."

He shakes his head in dismay, eyes on the floor. I get the feeling that in his mind, the one vestige of hope for me, the one thing that meant I was not a deliberate enemy of the Gospel, was my supposed helplessness. Now I'm telling him that everything I've done—from newspaper interviews that criticized Mormon leaders to this, this horrific treachery toward God's best-known apologist—has been deliberate. Born to one monstrous woman, he has spawned another.

Watching him, I lose my brief connection to the Stream and dive instead into self-righteousness. How dare he judge me, this man whose act of insanity damaged me almost beyond repair? I can feel my facial expression become a mirror of his; a portrait of irked self-pity, of a victim seeking to control a victimizer. Then, at almost the same time, we both raise our hands and rake them through the hair above our ears, and I catch myself. I almost start to laugh, because it's so clear that we're almost the same person, my father and I. Two broken children raised in the same strange culture, trying our hardest to make sense of our lives, screwing up every other instant. My choice now is the choice I've had all along, to fight the Stream or surrender to it. I choose surrender. Which means, of course, that I'm still very much in the fight.

CHAPTER 29

Purity

I never had any trouble understanding why Virginia Woolf killed herself. I'd read biographies describing how the writer was molested by a cousin during childhood and developed a classic case of posttraumatic stress disorder, which seems to have left her half sentient, never fully engaged with the events around her. She could see beauty but not feel connected to it, yearn for love but not participate in it. She experienced things flattened, diminished, once removed. She was anesthetized to physical suffering (she seems to have drowned herself without flinching) but also to happiness. Psychologists call it psychic numbing or, in Virginia Woolf's words "living behind a pane of glass."

This phrase fit my own experience perfectly for most of my first three decades. Before my initial round of therapy, in my late teens, I felt almost as though I were living in a sensory deprivation chamber. I sometimes stayed out in the snow until patches of my skin were frozen solid with frostbite, not really aware of the cold. I viewed cuts and bruises with distant curiosity, wondering how they got there, since I rarely felt the moment of injury. After therapy, I was more conscious of emotion and sensation, but at a distance. Until my second pregnancy, which uprooted much of my deepest psychology, I even experienced motherhood as though it were happening to someone else. I wanted to feel more; I simply couldn't. The world seemed strangely flat and gray, but instead of leaving me indifferent, this tepid reality made me long for something more. My steady-state emotion was a dull longing for the ability to experience joy. It didn't seem much different from being dead, except that it was a whole lot more work.

I am endlessly grateful for the fact that I was lucky enough to learn something Virginia Woolf never realized: glass can melt. It melted for me when I began allowing myself to know what I already knew, to feel consciously the pain I'd been ignoring almost all my life, to question the Mormon way of seeing the world. Call it awakening, call it being born again, call it whatever you like; but the sensation of my disowned self moving back into my body was so strange and delicious that it occupied much of my attention for many months. In the words of another female writer, Emily Dickinson, "to live is so startling it leaves little time for anything else."

All my senses became sharper and more intense—so much so that I wasn't sure exactly how to handle it. Having been numb a long time, I was unprepared for the vividness of life without my pane of glass. Colors looked so much more intense that seeing a sample of paint chips could reduce me to tears of wonder. I remember having to sit down abruptly after Lizzie patted me on the face, literally swooning with love at the texture of those soft little fingers. A bite of chocolate—or oatmeal, for that matter—was almost too beautiful to bear. Sensation poured back into my body the way blood flows into a limb after a tourniquet is removed, and for the first time, I began to understand something that had always baffled me: why so many people would rather be alive than dead.

I think this had everything to do with sex. Like Virginia Woolf, I'd numbed everything connected to sensuality, to physical sensation, because I associated it with trauma. But feeling is a package deal, and when a person avoids all things sexual, the ability to experience physical pleasure in any form becomes a ghost of its former self. Due to early therapy and John's patience as a lover, I'd managed to have an acceptable sex life before I remembered my childhood, but it had always been somewhat frustrating; I could feel present either physically or emotionally but never both at once. Now my body, mind, and heart seemed to be reconnecting. Not only was being with John dramatically more satisfying, I felt as though I were making love with the entire universe, all day every day.

I strongly suspected that this was a sin.

I might have simply numbed out again, except that the lion phase of my spiritual journey made me almost obsessively reexamine all my beliefs, from expectations about what follows death to the morality of consuming caffeine. At its simplest, this process was like untangling a huge mess of sticky, tangled yarn. When it came to sexuality, the tangle was so chaotic and tightly knotted that I had trouble making progress at all. My childhood trauma made me cautious of the suspiciously gasping pleasure I now got from feeling, seeing, touching, tasting, and smelling the most ordinary aspects of the physical world, and my early religious training pushed this caution almost to the point of phobia.

Mormon guilt about sexuality—and sensuality—is different from, say, the flesh-tormenting asceticism of Catholicism, with its celibate leaders, its history of whips and chains, its paintings of tormented saints whose bodies and faces are contorted by an agony that looks darn close to ecstasy. The Latter-day Saint attitude toward physical desire is more what you'd imagine hearing from Queen Victoria if she'd lived in the 1950s and joined the John Birch Society. Mormon leaders rarely speak out about sex, except to state that it is direly forbidden to anyone who isn't sealed in the covenant to that one special man (or forty-eight special women). When they do tackle some sex-related issue, these leaders spare no effort in encouraging Mormons, young and old, to repress their physical urges.

Let me show you what I mean by quoting a tract that was once widely disseminated (pun intended) among the Saints. It was written by one of Mormonism's twelve apostles to help flawed but well-meaning Church members (pun intended) avoid the insidious sin of autoeroticism. This selection is mild, compared to the whole document, but it will give you the general tenor of Mormon attitudes toward sex. The following is printed just as it was in the original document, capital letters and all.

- If you are associated with other persons having this same problem [masturbation], YOU MUST BREAK OFF THEIR FRIENDSHIP. Never associate with other people having the same weakness . . . You must get away from people of that kind.

- When you bathe, do not admire yourself in a mirror. Never stay in the bath more than five or six minutes. Then GET OUT OF THE BATHROOM AND GO INO ANOTHER ROOM WHERE YOU ARE NOT ALONE.

- If the temptation seems overpowering while you are in bed, GET OUT OF BED AND GO INTO THE KITCHEN AND FIX YOURSELF A

SNACK, even if it is in the middle of the night, and even if you are not hungry, and despite your fears of gaining weight.

- KEEP THE PROBLEM OUT OF YOUR MIND BY NOT MENTIONING IT EVER—NOT IN CONVERSATION WITH OTHERS, NOT IN YOUR PRAYERS. KEEP IT OUT *of your mind!* . . .

- A *Book of Mormon,* firmly held in hand, even in bed at night has proven helpful . . .

- In very severe cases it may be necessary to tie a hand to the bed frame with a tie in order that the habit of masturbating in a semi-sleep condition can be broken . . .

Even as a teenager, I rather envied other religious sexual archetypes—the nun rapturously faithful to Christ, the Hindu or Sufi mystic whose passion is wholly consumed by contemplation of the Divine. Instead, my Mormon friends and I were supposed to emulate the archetype of a chubby, utterly friendless Latter-day Saint adolescent, who gripped a Book of Mormon in a hand that was firmly lashed to a bed frame, while preparing and stuffing down midnight snacks with the other. Really, it lacked panache. It just wasn't *sexy*—which, no doubt, is precisely the way its author liked it.

But even this image was downright pornographic compared to the sexual attitudes in my family. My father was so prudish he never bathed at home, only at the BYU swimming pool, where he went for daily exercise. I assume he used the private dressing stalls there; either that or he was more comfortable letting indifferent strangers see his body than he was with his family. I remember attending one of his public lectures when I was eighteen, listening to him read aloud the scripture that says, "To be carnally minded is death, and to be spiritually minded is life eternal." "You see?" he'd said to the audience, breaking away from his prepared script to put special emphasis on his words. "Do you see what the Lord is saying here? Sex is death! *Sex is death!*" At that moment I'd been overwhelmed by a wave of nausea, rage, and intense anxiety, so sudden and severe that I'd had to run out of the lecture hall, though at the time I had no idea why.

I didn't hear my father give another speech on sex until the week before my wedding, when I stayed at my parents' house for a few days between returning from Harvard and leaving with John on our honeymoon. Fresh off a heartening year of therapy that had allowed me to relax my sexual neuroses (the only reason I'd been able to date, let alone fall in love and get engaged), I was trying to act like a normal, mature adult even in the presence of my parents. So when I went into the kitchen one morning and found my father already there, drinking the vinegar/cod liver oil/wheat germ concoction he called his *potion magique,* I didn't turn around and flee the room, as was customary. I just got myself a bowl of Shredded Wheat and sat down at the place I'd always occupied at childhood dinners.

"Sin is waste," said my father.

I looked around the kitchen to see who else was there, but found we were alone. It took me a moment to understand that his comment was meant for me, because I wasn't used to being addressed by my father directly and because he was looking at the wall across the room, not at me. When I realized he'd actually started a conversation, or at least a monologue, I listened very closely indeed.

"Sin is waste," he repeated. "Waste of energy, work, money, and so forth. Any waste."

I squinted at him. "Okay," I said slowly.

"So, of course," he went on, eyes glued firmly to the wall, "the same thing is true of life itself. The creation of life."

I munched my Shredded Wheat. I'd spent many hours discussing my father with my therapist and had become more or less comfortable viewing him as a cherished enigma, devoid of social skills but enormously admirable in other ways.

"That's why, if a child is conceived, well, nothing has been wasted. That's permissible. But other than that—no, that would be a waste. Only when conceiving a child."

Seeming exhausted by the effort of so much communication, he buried his nose in his mug. For me, the light dawned slowly, but it dawned.

"Are you telling me I can have sex with John, but only if we're trying to get pregnant?" Hours and hours and *hours* of therapy had worked their wonders, or I never could have blurted it out.

My father didn't respond verbally. He began jiggling back and forth a little, perhaps invigorated by his *potion magique,* muttering under his breath in a foreign language. In short, our relationship was back to normal.

I said nothing else, just let him think I planned to follow his paternal advice. I felt very strange about our conversation. It seemed to me that he'd been allowing me the option of pregnancy as some sort of special dispensation, as though I were meant to understand that barring his permission, I would never be allowed any sort of carnal knowledge whatsoever.

I threw away the rest of my Shredded Wheat and went to find one of my married sisters (the one who, despite her emotionality, was mysteriously free of warts). This sister had generously forgiven me for having a meltdown the night before *her* wedding. She still thinks that I began weeping uncontrollably to divert attention away from her and onto myself, but though I now see how horribly unfair to her my behavior really was, at the time I honestly couldn't help it. I remember telling my therapist, who sat with me for a few catatonic hours, that it was because I knew romantic love, marriage, and sex were forbidden to me. Not to anyone else, just to me. I didn't know who told me that, but it seemed somebody had. My father, I thought, though I didn't know how and when.

"Did Daddy talk to you about sex before you got married?" I asked my sister now. "Did he, like, give you permission to have sex, but only if you were trying to get pregnant?"

"What are you talking about?" she said.

I told her about my father's speech in the kitchen. She burst out laughing. For the rest of the day, as she used her impressive sewing skills to put the finishing touches on my wedding dress, my sister also sang a loud and lusty song, courtesy of Monty Python, titled "Every Sperm Is Sacred." My father escaped to his office, his shoulders hunched like a raven's inside his black secondhand coat.

· · ·

A few days after our Shredded Wheat conversation, as I sat in the temple initiatory booth dripping oil beneath my shift, I was prompted by two elderly lady strangers to vow that I would "follow the law of my husband."

John, last I'd checked, was emphatically in favor of nonprocreative sex, and I felt a slight sense of relief that my religious obligation to him now clearly overrode my father's instructions. That day, I thought I was already a fully functioning sexual being. I was certainly in better psycho-sexual condition than I'd been before therapy. But it would be another ten years before my pane of glass melted, before I realized how much my body could feel, how deliriously delicious physical sensation could be, in bed and everywhere else.

I was pondering all this one day as I cleaned the kitchen cupboards, wondering how much more intense my newfound sensuality was going to get and how guilty I should feel. I reflected on the many religious texts and precepts I was still studying (to evaluate them, rather than simply obey them). I thought about the "pure love" that is so commonly noted as an essential attribute of God. Mormonism had taught me that "pure" meant sexless, tame, and manageable, which is just how things had felt behind my old pane of glass. It perplexed me to realize that the more I pursued the pure love of God, the wilder, juicier, and more carnally delicious my life was becoming.

I'd taken all the bottles and cans out of the cupboards in order to dust them, and the sunlight from the window, pouring through the clutter of containers, made them sparkle like jewels. The sight took my breath away, and I had the odd feeling—it happened often, those days—that I was somehow falling in love. I wanted to touch the bottles, hear them clink against each other, see them in different arrangements. This desire, like any physical desire I experienced at the time, was so intense, so thirsty, that it felt confusingly close to sexual sensation.

I puzzled over this as I replaced some jars in the cupboard, then, without thinking, put my hand to my lip like Rodin's *Thinker*. Suddenly my mouth was filled with an explosion of peppermint. It started at the tip of my tongue, but within a second it had spread to my whole mouth, gone down my throat and up my sinuses, made my eyes water, set me coughing and wheezing. After a minute I managed to regain basic motor control, though the universe still seemed entirely mint flavored. I looked at the label on the bottle I'd just handled, which said PURE PEPPERMINT EX-TRACT. I swear I heard that bubbling laughter, that joyful silent voice in the ether. *That's what I mean by pure,* it said. *That's how "pure love" feels.*

Ever since that experience, I have done my best to follow pure love wherever it takes me. It is the opposite of living behind a pane of glass; it's raw and unorthodox and unpredictable and sublime, and it never fades. I still have to wipe tears from my eyes in art supply stores, where the colors are so clean and pure, the smells so strong and beautiful. I can still feel drunk with bliss at the sound of a friend's laughter. I say "Oh, God" a lot. Mormons believe that this is "taking the name of the Lord in vain," but it doesn't feel vain to me. It feels like prayer. People tend to say it when the divine aspect of their being connects with the divine aspect of everything else, when God within touches God without. What else could a physicist say, contemplating the way light curves through the vast continuum of space and time? What else could a human body breathe when its lips touch the skin behind a lover's ear? Every form of beauty perceived, every form of lovemaking, is God meeting God. And it is all pure.

That was what I decided, one morning in the kitchen when I was going on thirty and falling in love with life. And it was a very good thing, this newfound way of loving, because I was about to lose almost every other kind of love I'd ever known.

CHAPTER 30

The Gang Bang

Y ou need to get your sisters in here," said Mona one day as I sat under her dog, watching the icicles melt from the eaves outside her office window.

"Mm . . . no," I said. "I don't think so."

"They deserve help, too," she said. "They went through the same thing you did."

I frowned. "How do you figure that? You haven't even met them."

"Don't need to," said Mona. "Perpetrators never stop at one. Four daughters, four victims."

"I don't think . . ." My protest trailed off. I actually had thought about this possibility, but was trying to remain objective and evidence based in all my claims. My sisters knew about my memories—I had told the Wartless One, and my mother called the others to warn them I'd lost my mind—but they all denied having any similar experience, even though our entire family was filled with quirks that fit the characteristics of people in a sexually abusive system.

(For example, one of my sisters, a brilliant writer, had at one point told me she'd discovered that the real, underlying reason for all her written work was to describe rape. She wrote several stories on the themes of rape and incest, then, for reasons that are still unclear to me, became violently angry at me and broke off all contact between us. This and other odd behaviors displayed by my siblings convinced me that my memories were real, but I'm trained as a social scientist, which means that I try very hard not to jump to conclusions. I also wish to avoid violating my siblings' privacy by writing much about them in this account. Though some of them collaborated on a biography of my father that asserts that I am a liar and a victim of false-memory syndrome, none of them ever did anything to harm me as a child. On the contrary, I survived largely because of their awkwardly expressed love, and I prefer to give them as much privacy as possible, even at the cost of reserving information that would strengthen my case.)

At any rate, my therapist's theory—four daughters, four victims— would have given me a sense of company, validation, and solace, if I'd been able to believe it as wholeheartedly as Mona. Though I didn't want to believe that any of my sisters had been through such horror, sharing a history of abuse would in some ways have been a huge relief.

"You really need your sisters' support," said Mona, "and they need yours. Bring them in, and I guarantee I'll have them talking about their own abuse within an hour."

I thought about this for a long moment as Mona's dog breathed lovingly into my face. I believed that Mona was making a massive false generalization. Her assumptions were statistically grounded, to a point—most pedophiles do indeed go after any small and helpless person they can get. However, incest perpetrators often single out one child (as do physically or emotionally abusive parents), and what's more, my case didn't fit the most common patterns I'd read about in my research on sexual abuse. Molesters tend to be debauched bacchanalian types, prone to intoxication and lechery as a general rule. My father was the opposite. There was no alcohol in his history, let alone our home. His attitude toward sex made the Puritans, with their fancy-pants buckles, look downright salacious.

There was, however, one type of perpetrator profile that fit my father like a glove: the charismatic religious narcissist, a man who believes himself to be specially chosen by God to do things that are forbidden to others and who has a profoundly split horror/fascination response to sexuality. The abuse I remembered wasn't about lust. It wasn't even about sex, except as a form of torture or even symbolic death. No, it was all about religion. I didn't know how it affected other people in my family.

"C'mon," said Mona, smiling sweetly. "Trust me. There's a ton of circumstantial evidence. You need to come out of denial."

"I don't think this is den—" I began.

"Well, I don't know what else you'd call it," said Mona.

I looked at her with some irritation. It was becoming apparent to me that Mona had done a lot less reading about sexual abuse, repressed memory, and trauma than I had. She apparently hadn't encountered strict evidentiary training or conflicting theories about abuse in her two-year education as a social worker. It wasn't her fault, I thought. It's just that after *my* education, I couldn't be so flippant about making what's known in sociology as a "truth claim."

·   ·   ·

It was the second week of my doctoral program at Harvard. One of my professors, a world-famous sociological theorist, had assigned all of us first-years to write a paper predicting the most important social changes of the next ten years. I wrote up an essay that, in all modesty, would probably have been well received in the courses I'd taken as an undergraduate. The famous sociologist began our second discussion by holding up my paper between thumb and forefinger, as if it were a soiled nappy, then eviscerating every false generalization or unsupported extrapolation I had typed onto its miserable pages. I thought I'd been impeccably fact based, but it was clear that now I was in the big-boy arena, that the bar for data grounding had been jacked up a few nautical miles even since my undergraduate days.

After being scalded to a fine, pink tenderness by the famous sociologist's criticism, I became almost maniacally committed to the kind of precise wording and conditional assertion that give social science journals the zingy, mellifluous tone of a computer manual translated from Japanese. But while my writing suffered, my social science training seemed to flourish; at the end of the semester, to my immense surprise, the famous sociologist asked me to become his research assistant.

This strict sociological education served me well in investigating the return of my repressed memories. In the months since my flashbacks began, I'd read thousands of pages about the social upsurge in claims of abuse in North America, the possible neurophysiological mechanism of memory repression and recovery. I wanted to be absolutely sure that I'd covered all the research bases, considered every possible reason for my experience. I tried to become coldly objective about the likelihood of my abuse, looking for any other possible explanation for my vivid memories, physical scars, and rocky psychological history. I hadn't found one.

Some of the arguments I'd read (many written by accused perpetrators) pooh-poohed the whole notion of traumatic memory repression and recollection, pointing out that false memories of nonevents could be implanted in experimental subjects by suggestion. On the other hand, I'd watched films of World War II soldiers, stricken with psychosomatic paralysis after battles they could not remember, suddenly regaining full physical mobility as psychologists prompted them to recall the details of their experiences—events that had been witnessed by hundreds of others. On yet a third hand, I agreed with Oliver Wendell Holmes that it would be better to let a hundred criminals go free than convict a single innocent man on the basis of tenuous evidence. Even so, when I tried to dismiss the strange things I remembered, everything in my mind and body sent out the silent scream, It happened, it happened, it happened, it *happened*!

After months of absorbing passionately biased arguments on both sides of the repressed-memory debate, I wrote up a carefully worded statement I planned to make if anyone ever confronted me about the accusations that were surely zipping along gossip grapevines throughout Utah. I would say, "There is physical evidence that I was sexually abused. There is circumstantial evidence to suggest the identity of the perpetrator. I am not prepared to make any other evidence-based claims." This was how I'd made my case to Mona, the first day we began working together. I was so afraid she'd denounce me as a false accuser that I nearly choked on my fibrillating heart and was hugely relieved when she accepted my memories without so much as a twitch.

And what if Mona were right? What if something had happened to my sisters? What if, just by having one frank, honest conversation, I could get most of the people I loved more than anything in the world to back up my memories? It was achingly tempting.

"You set it up," said Mona, "and I'll get them talking. Guaranteed."

"But . . . well, you don't know my family," I said. I doubted Mona had ever done battle with a Viking horde. "They're smart. Really smart. And . . . um . . . . outspoken."

Mona smiled. "Oh, I think I can handle them. I'm pretty smart my-self, you know. And outspoken."

I marveled, as I often did, at her absolute lack of doubt.

"Believe me, Martha," she said, removing her fashionable horn-rimmed glasses and tapping her chin with one of the earpieces, "your sis-ters need this. Get them here. I'll take it from there."

. . .

So it was that in the spring of 1992 I found myself headed toward my therapist's abode in a minivan filled with extremely tense relatives: John, my three sisters, and one of my brothers. Two of my sisters were livid disbelievers. The Wartless One, along with my only available brother (the one who'd arranged for me to get therapy as an adolescent), seemed much more open. Both had initially said they believed me, then fallen silent on the issue; I wasn't sure what they thought now. Despite their differing opinions, the fact that they all showed up for the session was a testament to the genuine love they all had for me.

That minivan ride was one of the most nerve-racking experiences of my life. The anger and fear stuffed into the exoskeleton of the vehicle created approximately the same pressure that existed in the minuscule dot of the compressed universe right before the Big Bang. We rode in si-lence, broken by a few lame attempts at joking, followed by lame at-tempts at laughing. I'd never seen the Viking tribe so . . . pent.

Mona met us at her door looking very professional, dressed in a crisply tailored wool suit instead of the jeans and sweaters she usually fa-vored. I made the introductions as John, my siblings, and I found seats on the chairs and couches Mona had arranged in a circle. She sat in an im-posing leather armchair, looking sharp and polished. I smiled at her, grateful that I didn't have to deal with my siblings alone anymore. Mona was right; she knew what she was doing. I could relax. It brought tears of relief to my eyes. I narrowly managed not to shed them.

"Well," said Mona briskly, smiling at my family members. "I guess you all know why we're here. Martha, do you want to tell your brother and sisters what you remember?"

I squirmed. No, I did not want to tell my siblings what I remembered.

I didn't want to tell anybody. It would be nice, I thought, if we had an earthquake right now. I pictured the floor buckling, ripping, and falling away beneath me, letting me off the hook. I paused, praying for the deus ex machina that in any self-respecting Greek drama would drop in right now to resolve this whole horrifying situation.

And it happened.

The earth didn't part, but Mona's doorbell rang, which was enough for me. My therapist gave an exasperated sigh, went to the door, and jerked it open. On the steps stood a young man who was selling something—candy bars, maybe, or cleaning solvent. Whatever it was, Mona wasn't buying.

"Get off my porch, you son of a bitch!" she shouted. "We're in a god-damn meeting here, can't you see that? Get off my goddamn porch and stay off, or I'm calling the cops!"

She slammed the door. John looked at me, and I looked at John, and then we looked at my siblings and they looked at us, everyone wide-eyed. True, Mona wasn't Mormon, not even a native Utahan. Still, this level of Not Nice seemed extraordinary.

My therapist rushed back to her armchair, sat down, smoothed her wool skirt. "Sorry," she said. "Now, where were we? Martha, I believe you were telling us . . . ?"

So divine intervention hadn't helped me at all, any more than it had done when I was five. Fortunately, I could still call up my pane of glass when it was really needed. I slipped behind it, stared at a spot on the Persian rug, and choked out my story.

"Now," said Mona when I finished, "I assume you all know that I am a licensed clinical social worker—an expert in this field. Let me assure you, what Martha remembered really did happen." She gave my siblings a firm nod. "So, that should clear up any doubts you might have had. Let's discuss where we should go from here."

All the Vikings looked at her. They raised one eyebrow apiece. I did it myself. This wasn't exactly the tack I'd expected Mona to take. Simply asserting expertise, then swearing to the truth of her own beliefs, was way, way too facile to pass inspection among my siblings. She might as well have said that she was a Ghost Buster and that our childhood home had been possessed by the spirit of Humpty Dumpty.

"As an expert," Mona went on, "I also know that Martha is not the only one in your family who was abused by your father. I'm here to listen. You can tell me. What did he do to you?" She bent forward, looking with intense and sympathetic eyes at my sisters.

I felt the blood drain from my face. I'd been doubtful about setting up this battle of wits, but I hadn't expected Mona to arrive *completely* unarmed.

My oldest sister broke the stunned silence. "*What?*" she said. "We're here to help our sister—because she's lost her mind—and you have the audacity to tell the same kind of lies about *us*? *To* us? Where did you get the nerve? What kind of self-promoting, witch-hunting moron are you?"

The volcanic anger in my sister's voice response nearly blew out the back wall of the room. It hit Mona full on, making her gape like a light-blinded deer. There was a portentous pause.

Then all my siblings started yelling at once. Articulate, analytical, apocalyptically angry, they took Mona apart a chunk at a time. They attacked her logic, her looks, her educational background, her professional ethics, her personality, her suit, her treatment of the teenaged door-to-door salesman. The awful thing was, I agreed with them. Even the brother and sister who had been willing to listen to me were now convinced that I'd been hoodwinked by a two-bit Svengali whose magnetism they were totally unable to perceive.

At first, Mona tried to fight back, shouting a retort here and there. She was way, way out of her league. She couldn't finish a sentence, much less bend my family to her will. After the first five minutes, she crumpled up in her chair, clenched fists pressed to her heart, and just let the torrent of rage wash over her.

In the end, the person who brought order back to the session wasn't Mona, but John. Far brighter than my therapist, and obviously more accustomed to intellectual argument, he charged single-handedly into battle with the Vikings. Though outnumbered, John had one advantage: he was even more pissed off at my family than they were at me.

"You're not even listening to her!" John shouted, his voice rising above the general mayhem. "Could we please talk this thing through?"

Abruptly, the Viking horde left Mona in a bloody heap and turned its furious energy on my husband.

"My father would never do anything like that to Martha," said one of my sisters, "but I know who would: *John!*"

John and I looked at each other, confused, as the sister who'd just spoken began to cry.

"It's true," she sobbed through her tears. "He rapes her all the time. She doesn't say anything about it, but I know. From the time they were married, he's been doing it."

John was so incredulous he couldn't find words. He just looked at me and put his hands up in astonishment.

"Um . . . see, that really is impossible," I said, finding my voice. "Because you can't rape the willing."

"You can say that, but I know," my sister whispered, the tears running faster. "I've seen it. Not literally, but in my mind's eye. I *saw* it."

I found this very curious. Where did this sister, the closest to me in age, get her conviction that she had seen me raped? My other siblings fell silent for a beat, perhaps because they, too, thought this strange. Then a different sister, not wanting the action to slacken, took another run at John.

"Why are you even here?" she demanded. "This is about *us. Our* family. What makes you think you even have the right to be here?"

"*Because I love my wife!*" John burst out.

My siblings were struck mute. John's statement was an unorthodox—make that unthinkable—thing to say in our family. Our mutual esteem, our pack loyalty, was meant to be understood without words. Saying you loved someone, right out loud, was considered the worst kind of gauche sentimentality. Ordinarily, my siblings would have dismissed John's words out of hand, but under these circumstances they seemed impressed. At that moment I learned something I've relied on ever since: though memory can be challenged and evidence lost, though we may be dreaming our reality, rather than living it, and therefore every truth-claim can be challenged, there is one thing we can know for certain from the core of our being, and that is "I love." John meant what he said with every cell and fiber, and this indubitable fact silenced the horde.

We sat there, panting like winded wrestlers, until Mona's quavering voice broke the stalemate.

"So," she said (and now she was a humble therapist), "why don't we just talk about what life was like for each of you, growing up in your family?" She looked at my eldest sister. "Would you like to begin?"

My sister looked at Mona as if she were a bad cheese. "That's a pretty vague question. What do you mean?"

Mona shrugged timidly. "Oh, for instance," she said, "what was your house like?"

My sister paused for a long moment, her eyes on the carpet. Then she sighed and spoke quietly, calmly. "Unbelievable," she said. "Filthy. Dirty diapers in the corners, junk everywhere, I mean *everywhere*. Mint green walls with hunter orange chairs—indescribable, really."

Her manner had softened a bit, giving Mona the courage to sit up a little straighter. "Oh, come on," she said, with a cautious hint of a smile, "it couldn't have been that bad."

"It was." My sister gave an emphatic nod. Immediately, the rest of us Vikings backed her up. There was another minor hubbub as we all began describing our childhood home, recalling particularly hideous decorating features, laughing at each other's imagery. My siblings all agreed (facetiously, of course) that the condition of our house had been way more bizarre than a little psychotic child abuse. Mona lapsed back into her stunned-mullet pose, baffled at the suddenness with which my siblings and I had moved from conflict to consensus, rage to hilarity.

"This," she muttered, so softly I could barely hear her, "is the most dysfunctional family I have ever seen."

"Really?" said my brother. "The very most dysfunctional ever?"

"Without question," said Mona.

My siblings and I all regarded each other with some satisfaction. Then, in synchrony that needed no consultation, we all raised our forefingers in the air and began to chant, "*We're number one! We're number one! We're number one!*"

When the cheering had died down, Mona began questioning each of my siblings about their experience of life in the swimming-pool-blue house. Every story broke my heart. I hadn't realized that my eldest brother and sister had explicitly decided to take on the task of raising their six siblings, since my parents were clearly unfit for the task. I didn't know that my younger sister blamed her neglected childhood on living in my shadow (me?) or that my middle sister had repeatedly borne our parents' anger for defending the rest of us from various forms of attack. Every one of the Vikings had fought the battle of childhood in a different way, and therefore our wounds formed different patterns. Nothing more was said about abuse, but one thing was certain: we were all wounded. We all bore scars: badges of courage that represented the help each of us had tried to give the others, unsupplied and desperate though we'd been.

That session was the first and last time I battled the Vikings. (In the proud tradition of our number one dysfunctional family, we have barely spoken of it since—in fact, I haven't spoken with most of my siblings about anything. But if I were in their shoes, I think meeting Mona would have convinced me that she was a memory-implanting lunatic, proselytizing for a social fad.) Five hours after arriving at Mona's house, we quit talking and went to dinner together. There was less tension than before the session, more of the Nordic warrior rowdiness of our childhood, but I was ashamed, mortified, disgraced beyond recovery. I watched my siblings from behind the pane of glass, loving them, losing them. I couldn't unremember my childhood, and I couldn't remember it without violating Valhalla's rules of order.

The following week, I had one more meeting with Mona. She told me that I should have warned her that my family was so "cold" and that if I'd told my story better, the session would have gone exactly as she'd planned. I told her I didn't think so. I used the f-word—and I don't mean *feminism*—liberally. Loudly. She told me to shut my insolent mouth and run around the building until I could keep a civil tongue in my head. I told her she was fired. I have to say, it got me in touch with my anger.

John thinks that our family session (he calls it the gang bang) was a blessing in disguise. Mona shouldn't have forced the issue into the spotlight so soon, when I was still so raw, but she inadvertently spared me a long, slow, horrible period of awkwardness and silence. Years of unstated suspicions and innuendo between me and my siblings would probably have been worse than the gang bang, in the same way that losing a limb to leprosy would be worse than having it ripped off by wolves. Still, that afternoon was one of the very worst things that has ever happened to me. It would have been less painful to lose my family to war or natural disaster: less shame, less confusion, less personalized agony.

I did lose them, you see. I've never really been back. Though there isn't an official "no contact" rule between us, my siblings and I stopped most communication after that bloody battle. I hear from other relatives and friends that I'm the black sheep now, the traitor to our family's code of conduct, the enemy of everything we once stood for together. My father was our claim to fame, our saving glory. Turning against him in such a shocking way was like using a burning flag to set fire to our supreme commander. There is no doubt in my mind that my siblings will always love me; they have loved me since I was born, and real love is indestructible. But I will never again belong to the bold, brash Viking horde. I have left Valhalla behind. Sometimes I think there is not room enough in the universe for the sorrow of that exile.

CHAPTER 3 I

Dana

W
ould you like a glass of water or something?" I ask my father. I don't know what else to say. This conversation,
which I have rehearsed in my mind so many different ways
over the years, has dwindled down to the one thing I never expected:
small talk. We might as well be at a cocktail party, except that Mormons
don't have cocktail parties. They mainly have church-based leisure activities featuring a blend of soda pop and fruit juice called sparkle punch.
Perhaps if we had some sparkle punch now, we would be communicating
better.

"What?" says my father. "Oh. No, no, don't bother."

It's like an absurdist play, the two of us going through the rituals
of polite sociability when our history calls for something much more
intense—hate, love, a roller-coaster ride through both. But all I feel is
the same dull sadness I remember from childhood. In the ten years of silence between me and my parents, I have never missed either of them,
not for an instant. I miss my siblings, my erstwhile friends, the hair-
dresser who kept cutting my hair rebel-short during my days in Utah and
who gradually became a pal. But not my parents. When I hear friends talk
about actually wanting to be with their mothers and fathers, whether
they're remembering the past or musing about the future, I always wonder what this must feel like. I literally can't imagine it. I often wonder if
this means my emotional life is fatally flawed; I can't imagine my children
missing me, either, and what's that doing to them? Suddenly filled with
self-doubt, I put both my hands in my lap. I'm stumped.

And then, lo! Once more, the god drops from the machine. The
heavy hotel room door creaks, opens, and delivers an Athena in the form
of my cousin Diane.

Diane's father, who died several years ago, was my father's brother. He raised his three daughters in a small Utah town about eighty miles from my home, and we visited often. My relationship with my cousins was marked by extremism. Miranda, the youngest, who at the moment is curled into a silent ball in the hotel closet, was extremely shy. Diane was extremely feisty. Since we were only a few months apart in age, we were expected to be natural playmates, and sometimes we were. At other times we had violent, hair-pulling arguments, which ended when one or the other of us came up with a project—setting fire to something, for example, or jumping off a roof. I remember one busy day we spent carving our initials into the skin just above our knees, trying to create permanent decorative scars. Many years later, I would read that emotionally disturbed girls often cut themselves; the pain of the wound in the skin drowns out the pain of the wound in the heart. Diane and I never talked about pain when we were kids, though we now look back on our own behavior with the kind of appalled wonder you feel looking at *National Geographic* pictures of primitive scarification rituals.

"Hi, sweethearts," says Diane now, smiling her radiant smile. She and her sisters betrayed me in adolescence by growing to be unusually tall and extremely beautiful. As adults, they also developed an overflowing, effusive affection for almost everything in the world, from babies to lint. Based on our childhood interaction, I would never have expected Diane to become a tender maternal force, but she did.

"How are you, dear?" Diane says to my father. She drops to one knee so that her eyes, which are the color of maple syrup, can look straight into his. Her brow is delicately knit.

My father isn't quite sure how to react. He has every reason to be furious with Diane, but her manner is so kind it's difficult to resist. Plus, she's his only ride home. He doesn't answer, and after a moment Diane squeezes his hand, then comes to sit beside me on the sofa.

"I've been listening," she says, gently. The point was never to lie to him. We agreed on that before we came here. The point was just to let me speak with him one on one, but with witnesses to validate that the conversation had actually happened.

"It's all utter nonsense," says my father.

"But she has scars," says Diane. "How did they get there? At the very least, you have to admit that *something* happened—something bad enough to make her disappear for ten years. Why won't you talk to her about it?"

"*Utter nonsense!*" my father growls. "Parents do not do things like that to their children. It's all pure invention."

"Yes, they do, dear," said Diane patiently. "Parents abuse children all the time. You're not being rational."

"All the experts will tell you," says my father. "It's fantasy, mental illness. These things *do not happen*."

Diane shakes her head as if there's water in her ears. "There are people who swear the Holocaust never happened, either," she says. "There are experts willing to swear that the camp survivors are lying." With the fingers of one long, slender hand, she touches me reassuringly on the knee, right where I once carved my initials. "Martha loves you," she tells my father. "She has nothing to gain by making this up."

He doesn't answer. I'm feeling stronger by the minute, as though Diane is giving me a blood transfusion. It's wonderful to hear her talk about logic and evidence, even if my father isn't listening, even if he never will. Even if most of my people, from near-and-dear relatives to the most far-flung Latter-day Saints, will never listen, either. They will almost certainly judge me without hearing my case, and it's virtually impossible that anything will change their minds.

•   •   •

I realized this during the long, weary days and sleepless, grieving nights that followed the family gang b— um . . . session. I could see that my siblings' truth, as well as that of all other Latter-day Saints, would always be based on group consensus. I read psychology texts about the effects of socialization on perception, pondered the famous experiments by Solomon Asch that demonstrated how subjects who didn't know they were being tested changed their perceptions in order to agree with other people. Shown two lines, one long, one short, in the company of people who all claimed that the lines were of equal length, the naive subjects almost always agreed with the majority, rather than the evidence of their own senses. They not only *said* that the lines were equal; they often came to actually *see* them as being equal.

The more I read, the more isolated I felt. John, as always, was staunchly in my corner, but he was the only person I'd known for any length of time who had heard my whole story and sided with me. Everyone else seemed dangerous, even people I hadn't met.

At that moment, I wasn't the only Mormon who walked around feeling a little tense. In Salt Lake City, the highest officials of the Church were continuing what the newspapers called a purge of intellectual rebels. Every time I went to the BYU campus, I heard more accounts of faculty members being "called in," threatened with disfellowshipment, excommunication, and their attendant catastrophes. Rumors of Church-sponsored espionage continued to fly. Two university administrators told me they'd been "called in" after their home telephones started making strange clicking sounds and that the religious authorities who reprimanded them knew things they could only have gleaned from listening to the administrators' private phone conversations. I didn't know whether to believe these accounts. I didn't know what to believe.

I was now teaching Sociology of Mormonism, possibly the only course at BYU with the potential to be more controversial than Sociology of Gender. I'd long ago given up any pretense of communicating actual sociological theory. My one and only goal was to teach my students the difference between a scientific fact and a value-based belief. I wanted them to realize that from a social science standpoint, there was no way to either confirm or disconfirm religious dogma. I created the midterm exam for the course to emphasize this. I made a long list of truth claims familiar to every Mormon boy and girl, then asked the students to determine whether each statement was true, false, or impossible to determine from empirical evidence. For example:

1. *God has blue eyes. (true, false, scientifically indeterminable)*

2. *The Three Nephites live in the United States. (true, false, scientifically indeterminable)*

3. *Polygamy is the eternal order of marriage. (true, false, scientifically indeterminable)*

And so on.

The answer to each and every question on this test was "scientifically indeterminable." That was the whole point: I wanted the exam to remind them that religion and science occupy different corners of reality. Three of my forty students got it. The rest marked each question with the answers they'd learned in Sunday school, defending Mormonism as empirically true, down the line. One of the students who failed the test, a twenty-one-year-old returned missionary, stood up in class and patiently explained that I was wrong, and his answers were right.

"You see, Sister Beck," he told me in an earnest voice, "I hold the priesthood, and that means I'll *always* know better than you." Most of the class nodded sagely in agreement.

I briefly considered responding, "And yet, Brother Boswell, you're as dumb as a sack of hamsters, and that means *I'll* always know better than *you*." But I thought better of it. In the context of a Mormon worldview, his argument was flawless. I thought about one of my friends who'd told her bishop that Church doctrine made her feel like a second-class citizen. He'd looked at her with wounded confusion and said, "But, Sister, you *are* a second-class citizen." So I politely asked the missionary to sit down, then explained to the class—*again*—that as long as we were in an academic setting, untestable religious tenets did not rule the day.

They didn't get it.

· · ·

After class, I went back to my office and tried to work on my dissertation. It wasn't easy, because I was distracted by the sound of a piped-in "devotional," one of a series of speeches given every month or so by the major Mormon leaders (the General Authorities) to the BYU community. The sound systems in the social science building (and all others, as far as I know) had been set with a central override switch so that it was impossible for faculty members to turn the sound in their offices off—or even *down*. As I tried to focus on interpreting data, the sonorous voice and lugubrious cadence assumed by all General Authorities (John and I called it pulpit-speak) resonated from the speaker in the ceiling. I was sure it was calculated to sound like the voice of God, though to me it seemed closer to Big Brother. "Of course the leaders of the Church trust our scholars," said the voice. "That is precisely why we must make sure our trust is merited."

I put my elbows on the desk and my face in my hands, shaking my head in something very close to despair. Did anyone else hearing these words realize that they were self-contradictory? The speaker droned on, trusting (because he'd made sure) that no Mormon scholar would contradict him.

I heard a small rustling sound behind me. When I turned toward the door, I saw that a folded piece of paper had been pushed under it. It was written in red Magic Marker, which had seeped through the paper, like blood. I went to the door, opened it, and looked up and down the corridor outside. There was no one there (almost everyone on campus was in the basketball arena, where the General Authority was delivering his "devotional"). Cautiously, I picked up the folded page and opened it. Scrawled in large, sloppy letters were the words "You've gone too far. You are the Antichrist."

It was such a ridiculous assertion that I probably should have laughed, but I couldn't. I checked the hallway again (still empty), then closed the door and sat down, shakily, at my desk. My mind raced, trying to figure out who had sent the note, and why. Was it the returned missionary who'd just spoken out in Sociology of Mormonism? Was it a fanatic who'd read something I'd said to a newspaper reporter about the purging of feminists and intellectuals? Either of those explanations would have been comforting compared to my strongest suspicion: one of my father's more loony acolytes had finally heard that I claimed to have been abused.

My father had attracted a steady stream of such people, along with genuinely lovely Mormon devotees, for as long as I could remember. I recalled an employee from my father's publishing company who came to our house wearing a sweatshirt with the great man's name printed on it, kneeling reverently on the floor in our living room while my father checked some bound galleys. Another time I recalled five polygamists, one man and four wives, sitting in our living room while the man discussed doctrine with my father. I remembered that the visitors smelled strange, like sour milk, and that their clothes looked like relics from the nineteenth century. Not long after their visit, the husband shot himself in the head and his wives pushed their children from a tall building in Salt Lake City, then jumped to their own deaths.

Along with all the other foul play perpetrated by Mormonism's lunatic fringe, which popped up in the back pages of Utah newspapers on a regular basis, incidents like these had left me a tad skittish. I tried to dismiss the note as the work of a prankster, but it wasn't easy. In fact, it wasn't possible. It infuriated me that the writer of the note managed to scare me, but scared I was. I fled my office, where the devotional was still droning on, and picked up Elizabeth from day care. (Mormon women weren't supposed to work, let alone use day care—was that why someone thought I was the Antichrist?) Then I collected Adam and Katie from their respective schools. Once we got home, I closed the curtains and turned on all the lights. John was out of town on business; I wondered if the note writer knew that. I felt desperately alone.

Being with my children helped a little. I gave them frozen waffles for dinner (another Antichrist behavior?), then assembled them on my bed, where we all watched cartoons (Antichrist) until the kids fell asleep. I didn't put them in their own rooms, partly because I needed company, partly because I was afraid to let them out of my sight. There was no iron-clad reason to believe that any of us was in any danger, but I had a colossal case of the creeps. I was still haunted by nightmares, though they were becoming less violent, and the atmosphere at BYU, topped off by the anonymous note in bleeding letters, wasn't exactly tranquilizing. I felt friendless, orphaned, adrift, and vulnerable. It took me until the wee hours, after crying for a while and being soothed by my children's soft, peaceful snoring, to remember that I wasn't alone.

I'll be here. Always. I will always be right here.

I sat up on the bed, crossed my legs, straightened my spine, and let myself be still. These days, no WHAM! interrupted the slowing of my thoughts; there was a flurry of fear and anger, and then my mind let go and my heart began its customary seeking. I was listening for my next prayer, feeling for the direction of the Stream.

And then, quite unexpectedly, something—a chunk of information, like part of a computer code—simply appeared in my mind. One instant it wasn't there at all, and the next instant it was completely present, as though I had known it my whole life. It was the knowledge that someone was coming to help. To be my friend. I got a sense of a woman about my age, very warm, generous, and smart. The impression of a name came to me, just as though I were a bad TV psychic. I could "hear" it just well enough to think that it had a *D,* an *A,* and an *N* in it. Dana, I decided. That was the name. I didn't know anyone named Dana, but if I met such a person anytime soon, I'd pay attention. The thought made me feel calm, almost happy. I fell asleep right away.

· · ·

Two days later, I was home working and drinking a Coke (Mormon women are reprimanded for doing any paid labor or consuming any caffeine-containing drinks; Antichrist, Antichrist . . .) when the doorbell rang. I had stopped simply yanking it open; I always peeked through a window first, like Boo Radley, to see who was there. That day, I was glad I checked, because although I hadn't seen these visitors for at least ten years, I recognized them instantly. They were related to me. Through my paternal line. Not good. And yet . . . their names were Diane and Miranda—two *D*'s, three *A*'s, and two *N*'s—and they were just about my age. Heart thumping, I opened the door.

"Hallo, Martha!" Diane shouted. Miranda, still the quiet one, gave me a shy smile.

"Uh . . . hello," I said, nervously.

"We're on a mission!" Diane said. I winced at the word, but she made it sound like the best party ever thrown. "We're here to find out why our family is so totally and utterly screwed up!"

"We thought you might be able to help," said Miranda. Now that she'd brushed back the waist-length hair that had curtained her face in childhood, she turned out to look like a hazel-eyed Gwyneth Paltrow.

I just stood there, staring at my cousins, mouth agape.

"Unless . . . oh, I'm so sorry," said Diane, dropping her smile. "Did we offend you? I mean, it's not that we don't love the family, it's just that, well"—she shrugged regretfully—"they are . . ."

"Totally and utterly screwed up," Miranda repeated helpfully.

"No, no, I'm not offended at all," I said. "If you only . . . I mean, please, come in."

I stood back to let them enter. The temperature of the house seemed to warm slightly as they sat down on my living-room couch and I took a chair across from them.

"Here's the thing," said Diane, as though the break in contact between us had never happened, as though we were all still sitting under a tree in Ephraim, Utah, where they'd been raised. "We're not really sure what happened in our fathers' house, when they were growing up, but we think it must have been bad."

"Colossally bad," said Miranda, nodding.

"And since they didn't have any psychological literacy, we're the generation that has a chance to fix things," Diane went on. "But only if we more or less know what happened—what's still happening—in our family."

My lips had gone dry. I tried licking them, but my tongue was dry, too.

"You guys are here because you know about what I've been saying, aren't you?" I asked them. "What I've been saying about my dad."

Both my cousins looked at me with so much compassion in their eyes that I almost stopped trembling.

"Well, sweetie," Diane said, very softly, "we haven't heard anything specific, but we were kids together, right? So we've pretty much always known there had to be something."

"Happy kids really don't act the way you acted," said Miranda, smiling a smile that managed to be both sad and very cheering. "Of course, they don't act the way *we* acted, either . . ."

"You know it was sexual abuse?"

They both shrugged and sighed, appearing not even slightly surprised.

So I told them everything.

We were up most of that night, talking as fast as we could, comparing notes that clarified the past for all of us, laughing uproariously at things that should have been the opposite of funny but became hilarious in the presence of staunch companions. The whole world would feel safer to me forever after, partly because learning more about Diane and Miranda's father (one of my own father's brothers) convinced me even more thoroughly that both men were raised by a mother who could have earned a merit badge in child abuse. My father had apparently been his mother's favorite, a mixed blessing to say the least, since her frankly creepy attentions (I kept remembering how she'd told my mom, "He'd make such a good lover") seem to have pushed him to complete dissociation, a huge case of narcissism, and what the textbooks call "fugue phases of perpetrator behavior." My uncle, on the other hand, had not found favor in his mother's eyes. He'd grown up to be a thoroughgoing victim, kind and bright, but utterly psychologically helpless. The aggressor in Diane and Miranda's life had been their mother, who (in just one example of motherly attentiveness) had her daughters' cats killed one day because the girls forgot to feed them before school.

In the years since my cousins reappeared to light my life, we've spent many a night telling these stories, along with other harrowing tales from our early years. I've also heard the backstory to our unscheduled reunion, which is a little spooky: the day I got my first threatening letter, Diane and Miranda, who lived fifty miles away in Salt Lake, felt peculiarly driven to seek me out—so much so that Diane called Miranda and simply stated, "We're going to find Martha," and Miranda, without asking a single question or missing a beat, answered, "Yes, we are."

One of the things I love most about my cousins is their refusal to see our heritage as anything but fabulous, a series of unfortunate catastrophes that ultimately put the fun in dysfunctional. They are not only open about airing family problems; they're downright jolly. Their only condition for letting me write about them here was Diane's request that I describe her as having large, perfectly formed breasts. Fine with me, although I've never really noticed her breasts. Usually—right now, for instance—my attention is drawn to Diane's clear, intense auburn eyes, to the high, bright energy that seems to fill her body and radiate several yards beyond it.

"Do you see," Diane is saying to my father, "that when you deny things so globally—when you say *no* parent *ever* sexually abused a child—you aren't actually looking at the evidence? Do you see that isn't rational?"

My father retreats into another language, grumbling at his hat. Diane regards him with frustration and tenderness. She grins at me and mouths, "You're doing great!" as though I'm playing the role of the Radish in a kindergarten play. Her maple-syrup eyes sparkle above her large, perfectly formed breasts. Then—Diane just can't help it—she begins to chuckle at the absurdity of the whole situation. Her laugh, impossibly infectious, makes me smile almost against my will. My father looks up, confused, but then he smiles as well, and I'm overwhelmed all over again with how lovely and crazy my family is. I am seized with a fierce, proud, possessive happiness that each of my relatives exists, even knowing that every one of us has lived through times when we wished we'd never been born.

CHAPTER 32

Dissidence

R eally, truly, be careful what you pray for. By spring of 1993, my spiritual quest had led me to exactly what I'd wanted most: a deep, warm sense of love and meaning in the universe, an inner moral compass by which to direct my actions, a daily life filled with a steady stream of small miracles. The problem was that my newfound faith was driving me straight out of my religion.

Mormons who leave the fold, unlike apostates from other faiths, tend to avoid joining any other church. I think there are at least two reasons for this: first, because Mormonism is so all-pervading, so exclusive of other creeds, and, second, because Latter-day Saints are actually taught to test religious claims against their own sense of truth. This approach to learning, encouraged by Joseph Smith and his successors, made Mormonism very appealing to the religious seekers of the nineteenth century—but, of course, it has its exceptions. One day, when I mentioned Mormon truth seeking to a non-Mormon friend, she said, "Wait—I'm utterly confused. Wouldn't that mean they'd encourage discrediting Church claims that aren't true?" "Utterly confused" is exactly how I felt most of the time I was Mormon, because the "seek your own truth but believe in the Gospel" tradition is one huge double bind. It goes like this: Before you accept any religious claim, you must scrutinize it to see if you really believe it's true. However, if it's an official Church doctrine and you feel that it *isn't* true, this is the work of a sloppy soul or, worse, the devil. On the other hand, if you accept the advice of a Church leader, which then turns out to be wrong, it's your own fault for not "discerning" that in this particular case, the leader was mistaken.

To deal with these contradictory instructions, Mormons are advised to use something called "the shelf." "Put it on the shelf" is the phrase used to describe the tidy act of deliberate denial that allows the Saints to keep occasional surges of disbelief from troubling them. If it bothers you to know that Joseph Smith said the moon was populated by small humanoids who dressed like Quakers, "put it on the shelf." Likewise if you find it improbable that God gives his favorite Latter-day Saints their own special magic rocks, called "seer stones," which allow them, among other things, to find buried treasure. Or if you don't wholeheartedly believe that there is a trio of immortal pre-Columbian American Jews, known as the Three Nephites, who were spared by Jesus from the curse of death and have spent centuries wandering the American continent, assisting Latter-day Saints with anything from missionary work to flat tires. The improbability of these ideas needn't inconvenience any Saint who has a sturdy, commodious, and well-maintained shelf.

As a spiritual camel, I had installed many, many square yards of shelf space in my mind. During my lion phase, I compulsively tore them all down. Day after day, I yanked stacks of stored beliefs off the perches in my subconscious moral system. Once they had tumbled into consciousness, I would subject these beliefs to examination by both my mind and heart, deciding what I thought was worth keeping, and what would no longer fit onto the drastically diminishing storage area in my brain. Though I maintained an abiding respect for the close-knit communities and wholehearted goodness of most Latter-day Saints, the actual doctrines on which the faith is founded just kept crashing down.

Since my family and I were no longer communicating, I was free to pursue this process without much pressure from my nearest and dearest. John, however, was trying to do the same thing while remaining connected to his very caring, thoroughly Mormon parents.

"It just doesn't make sense," John told his mother one day as we sat in my in-laws' home, eating homemade chocolate-chip cookies. "A lot of stuff about the Church seems wrong to me."

"Have you prayed about that?" John's mother asked, unable to keep the shrill edge of anxiety from her voice. "The Lord will tell you the truth, you know. You'll get the burning in your bosom." (The "burning in the bosom" is a classic quote from Mormon scripture, the sensation by which God confirms one's "testimony." I always wished the phrase came with an illustration of a flaming brassiere and perhaps a sample-sized pack of Rolaids.)

"Yes, Mom, I have prayed about it," said John. "And I really, truly feel that a lot of it's wrong. For me."

"Well, I don't see how you'd get *that*," said his mother, voice crackling.

"I *feel* it, Mom," he said. "I think it, and I feel it."

"Are you sure those feelings are in line with the Gospel?"

"No," said John. "They aren't. That's just the point. I'm trying to find out what's true for me."

"Well," snapped his mother, with more anger than I'd ever seen her display, "that's just sign seeking. You go praying like that, you could end up believing anything."

"I know," said John quietly.

His mother didn't reply, just set her jaw the way her pioneer forebears had when their babies died on the long walk across the Great Plains. I could see a delicate blue vein throbbing near the line of her silver hair, and I knew she was terrified. Before John came along, she'd lost two babies herself, one at birth, one at six months. But what she saw happening now was far worse. She'd see her other lost sons in the celestial kingdom, but her youngest seemed ready to disappear into outer darkness, where she would never, ever see him again, where he'd float as a ghost for eternity. We ate the rest of our cookies in nerve-racking silence.

•   •   •

For months, John and I had variations on this conversation over and over again, with many different authority figures. Since we were both working at BYU, our regular job evaluations included questions about our religious practices and beliefs, the state of our "testimonies." Did we believe that the Mormon president was the world's one true prophet? Did we support the General Authorities in all matters? Did we refrain from studying or teaching anything that might undermine the teachings of the Church?

Hints about how to make it through these interviews without hating ourselves swirled through the BYU community like drowning cats in a tidal wave. Some faculty members pointed out that one could support the social system of the Church without really believing that the doctrines were empirically true. In other words, you could stand behind Latter-day Saints leaders in the knowledge that all human representatives of God are bound to be flawed. But the most common piece of advice John and I got from our peers was very simple: Lie. Claim to swallow the whole shebang, then believe what you damn well please. Keep your thoughts to yourself and your pie-hole shut.

This would have made perfect sense to me, except for two things: I had already discovered that hiding my real self was a form of slow psychological death, and I actually believed in God. Damn. I hate it when that happens.

At least I wasn't alone in feeling skittish and under threat. Many of the younger faculty members at BYU had stopped eating lunch on campus and started going to small cafés where they could talk freely. "Lunching with known dissidents" became the thing I liked best about my job. Over clam chowder or bagels, we rebels discussed the impossibility of teaching the latest developments in our fields of study without contradicting Mormon dogma. We'd shake our heads over the way the General Authorities were destroying the careers of BYU's best young professors, firing them for "shoddy scholarship" when, in our view, their work was the only publishable material coming out of the university.

Almost everyone I knew and liked seemed nervous. If the General Authorities in Salt Lake happened to interpret something they said or did as heresy, their whole lives could be turned ass over teakettle: incomes dropped to zero, connections with friends and family attenuated or broken. One of my closest friends from our neighborhood ward, a therapist with a politically liberal professor husband, told me she prayed every day for protection from the leaders of the Church. "A couple of nights ago," she told me one morning as we watched our toddlers play in a neighborhood park, "it finally occurred to me how paradoxical it is. I'm praying to God for protection from the servants of God. Could that be right?"

As tensions continued to mount, most BYU employees kept a tighter and tighter rein on their tongues. Casual dissident lunches became fewer and farther from campus. Anything one said could be overheard and reported; it did not pay to trust. Even friends could turn state's evidence, reporting on their colleagues' heresy in order to save their own jobs, their families' reputations, their standing in the community. In particular, no one said anything that might be reported in the press. Of course, for this very reason, the press in Utah seemed obsessed with getting BYU professors to talk. Reporters skulked around campus, looking for men whose grooming was slightly more rumpled than Ken doll perfection, for women with very short hair. But even these people usually wouldn't open up. Dissidence was one thing; social and financial ruin was another.

John and I were exceptions to this rule. We decided that we should stand up for our colleagues, since we trusted our job prospects outside the Mormon community more than the majority of them seemed to and since, as Aleksandr Solzhenitsyn said, "there are times when silence is a lie." Plus, we had become almost used to sitting on a secret so large and potentially explosive—my memories of abuse, the domino effect they might have on other Mormons' opinions of my father, his personal credibility, the credibility of his work, and finally the Church doctrines he spent his life defending—that political and philosophical differences with Mormonism seemed tame by comparison. So we decided that when it came to defending other academics or declaring our real thoughts about the Church or its policies, we would not keep silent. Not even with the press.

We were so rare in this regard that we seemed to get calls every other day from reporters who were writing or broadcasting stories about the Church's "purge" of intellectuals. One day the Salt Lake Tribune quoted me as saying, "Trying to force someone to have faith is like putting a gun to his head and saying, 'Love me or I'll pull the trigger.' It's counterproductive." The next day, when John called me from his office at BYU, we both noticed a strange, intermittent clicking sound. After a few minutes of testing, we determined that our home phone was the one doing the clicking. When the sound persisted for several days, we called the phone company, who sent out a repairman. He discovered that our phone line had been crossed with another line inside a phone junction box at the nearby Mormon chapel—something, the repairman said, that could not have happened accidentally. He separated the wires. The clicks went away. A few days later, they came back. We didn't even bother to get the phone fixed again. Instead, we started saying howdy to the good brothers on the Strengthening the Membership Committee. Just in case.

One day I picked up our clicking phone to hear a strange, rasping male voice. "Now here's what I think," said the voice. "I think that people who speak out against the Gospel shouldn't be Church members. They should be dis-membered." The voice paused to let this clever word play have its full effect. "I'd be happy to dismember you," it concluded. There was a click (I presumed that was Strengthening the Membership hanging up) and then another click (that was the caller bidding adieu).

I started having nightmares in which jarring hints of my father's presence kept cropping up in an otherwise ordinary day: his hat sitting on the roof of my car, his sunglasses in the bathtub. They left me jumpy and insomniacal for days. I decided I could use more therapy.

Before I'd had my falling-out with Mona, she'd given me the name of a therapist she said was "the best in Utah Valley." Rosemary Douglas had mentioned the same name when she was looking for a counselor to help another ward member. Both recommendations actually put me off: I wasn't interested in another round of Mona-style analysis, and Rosemary's referral almost certainly meant that the therapist was Mormon. After all, I'd promised my mother to keep my secret from all Church members, to spare their testimonies. Then I reflected that despite my sense of impending doom, I felt much saner and happier than I had before my own testimony took a sharp southward turn. I dug through my purse and found the therapist's name. Let's call her Dr. Rachel Grant.

The day I called Rachel Grant's office, her client list was full— almost. The receptionist told me that a spot had just opened in a group therapy session Dr. Grant ran in the evenings. The receptionist suggested that I take the spot, if only for one evening, to see what I thought of Grant's methods. I hesitated. *Group* therapy? That would mean other people would hear my story. Possibly no one in the group would recognize me, but if they did . . . I was startled to hear my own voice telling the receptionist I would be there, that very evening. It felt as though someone else had borrowed my vocal cords. Strangely enough, it left me very calm.

By that evening, when I arrived at Rachel Grant's office, the calm had dissipated. I sat in the waiting room second-guessing my decision, wondering if I should bolt before I made things even worse. I wondered if Dr. Grant was descended from former Mormon president Heber J. Grant.

That particular prophet was born completely tone-deaf, but after literally years of effort, he'd learned to sing a single Mormon hymn perfectly by feeling the sensation in his throat. He liked to inspire congregations of Latter-day Saints by describing his handicap, then performing the hymn. The accompanist President Grant took with him to these events was my father's father, a talented pianist, who (family legend has it) frequently got bored and changed keys in the middle of the prophet's performances, creating excruciating discord as the prophet sang obliviously onward. If this therapist was the grandchild of Heber J. Grant, maybe she would want revenge.

My first glance at Rachel Grant deepened my suspicions: she looked cut from the same bolt of pioneer gingham as any other Saint sister: fair-skinned, blue-eyed, fiftyish, dressed neatly and conservatively in slacks that showed a thin seam of sacred garments just over each knee. But her manner didn't fit the look. As she invited me into her office, she was congenial but rather cool, almost brusque. She did ask me to call her Rachel, instead of Dr. Grant, but the sugary voice and unctuous cadence I'd come to expect from women in Utah were conspicuously absent. She talked, in fact, like a dissident. Despite myself, I was intrigued.

Rachel began the session by introducing me to the other seven women in the group, then invited me to watch in silence until I felt comfortable enough to talk. For the first thirty minutes I sat with my eyes half closed, trying to hide my thoughts as I sized up the situation. Almost everyone in the group seemed to have been sexually abused by someone—neighbor, foster brother, mother's boyfriend, all of the above. I was startled by how skeptical Rachel's reactions seemed to be. Mona had seemed overeager to believe abuse stories; by contrast, Rachel asked for evidence. After one woman breathlessly speculated that she might have been ravished by her dentist, her driving instructor, and a cable repair guy, all in one day, Rachel mildly asked her if she read a lot of comic books, since her allegations sounded like slightly skewed accounts of a superhero cartoon. I remember being a bit scandalized (in those days, it wasn't considered politically correct for any therapist to question a sexual-abuse story) but also relieved. The woman's story had sounded disingenuous to me, too, though all the other women's words rang true.

When Rachel began asking me questions, I set out to make a brief, antiseptic statement about my situation, something no one in the group would find interesting enough to repeat. This is how I'd always talked to Mona, and I'd never experienced much emotion in her office. But as I began speaking to Rachel's group, I once again seemed to lose control of my voice. Suddenly I was telling the whole story, crying like a wino at a wake, barely managing to fudge the details in order to disguise my father's identity. I was horrifically embarrassed, but I also had that sense of a boil being lanced, of poison escaping, that I'd felt during my first flashbacks. When I babbled to a stop, Rachel Grant was regarding me with direct, unsmiling eyes.

"I know who you are," she said. "And I know your father."

One of the other women in the group, obviously curious, whispered, "Who?"

"I don't think I'd better mention any names," Rachel told her, in a tone that was at once mild and final. "A great moral authority in the Church. And please remember, what's said in this room stays in this room."

Terrified that Rachel was about to side with my father, I braced myself for a whole 'nother kind of gang bang: seven Mormon women and their saintly leader. But my new therapist surprised me again.

"I also believe you," she said. "And I'll work with you. But it's going to be a hell of a process, and make no mistake about it: If you do what it takes to get over this thing, the Mormon Church is going to ruin your life."

I remember thinking this should have upset me, but in fact, it made me feel good. Really good. In fact, I wasn't sure I'd ever heard anyone say anything that made me feel better. Certainly, this wasn't because my new therapist's analysis was happy news. It wasn't that she'd delivered it in the loving tones I expected of someone matching her age, religion, and physical description. It was because of something I would learn over and over in that office, with the cool-mannered, warm-hearted Dr. Grant: that no matter how difficult and painful it may be, nothing sounds as good to the soul as the truth.

CHAPTER 33

The September Six

The letter was printed on a college student's cheap computer. Two pages, single-spaced. The bottom of the second page, the part that bore the signature of the writer, had been scissored off. Anyone in either of my classes could be the author.

"You know I don't want to be having this conversation," said the chairman of the sociology department, looking at me with genuine pain in his gray eyes.

"Yeah, I know," I murmured, scanning the letter for the second time. It had been sent by a student to one of the General Authorities in Salt Lake, who had forwarded a copy to the department chairman, along with a recommendation that I be "called in." The letter accused me of many crimes against the kingdom of God: I had paraphrased a speech given by the prophet that made him sound like a chauvinistic jerk. I had told students that there was no logical way to ascertain absolute truth, that they should make their own best guesses and keep their minds open. I had told them to cherish the parts of Mormonism they loved and believed but feel free to question anything that seemed immoral or absurd. In all these ways, I was leading young Saints astray. The letter writer wanted to see me disciplined. I mean *really* wanted it.

"It reads like a sixth-grade hate note," I said.

"I know," the department chairman nodded wretchedly. "They all do."

I bit my lip, surprised at how sick I felt. After all, I'd known it was only a matter of time until the grinding cogs of orthodoxy caught me and dragged me into the Latter-day Saint Purge-O-Matic. My academic friends were getting disciplined right, left, and center, and I was far more vocal about my beliefs than most of them. Still, it was queasily unpleasant to wonder which of my smiling, well-coiffed, incredibly nice Barbie/Ken students had put in so much time and effort to make sure I was punished.

I told myself that I should be able to let this run off me like water off a duck. I'd spent the summer rebuilding my optimism and courage, talking with John, my dissident friends, the women in Rachel Grant's weekly therapy group. I'd become very fond of these women, once the patient with the comic-book rape speculations dropped out (not long afterward, she appeared on a daytime TV talk show, wearing a wig and dark glasses, to report that one of her therapists had implanted false memories in her six ways from Sunday).

I'd also started having individual sessions with Rachel, because we both knew I could say only so much about my father or the Church during group sessions. I couldn't expect all the other clients to refrain from leaking information about me into the Mormon gossip system. I wasn't worried for my own sake (there was little doubt my allegations were widely rumored by now), but if Church authorities learned I was Rachel's client her career and reputation would certainly be in jeopardy.

There had been a time when this kind of caution had struck me as irrational. Not anymore. The Mormon Church was in full-on purge mode, disciplining or threatening all sorts of Saints for all manner of heresy. The newspapers and television news ran daily stories on intellectuals who had been "called in" and warned to conform. Right now, I was in the first stages of this process. Being cautioned by the sociology department chairman, a freethinking intellectual himself, wasn't nearly as oppressive as an interview with my local ward leaders, which would be far less stressful than an encounter with authorities higher up in the chain of command. Some of my friends, who had been questioned multiple times, by loftier and loftier commanders, said that the full-fledged process felt like "spiritual rape."

I'd thought this was an overstatement, but now, rereading just one little letter that described me as a disseminator of evil, I understood. The student made sweeping statements about my lack of moral fiber, my unholy personal thoughts, my obvious inability to exercise any form of honor or self-discipline. Rage and condemnation seethed from the pages. It was just a ridiculous rant from a grumpy teenager who'd probably funneled a few years' worth of adolescent frustration into a crusade against a random authority figure, but even so, I felt as though someone had killed my cat and left it on my pillow. Teaching had always been a kind of sanctuary for me; I loved watching students grow and challenging them to think for themselves. I'd never do it again without wondering which one was the mole, without suspecting every student.

I told the chairman that I intended to continue teaching exactly what I believed, though it wouldn't be fun anymore and would almost certainly get me in more trouble. He responded with the obligatory warning, but his eyes shone with equal parts protectiveness, encouragement, and envy. The chairman's age and career level meant he was basically stuck at BYU. I had more freedom. As we ended the conversation, I remembered Toni Morrison's statement that "the function of freedom is to free someone else." Utah wasn't the Deep South, and we Mormon dissidents were hardly the Underground Railroad. But I did believe that our culture had trapped us, that many Latter-day Saints lived in mental and social prisons that perpetuated precisely the kind of insanity with which I'd grown up. It wasn't slavery, but it was a powerful form of bondage: the belief that God had ordained a pattern of secrets and silence, that religious authority always trumped one's individual sense of right and wrong, that the evidence of the senses must bow to the demands of orthodoxy, no matter how insane. It was a kind of institutionalized madness, and its shackles were all the more confining for existing almost entirely in the human mind.

That night, the local news led off with a report that leaders in several different Mormon wards had simultaneously organized courts—sorry, Councils of Love—to try six Latter-day Saint intellectuals on charges of heresy. If convicted, they faced possible excommunication. To the Mormon community, this was worse than the death penalty; it could mean that the accused would spend eternity in the telestial kingdom (an ignominiously low level of the afterlife, without even visitation rights to the better kingdoms). More immediately, it meant literal excommunication, exclusion from community, from connection. Like Sonia Johnson, the feminist heretic of the 1970s, excommunicated Saints might be blotted from the history and company of their people. If they humbled themselves, waited a year, and applied for rebaptism, they may once again become members of the Church, but they could never really redeem their tarnished reputations. For a pioneer people, accustomed to a level of interdependency rare in the United States, this was a horrifying prospect. It was similar to the penalty of *mura hachibu,* "expulsion from the village," in feudal Japan, where many people found suicide preferable to living as exiles.

Throughout Utah, educated Latter-day Saints were up in arms. Excommunication was rare, even for rapists and murderers, and the accused heretics had broken none of the Church's commandments except for the unspoken eleventh ("Thou shalt not commit publicity"). They hadn't even done much of that. Each had published academic or political articles about Mormonism, either in obscure academic journals or in periodicals circulated among intellectual Latter-day Saints. All would probably agree that they had feminist inclinations. But each professed full belief in the Church and support for the Latter-day Saint leaders. Their real crime was excessive knowledge—having it, communicating it.

Throughout Utah, prayer groups formed to support the accused heretics, who quickly became known as the September Six. Demonstrators picketed Church buildings, wrote letters, and chanted slogans, hoping to convince Latter-day Saint leaders to call off the Councils of Love. Mormon authorities countered by privately hinting that all the accused were adulterers and by making public statements that likened the intellectuals to "ravening wolves among the flocks."

I kind of liked the wolf analogy myself. After all, wolves are cooperative, sociable beasts who control rodent populations, babysit each other's puppies, and develop lifelong friendships. I decided I vastly preferred being a wolf to being a Woman Who Runs with the Sheep.

For weeks, as the Councils of Love prepared their cases, the September Six were constantly in the news. I had no doubt that the Church had decided to use these half-dozen scholars as examples to keep other potential intellectuals in line, and they simultaneously ramped up the pressure on the BYU faculty. Many professors began to hear flat-out threats from academic or religious leaders. Very few of them met with the kind of sympathy I'd gotten from my department chairman. As far as the Church was concerned, the "purge" strategy was beginning to work; more and more intellectuals agreed to keep their mouths shut rather than face *mura hachibu.*

Through all of this, John and I kept our pledge to talk openly, to any-one, about what we really thought. Quotations from both of us appeared frequently in the newspapers. Any day, I expected to get a call from my bishop, inviting me in for a Council of Love, a big flat hammer embedded in a silky casket of pulpit-speak. But the Church left me alone, possibly because of my lineage. The phone calls that did come were unofficial, anonymous. "I've got a pickup truck," one caller whispered, "and I could tie you to the back of that pickup truck and just drag you right out of Utah. Would you like that?" More letters arrived, both at my home and my BYU office. "Your attacks on the Gospel will be punished," one said. "Those enemies of the Lord who murmur against the prophets will be cut down," read a photocopied note, which had apparently been dupli-cated for mass mailing.

All over Mormon country, even outside of Utah, born-and-bred Latter-day Saints (who began to call themselves DNA Mormons) were catching this kind of flak. A whole generation of Latter-day Saints had been educated in secular colleges and graduate schools, and times being what they were, many of these people were kicking up their own private fusses. In Arizona, a journalist named Deborah Laake published a de-scription of her bad Mormon marriage, which, in her view, began with a bad Mormon temple ceremony. She discussed the ceremony at much more length than I have and was excommunicated in a Council of Love she didn't even attend. Laake called me to check some sociological facts after she read my name in the papers. She told me that the letter inform-ing her of her expulsion hit her harder than she'd expected. I thought about the hate mail I received every now and then, about my student's righteous epistle, and told her I understood.

One of Laake's acquaintances was Steve Benson, a Pulitzer Prize–winning cartoonist for the *Arizona Republic* who also happened to be the grandson of the reigning Mormon prophet. During the insurrection of 1993, Benson began giving speeches and media interviews in which he mentioned that his grandfather, God's "mouthpiece" to all the earth, was too old and frail to recognize family members, let alone receive revela-tion for every human on the globe. Though many of Benson's local lead-ers tried to dissuade him from continuing to speak on the subject, he wasn't officially put to trial. It was impossible for the Church to find grounds for excommunication: not only did the prophet's grandson have a squeaky-clean record, but trying him might lead to a media investigation into the state of the great leader's actual physical condition. Perhaps to compensate for this regrettable lack of official traction, Benson received especially violent threats from anonymous sources. When I met him, about halfway through all the ruckus, Steve described some of these threats to me in his typically understated way. I didn't worry much about him until I learned that he'd been placed under police protection, his home and car repeatedly swept for bombs and booby traps.

It all made for lots of excitement in Mormon country, which, I have to say, could use it. Not since I'd studied Chinese, using textbooks written by the Communists, had I run into more careful censoring, more suspicious questions, more timid conversations between people who hoped they might actually be true friends. On the BYU campus, normal social interaction became a peculiar dance, like a mating ritual between storks, as each party delicately sized up the other's level of religious conformity, and opened up or closed down to reveal or conceal their own beliefs.

To me, the Latter-day Saint community felt more and more insane, a multimillion-member extrapolation of my own dysfunctional family. Strangers still stopped me on the street to gush about my father's impact on their testimonies ("Especially," they would say, "in these troubled times"). On the other hand, when I chanced to pass a distant relative or childhood friend on the street, they often turned quickly away, becoming obsessed with cracks in the pavement or tree trunks until I was safely out of range. I didn't know if they had decided to "shun" me, or if they were simply afraid someone would catch them speaking to me. What I did know was that my life was coming perilously close to the condition of *mura hachibu*. Even though I knew this was a result of my own choices, my own failure to conform, it felt strange, alienating and confusing, to be a pariah.

•   •   •

All this time, I kept driving my children to school, teaching my classes, working on my (now nearly finished) dissertation. On the surface, my life was exactly the same as it had been four years earlier, when we'd moved back to the sanctuary of Zion. But everything had changed. Everyone was dangerous. Nowhere was safe.

During one warm week in the fall of 1993, judgment fell on the September Six. All were found guilty of heresy. Five were excommunicated, one "disfellowshipped," a milder but still dreaded punishment. That Sunday night, John didn't come to bed. When I got up Monday morning, he was sitting in the kitchen, drinking orange juice and scrutinizing a letter he had apparently just signed. It was much shorter than the one my student had written about me. John handed me the letter, his face pale but determined. I read it. It was his official resignation from the Church of Jesus Christ of Latter-day Saints.

"You're really going to do this, huh?" I said, half in awe, half in trepidation.

"Look," said John, "they've drawn a line in the sand. They exed those people to say that if you don't believe certain things, if you know too much, you aren't Mormon anymore. And, well, I don't believe those things. I know too much." He looked at me nervously, half expecting the good Latter-day Saint sister in me to come out of hibernation and say whatever his mother might say.

"I can't be part of it anymore," he went on, sounding a little desperate. "It's like leaving my name on the roll of some kind of sexist, racist, psychotic political party. I can't do it."

"Don't worry, John, I'm with you," I assured him.

His brow cleared. "Do you want me to put your name on the letter?" he asked. "We could leave together."

I considered it, stilled my mind, and checked how it felt. "I don't think so." Becoming a Daughter of Perdition is like getting married; you only plan to do it once, and you want it to be just right.

"Why not?" He clearly wanted my company.

"Stream," I said.

John nodded and fell silent. One thing we had both come to believe was that each person's path to God is unique, that we all follow a slightly different trajectory as Leaves in the great Stream, and that each human being's operating instructions are therefore different. John accepted my staying Mormon, at least for the moment, in the same way I accepted his quitting the Church.

"Anyway," he said, "it's not a big deal. I just give the letter to the bishop, he takes my name off the records, and it's done. No one will even know until I decide to tell them."

Okay, so he was wrong about that.

CHAPTER 34

Committing Publicity

This isn't going anywhere, is it?" says Diane to my father. She looks frustrated, but she's smiling, too, like someone trying to photograph a basket of kittens that keep bouncing off in opposite directions. Healing our clan is one of Diane's central preoccupations (psychologists would say that this makes her typical of oldest daughters in emotionally wounded families) and though she agrees with my old therapist Mona that we're among the most dysfunctional tribes in history, she seems to genuinely enjoy every moment of contact with any of us.

"Godamighty," she says, reaching back through her years of city living for her favorite small Utah town exclamation. "Don't we have the most *interesting* family discussions? Really."

"I have to get back to work," my father tells her, and once again I hear the struggle in his voice, half of him still in the role of the adult commanding children, the other half helplessly dependent on Diane for transportation.

"Oh, sweetie," Diane says to him, "don't you know that this is the most important work you'll ever do? This, here, talking to your daughter and your niece?"

"I need to get back to the book," says my father angrily.

"But Dad," I say, "nobody cares about your silly book. Nobody cares about *my* silly books. Diane's right; what we write doesn't matter half as much as how we live, how we love each other." God, Godamighty, it feels good to say these things out loud. I've been waiting to do it all my life.

"Well, yes . . . but we must serve the Gospel first," my father says sternly.

This makes me laugh, not because it's funny but because I feel so free.

"Don't you get it?" I say. "I'm not Mormon anymore, Dad. I don't think God has anything against Mormons, but they're not special favorites. And I'm not one of them. Of you."

I assumed my father knew all about my apostasy. Apparently not. My statement seems to hit him harder than anything else I've said. He opens his mouth but says nothing, just sits there looking thunderstruck. It's odd that he's so worried; after all, he didn't seem nearly so concerned when I was trying to kill myself. Then I realize that my father's expression looks like one of personal insecurity, not alarm on someone else's behalf. He looks nervous, a glib preacher who has just realized his audience is deaf. He may be somewhat concerned for my lost soul, but I strongly suspect that he's much more worried about what a sociologist would call "loss of legitimacy." If I'm not Mormon, then his work, his fame, his position mean nothing to me. I've chosen to ignore both filial and religious piety, so with me, he's lost his foundation.

"Oh, I'm sorry, Dad," I say, watching him open and close his mouth a couple of times, too shocked to speak. "I thought you knew."

Really, how could he have missed it? Everyone else in Mormon country knew about it. Especially after what happened with John. You can't get much more public than that.

·   ·   ·

It was the day after John hand-delivered his letter of resignation to our ward bishop. I was getting ready to head for work when I heard a minor commotion on our front porch. I peered through the window to see a TV news crew parked on the steps, lugging a full array of cameras and sound equipment. The reporter with the crew, whom I'll call Doug Patterson, was well known for his stories about the Mormon purge, the September Six, and the groundswell of Latter-day dissidence.

Doug had interviewed me before. Talking to him was like fencing: he stabbed every which way, trying to elicit sensational statements. I worded my answers delicately, determined that nothing I said could be taken out of context. I'd made a commitment to answer questions from the press, but not in a way that would misstate my real position. Doug and I were both allies and adversaries, respectful and cautious of each other's methods.

I decided to open the door, bracing myself for another fencing match, wondering what Doug's topic would be this morning.

"How are you?" the reporter asked.

"Fine." I didn't invite him in.

"Have you heard that BYU just fired some of your colleagues?" Doug named two of my friends, an English professor and an anthropologist, both excellent scholars.

"No," I said, feeling my heart sink for my friends. Like the September Six, these two would have to start their careers all over again.

"The authorities are saying their work wasn't up to the academic standards of the university," said Doug.

He watched for my reaction, and he got one: I couldn't help shaking my head in disgust. First of all, the fired professors were some of the smartest, best-trained scholars I knew. In addition, BYU's "academic standards" were, to put it charitably, spotty. I'd recently reviewed an article, supposedly written for a mainstream sociology journal, that examined the "decline of American Indian culture" by comparing modern tribes with the populations described in the Book of Mormon. Back around the time of Jesus, according to Mormon scripture, the Indians were good Christians, without all those heathen rituals. Many had even been "white and delightsome," their skin bleached by religious obedience and God's favor. The professor who'd written the article spared nothing in decrying the sorry decay of these high standards, quoting liberally from the Book of Mormon as the paper's only historical source.

"So," said Doug, watching my face, "are you willing to go on the record to say these two are actually decent scholars?"

"Absolutely," I said. I wasn't sure my speaking out would help my friends' badly bruised careers, but it might.

"What about your husband?" Getting a man to speak out on camera was a special coup, since female opinions are much more easily dismissed in Mormon culture.

"I'll check with him." I ushered the camera crew into my living room and went to find my newly non-Mormon husband. Like me, John was crushed to hear what had happened to our fired colleagues and willing to say so on the record.

Doug set up an interview site in our backyard, posing us on a bench and the camera crew around the periphery of the patio. For ten minutes or so, he grilled us about our perceptions of the BYU firings, the September Six, and the Mormon purge. Then the cameraman stopped to change film, and Doug got a little more personal.

"So, how do you think talking to me today is going to affect your Church membership?" he asked. "I've had trouble finding anyone who will talk, now that they're actually excommunicating people. The Church is playing serious hardball. Are you afraid you may be exed as well?"

I said nothing, just looked at John, who fidgeted for a long moment, then said slowly, "I guess I should tell you something. I quit the Church yesterday."

"Jesus Christ!" Doug started violently, dropping his clipboard and pen. "Are you serious?"

John nodded. I nodded.

"You mean it? Oh, holy *shit!*" Doug scrambled to pick up his belongings. "Well this, now, *this* is the story. *This* is what's going on the news."

The color drained from John's face as though he'd severed both carotid arteries. "What . . . I mean, Doug, I don't think so. It's not anybody's busi—"

"Look, dude," said Doug, writing furiously on his clipboard. "You tell it your way or I'll tell it mine, but this *is* the story. This *is* going on the news."

"Oh, man," John breathed. He looked at me, eyes wide with panic. I couldn't help him. I was already late for a doctor's appointment, and there was nothing I could do about Doug even if I stuck around.

"Just tell the truth," I whispered. "It'll be okay."

John nodded. I sat with him for a few more minutes, while the cameraman fumbled with his film. Then I gave John a hug and left him to the questionable mercy of the press.

•   •   •

I rushed home two hours later to find John sitting in the basement, staring at the wall, wringing his hands. You rarely see folks literally wring their hands, but that's what he was doing.

"They won't air it," he said when I walked into the room. "It's not important. It's not news. Why would they air it? They won't air it."

I put down my purse. "John, I think they might."

"But at worst, it will only be on that one channel," he said hopefully. "No one will watch."

"It's the top-rated channel in Utah," I said.

"But it's such a ridiculous thing," he reiterated. "I mean, who cares? Why would they even bother talking about me?"

The TV's remote control was sitting next to him on the couch. I picked it up and turned on the set. We saw the last thirty seconds of a soap-opera segment, and then, with timing almost too perfect to be true, John's face appeared on the screen.

"Dismayed by recent police actions within the Mormon Church," said Doug Patterson's voice, "a BYU professor has quit the religion. Story at five and eleven."

My knees felt wobbly. I turned off the television and sat down on the couch beside John. "Honey," I said, "you need to call your parents."

John's eyes widened. He hadn't thought of that. "They won't see it," he whispered.

"Their friends will. They'll get calls. They shouldn't have to find out that way."

He nodded like a robot. "Okay," he whispered. "Okay."

Five minutes later, still in robot mode, John had both his parents on the phone. I knew exactly how he felt, the mechanical way he was forcing air through his vocal cords, as though his lungs were a pair of bellows that belonged to someone else. "So, Mom, Dad," he said, "there's something you should know. I left the Church yesterday."

From across the room, I could hear the tinny, telephone-munchkin version of John's mother screaming—not in anger but in absolute horror, as though she'd been bitten by a nest of rattlesnakes.

"And," John went on, like a truck with no brakes, "it's going to be on the news."

There was a complicated clattering noise from the phone. John was silent, the earpiece pressed to his head. Then, without another word, he slowly lowered the receiver into its cradle.

"I think I killed her," he said hoarsely. "She fell down."

"Oh, honey!"

"My dad had to go help. He said he's never heard her make a noise like that."

My in-laws had been married more than sixty years. John's mother had borne eight children, watched two of them die, survived Depression poverty. For the past several years, she'd handled heart disease and cancer without complaint. She was the definition of grace under pressure. Through it all, through a long and often difficult life, she never screamed and fainted until her lastborn announced that he had become a Son of Perdition. And that it was going to be on the news.

"I'm sorry, John," I said helplessly. "I'm so sorry."

John looked like something a homeless person would scrape off his shoes. It's the way one looks when one has betrayed one's parents and one's people. I should know.

That night, at five and eleven, we watched as John, the top news story on the top-rated Utah channel, haltingly explained why he had taken leave of his faith. The reporter included me in the initial shots, putting up a caption that prominently displayed my maiden name, which every Mormon in Utah would recognize. But the focus was on John's apostasy. He explained it briefly, clearly. He didn't use the phrase *Leaf in the Stream*. He didn't talk about my father, about watching me fall apart while trying desperately to hold me together, about the strange fictions that pose as Mormon fact, about all the friends who'd seen their lives ruined by the purge. He only said that in his heart he felt that being Mormon was wrong for him. Really, nothing else mattered.

"You were great, honey," I said when the story was over. "I'm so proud of you."

John just stared at the screen, shaking.

· · ·

It would be years before we realized how far the ripples spread from John's hot-press apostasy. The immediate effects were obvious: *mura hachibu*. When we walked through our neighborhood, the people who had embraced us at church meetings now turned away, showing us their backs until we were out of sight. On the BYU campus, few people were brave enough to speak with us, much less do lunch. Our close friends were few, and we had no casual collegial relationships. When neighbors came for a visit, it was always an undisguised effort to convince us to repent, followed by stories about others who had left the fold and lived (though not long) to regret it. "My nephew did what you're doing," one neighbor told me, "and a week later he died of a ruptured spleen." "Our bishop's son left the Church," said another, "and now he's bankrupt in prison."

Even people whom we knew were having their own religious doubts, people who had shared dissident views with us or spoken up in Sunday school lessons about their disagreement with Church policy, seemed to draw the line at connecting with actual apostates. Former buddies awkwardly pretended we weren't sharing the same sidewalk, using adjacent gas-station pumps, lining up at the same cash register. When we initiated conversations, they would sometimes give a frightened smile and a quick "hello," then all but run away. Mostly, we were simply ignored. We had become ghosts.

On the other hand, all over the kingdom of Zion, some individuals rejoiced in John's defection. They began calling or visiting us at home, walking from several blocks away to avoid leaving their cars parked nearby (one never knew which license plates were being written down by the Strengthening the Membership Committee). We'd talk until one, three, five o'clock in the morning, listening to these people expose their souls and wonder aloud if they could possibly find jobs and build lives outside the community of Saints. Most concluded that they couldn't. Still, I was intensely grateful for their willingness to tell us about the struggle we all shared.

Of all the visits we received after John's TV news debut, the most surprising was from his parents. The very day after the news story ran, their large, seldom-used Cadillac pulled into our carport. My father-in-law, though elderly, was still reasonably healthy at the time, but John's mother was in failing health, so frail she was basically immobile. Though we often visited their home, she hadn't been well enough to reciprocate for many months. Now, here she was, apparently having survived her initial shock over the phone, her husband holding her arm, her hair and makeup perfect.

No one talked about the Church, about John's apostasy, about the news. Instead, we discussed John's recent travel, the house, the weather. We all knew that this was code for an entirely different discussion. "I see you've recarpeted," said my mother-in-law, but what she really meant was *You are my son, and that will never change.* "Those shingles should hold for another ten years," said John's father, meaning *I've trusted you to make your own choices since you were a boy, and I'm not about to quit now.* My in-laws got up to leave, no doubt exhausted, less than an hour after they arrived. But the message they'd come to deliver would stay forever. *No matter what you do, you will always belong with us. We will never stop loving you.*

So, in a way, my in-laws ended up adhering to the same religion John and I had adopted. The word *religion* comes from the Latin *re-ligos,* meaning "to tie together again." On a grand scale, I think this means the reconnection of all souls, all spirits, all the bits of divine creation that briefly imagine they—we—are separate and alone. This was the religion my parents-in-law chose to serve, even as their Church was severing ties with those who challenged authority, using excommunication as the chainsaw of God. Talking with John's parents, it seemed so obvious that the power of cutting, of force and threat, pale in comparison to the power of the compassion that connects. In 500 BC, Lao-tzu wrote that "when two great forces collide, the victory will go to the one that knows how to yield." John had yielded to his heart's best guess at the right thing to do. Now his parents, under dire pressure, had done the same. Watching them interact, I didn't think I'd ever seen three more victorious champions, or any more beautiful example of re-ligion, the tying together of separated souls.

. . .

That visit comes to mind again in the hotel room, ten years later, just after I drop my regrettably casual comment concerning my own apostasy. My father still looks so shocked that I realize that family and friends must have somehow protected him from the knowledge that I actually left Mormonism.

"Well," he says, finally catching his breath. "This will never do. You'll regret it, I'll tell you that. You'll get hit by a ton of bricks for abandoning the Gospel."

"You could be right," I say mildly. So far, abandoning the Gospel has brought me out of pain and isolation into happiness and love, but I can't be empirically sure whether his statement is true or false; it is scientifically indeterminable.

"There are penalties for that kind of thing," says my father.

"Could be," I say again. This response does not appear to be making my father feel better. He seems anxious and angry, unsure how to proceed with someone outside the system in which he is revered.

"Well," he mutters under his breath, "that's how you can tell the Church is true—people leave it, but they can't leave it alone. Always attacking, always lashing out, because you can't get away from the fact that it's the Lord's work."

He used to say this kind of thing often in speeches, even when I was a child. It occurred to me at a fairly young age that according to this logic, Frederick Douglass and Elie Wiesel must have believed that slavery and the Holocaust were God's work, too—after all, they just kept on talking, talking, *talking* about these systems, even after they'd left them behind. It's one of my father's favorite rhetorical techniques, the old double bind: if you profess that the Mormon Church is true, that's because you know it's true; if you profess that it isn't true, that, too, is because you know it's true.

"Could be," I repeat blandly.

My father is now thoroughly upset. "You've kept me from my work long enough," he says to Diane. "Let's end this foolishness now."

Diane looks at me, and I shake my head. It's the same head shake Rachel gave me one day in her office, when I'd been racked by nightmares for weeks, and my father had just been given yet another award for his righteousness. "I want to at least fight him!" I almost shouted during my private session. "It's not fair that he can just get away with it. How can he just *get away with it?*"

"He hasn't," said Rachel. "He's earned everything he's been given by the Church—just think what your life would be like if you'd been willing to do what he's done."

"Oh, God," I'd said, blinking away angry tears. "He's in hell, isn't he?"

That was when Rachel shook her head. "I don't even know where he is," she said. "I can't even imagine it."

So now, even with Diane looking as though she wishes I'd put up more of a fight, I decide to stop struggling against what is. My father's core belief is that he is always right, and mine is that I may always, in any circumstances, be wrong. That's as close to tying us back together, as close to the same re-ligion, as my father and I are likely to get.

Personal Priesthood

At a key point in the Mormon temple ceremony, which is supposed to be a literal rehearsal for what happens after death, each Church member gives a long, complex, secret password to a man hiding on the other side of a white curtain. If the password is given correctly, a hand emerges from a slit in the curtain, and, after a couple of secret handshakes and one brief, rather tangolike full-body clench, ushers the supplicant into the "celestial room."

When a man goes through the ritual, the hand from behind the curtain supposedly belongs to God (usually played by an aged temple worker with luxuriantly furry knuckles and, due to the high number of farming accidents in Utah, at least part of a finger missing). When a woman takes her vows, however, the hand that hauls her into heaven must belong to her husband. In the long run, the husband's hand is the same as the hand of God, because of the doctrinal belief that good Mormon men will eventually become Gods themselves. Unlike the vague, cloudlike nature of many a Christian heaven, Mormon salvation is very astronomical, centered near the planet Kolob for the God of this world, and the as-yet-unspecified planets that will be assigned to righteous Latter-day Saint men once they have completed all the Mormon ordinances, lived righteous lives, given up their mortal bodies, and then gotten those same bodies back on the morning of the first resurrection.

Women get to share their husbands' planets—not only with the husband himself, of course, but also with his other wives. Latter-day Saints believe that no woman will ever get to the celestial kingdom on her own—both her connection to the present God and her passage to eternal glory rely on her soon-to-be-divine husband. If a woman dies unmarried, she must be "sealed" to a worthy Mormon male (it is to be hoped that she'll catch a live husband, but if necessary, she can be posthumously sealed to the partner of her descendants' choice) before she can proceed toward salvation. Women were said by Joseph Smith to be more righteous than men by nature, and most converts to the Latter-day Saint religion are female. This means that more women will attain salvation than men, so it stands to reason that polygamy is inevitable in the higher kingdoms of the afterlife. This is why when I was a child, cynical Latter-day Saint "old maids" (that is, unmarried women over the age of twenty-one) used to sing the following song:

> Some day my prince will come,
> In the Millennium,
> And he will say to me,
> Come marry me,
> Be number three.

So John's apostasy had left my religious leaders in an awkward position as far as I was concerned. On one hand, Mormons are passionate about the sanctity of marriage and would never openly recommend divorce. In particular, dissolving a temple marriage requires a temple divorce, which is done only in extreme cases, with enormous reluctance. (Until the temple divorce occurs, the couple is still seen as married in the eyes of God, and the woman can't marry another man in the temple. The man, on the other hand, can marry again, because polygamous men are A-OK. The same is true in the case of death: a widow can't remarry in the temple without divorcing her late husband, but a man can keep adding wives even if the living ones keep dropping like flies.)

On the other hand, though no Mormon leader would push me into divorcing John, I was now attached to a man who, unless he mended his ways, was headed directly away from all the kingdoms of the afterlife, even the ignominious telestial. Technically, this meant that in order to be saved, I would have to dump John and marry a "priesthood holder" (any Mormon man in good standing). Only one thing was certain: Until John repented or I remarried, my bishop and the men above him in the Mormon chain of command had become my only links to God. They could only save me by somehow changing either my marital situation or John's mind.

This, perhaps, is why I was allowed to stay in the room when various Latter-day Saint leaders showed up at our house to have "personal priesthood interviews" with John, before punting him into outer darkness. First our bishop (who asked us to call him by his title and his first name, which, let us say, was Harry) and then the president of our regional, multiward grouping (President Dick) showed up to try to dissuade John from going through with his defection and to offer me salvation if John couldn't be persuaded to see reason.

"You understand, John," Bishop Harry said, leaning forward on our living room sofa, his bald head filmed with nervous sweat, "that if your name is taken off our records, you will no longer bear the priesthood of God?" He looked at John intensely, as though unable to believe that he comprehended the horrific nature of his actions. "You understand you'll have none of the special powers and authorities that come with the priesthood?"

"I understand," John nodded, his face impassive.

"But," said Bishop Harry, brightening up just a little, "you will still be allowed to give 10 percent of your income to the Church. You'll still have that blessing."

"Yippee," said John.

Appalled, Bishop Harry turned to me. "Martha," he said, "you can come to me when you need priesthood advice or assistance. We'll get you through this. Is there anything I can help you with right now? Any questions you want to ask?"

I looked at him wearily. Where to begin? "Well," I said, "I guess I'd like to know why the Church keeps attacking anyone who has material evidence disconfirming Mormon scripture. I'd like to know how people who talk all day about Truth can spend all their time trying to hide it. I—"

But there was no point in going on, because the good bishop had literally stuffed his forefingers in his ears. "I can't hear you, I can't hear you, I can't hear you," he chanted.

I am not making this up.

Some days later, when President Dick came to counsel John, the mood was even more tense. President Dick was a much higher authority than the bishop, and he seemed determined to use every ounce of influence to keep John in the kingdom of God. At first he acted sorrowful, but fairly quickly John's lack of remorse curdled his compassion into fury.

"Were you wearing your garments when you made this decision?" he asked, glaring at John. Where were you on the night of June 7, when Professor Plum was murdered in the study with the lead pipe?

"Yeah, I was," said John.

"Were you reading the scriptures daily?"

"Yes," John nodded.

President Dick worked his jaw in exasperation. He turned to me.

"And where were *you*?" he said. "What have *you* been doing to support John's testimony?"

"It never occurred to me that his testimony was my business," I said.

"And what's the state of *your* testimony?" President Dick continued. "Exactly what do you believe?"

"I believe that there's a lot of good in Mormonism," I said, slowly. "I believe that the leaders are probably very good men. And if one of them ordered me to do something that I felt in my heart was wrong, I would refuse."

President Dick was silent for a long moment. "Well, privately," he said leaning toward me, his voice somewhat softer, "I agree with you." Then he reared up again. "But if you ever make a statement like that in public, the Church will have to take action against you."

"I believe the same things in public that I do in private," I told him.

The president sat back, pursing his lips, shaking his head. "I used to be like you," he said. "I used to think it was all so simple. Now I know that running the Church organization is a complicated thing. Trust me, you're still too young to understand. You need to be obedient until you realize that."

"Well, gee," I said, "maybe you should stop telling people to model themselves after a guy who died when he was thirty-three."

President Dick narrowed his eyes. He turned back to John.

"How old are your children?" he said.

"Eight, six, and four," John told him.

The president nodded slowly. "You know, it's a terrible thing for children to grow up with apostate parents. Bad things happen to them—you know, bullying, ostracism. Problems at school. There's nothing we can do about that."

John stood up. "I think it's time for you to leave," he told President Dick. "Get out of my house."

And President Dick did leave, but not before casting me a meaningful glance. "If you need counsel, Sister," he said to me, "just call. And remember what I said about speaking publicly. Your children have too much to lose."

·   ·   ·

Strangely enough, encounters like these did not strengthen my belief in the truth of the restored Gospel. I was becoming more and more disillusioned with every personal priesthood interview, every suspicious click of our phone, every walk past the bluntly presented back of a former friend. Every day I considered writing my own letter to Bishop Harry, ending my membership in the Church. But something held me back. During the long daily sessions I now spent meditating and praying, trying to sense the current of the Stream, I still didn't feel quite ready to leave, to commit the sin more terrible than murder.

I stayed in this religious limbo for a few months, rationalizing my continued Mormon membership by telling myself that, practically speaking, I might be able to do more to help my people from within the religion than from the cursed perspective of an apostate. Now that John had left Mormonism, he could no longer work at BYU, or speak at formal gatherings of Saints. I, on the other hand, was still technically a Latter-day Saint in good standing. Because I believe in practicing what I preach, I had been scrupulous in keeping every rule of Mormonism, from the Ten Commandments to the Roughly Four Hundred Thousand Suggestions. Authorities might excommunicate me for my beliefs, but they couldn't justifiably do it for my actions. They'd also have a hard time legally firing me from my job. I was a known rebel, but still a member of the BYU faculty. Lion-style, I intended to use this position to do whatever good I could.

For example, part of my professional role included helping manage the Women's Research Institute, an organization that was expected to help BYU keep its formal accreditation by giving support to issues of feminine (though of course not feminist) concern. The institute, run largely by women whose earrings were longer than their hair, funded studies of things like gender-specific social pressures and the history of female life in Utah. Female students at BYU were also known to show up at the institute looking for various kinds of psychological support. Despite my continued disclaimers that I wasn't any kind of professional counselor, students kept knocking on my office door, closing it behind them, and then pouring out their hearts. A few had academic issues; some wanted advice on future careers. But the vast majority of the stories I heard had just one, cruelly monotonous theme: sexual abuse.

I still don't know why so many women came to talk to me about this. Perhaps they'd heard rumors that I claimed to be one of them. Maybe I projected some kind of sympathetic mien that drew them like iron filings to a magnet. Or maybe—this is, I think, the most likely explanation—there were simply a lot of Mormon women with a history of sexual violation, who were seeking everywhere for comfort, and I just happened to drift onto their radar screens.

The stories I heard in my office, day after day, were rarely of the repressed-and-recovered variety. In fact, I think most of the women who confided in me would have been thrilled to forget what had happened to them, if only long enough to get a good night's sleep. The daughter of a man well known for his work on the famous Correlation Committee had been molested by her three older brothers almost daily from the age of four. Another woman told me that her father had gone to his bishop every six months, confessed that he was having sex with all five of his children, repented, and was sent home with a clean record and a stern admonition that this time, he really did have to stop. A teenager cried in my arms after her doctor told her she'd never have children; when she was seven, her father had raped her with a pair of scissors, puncturing her uterus.

Though I sometimes dropped sympathetic hints, I never responded to these horror stories by confiding about my own abuse. These women didn't want to talk to someone who was (literally) as screwed up as they were; they were looking for someone strong and undamaged, a champion to comfort them and fight on their behalf. Many of them mentioned that because of my father's fame, the General Authorities would listen to me if I asked them to take stronger steps to prevent sexual abuse and heal its victims. I did try this approach. When a graduate student put together a presentation for Church authorities on sexual abuse and its effects, I helped deliver it. When an assistant professor began working on a field study to see how Mormon leaders reacted to reports of sexual abuse— though some were kind and responsible, most either ignored the women, assisted in the cover-up, or punished the victim as a sexual degenerate— I helped write up the results. In both cases, I explicitly avoided doing anything that might taint the field research with my own bias as a survivor of abuse.

Some of this research, as I've already mentioned, would eventually be published in newspapers or mainstream social science journals. In one case, an article I'd contributed to drew enough press attention that one of the twelve apostles, a former lawyer, took the time to speak with newspaper reporters, personally attacking the methodology of the research. Since the cases of abuse under study weren't taken from random samples, he said, they meant nothing. He ignored the fact that none of the research used methods that required randomness to ensure accuracy (for example, analyzing speeches by leaders and manuals published by the Church showed a systematic bias against supporting victims' accusations when they contradicted the claims of a "priesthood holder"—in other words, pretty much every man in Mormonism). Even after receiving quite a lot of hate mail, it felt all new and fresh to be on the crap list of an actual apostle.

I wish we could have done effective research to establish whether child sexual abuse is more common in Mormon country than in the rest of the United States. But you can't very well expect perpetrators to answer, "You betcha!" when asked, say, in a phone survey, if they molest children. So, short of divine omniscience, there's no way to determine whether the Latter-day Saints are unusually incestuous. Personally, I think the answer is yes, particularly in the core population of Mormons who are descended from polygamous ancestors. Since moving away from Utah and working as a life coach for hundreds of people from all walks of life, I have encountered only a handful who say they were sexually abused as children. In Provo, at the Lord's University, it seemed that I couldn't open my car door without smacking an incest survivor.

As I sat in my office at BYU hearing tales of predatory priesthood holders, wondering about the clicking on my phone, receiving the occasional death threat, and worrying about what would happen to my children, I often asked myself why I couldn't leave the Church as John had done. I still clung to the excuse that for real change to occur in any group of humans, pressure must come from both inside and outside the group. Maybe I was actually helping people by listening to their tales of rape and torment—after all, these people were faithful Mormons, which meant they were unlikely to trust anyone outside the Church. One of the nifty paradoxes of dysfunction is that the crazier the system in which you grow up, the more afraid and less equipped you are to leave it and stand on your own.

So, like my father and other Mormons of royal blood, I justified my continued allegiance to the Church by seeing myself as a servant of my people. Now that I wasn't even married to a Latter-day Saint, noblesse oblige was the one thin strand connecting me to the faith that my parents had cherished, the faith for which martyrs had perished. Day by day, I could feel that cord stretching, weakening, fraying. I knew it was going to break. I just didn't know that, once again, it would happen in front of so many people.

CHAPTER 36

The Child

Every spring, BYU plays host to one of the most popular events in Mormon country: the annual Latter-day Saint Women's Conference. Thousands and thousands of Sister-Saints come from all over to attend, walking to campus from the neighborhood where I once lived, driving from small towns in Idaho and Arizona, jetting in from big cities back east. For a few days, the university is a sea of X chromosomes, filled to bursting with maidens, matrons, and crones in boiled-wool jackets and control-top panty hose. You've never seen so many heads of helmet hair in your life.

In the spring of 1993, the Latter-day Saint Women's Conference was especially well attended. Feminism was a hot topic in the Church's ongoing purge, and Mormon females were torn between the increasingly egalitarian ideals of American culture and the staunchly traditional role demanded by their religious leaders. They came to the women's conference for guidance, inspiration, comfort, and the occasional pastry snack from the Cougareat Cafeteria.

Because of my education, my position at BYU, and above all my father's name, I had been asked to speak at several annual women's conferences. After John's kamikaze departure from the Church, I didn't expect to be invited in 1993, but I was. Truth be told, some of the organizers of the conference were quietly seditious themselves. I suspect they asked me to participate not in spite of the fact that I was a known dissident, but because of it.

As if merely putting me in front of a crowd weren't enough, the women's conference organizers asked me to moderate a panel discussion on the explosive topic of domestic violence. The speakers included the daughter of an apostle, a man who was currently serving as a midlevel

Church authority, and a Utah doctor who told me he'd become obsessed with preventing sexual abuse after seeing visible evidence of it in more than a third of his female patients. He had taken his case to the General Authorities, one of whom had heard him out and responded with a single sentence, "The Church is not run by doctors." "It really reminded me not to interfere with God's authority," said the doctor earnestly, meaning, I suspect, in the doublespeak of Mormon dissidence, *I hate those controlling bastards.* These were all devout Latter-day Saints committed to acting on the spirit of their faith, willing to summon whatever grit and grace they could to serve anyone in need. All of them were good, and all were brave.

I didn't feel particularly brave myself. I was still powering through the lion phase of my spiritual quest, testing all religious claims and finding many of them untenable. In hindsight, it seems silly that the prospect of doing this at a Latter-day Saint conference scared me. After all, I was only a panel moderator; I wouldn't be asked to state any opinions, just hand things over to the speakers. But the anonymous phone calls and threatening letters had done their work: it terrified me to think about standing up in front of a gaggle of strangers who might know my secrets, who almost surely venerated my father, who were likely to think me a liar and an enemy to faith. I thought about saying no, but the lion in me chafed at the thought of staying meekly in its den. So I agreed to moderate the panel presentation and began mentally preparing to withstand hostile questioning from the twenty or thirty women who might attend.

The volume on my anxiety dial went up several notches a couple weeks before the women's conference when I got the schedule in the mail and saw that my panel discussion had been assigned to a large, amphitheater-style classroom that seated between two hundred and three hundred people.

"They won't fill it up," I told Rachel Grant during one of my therapy sessions. "I'm sure we'll be talking to a bunch of empty seats."

The trace of a sardonic smile flickered over Rachel's usual poker face. "Uh-huh," she said. "And I'm sure you're in denial."

"Come on, Rachel," I said. "These are Mormon women. They'd rather die than show up at a session on domestic violence. We might as well call it the dirty laundry session, ask them to show us their armpit stains."

"I've been helping people wash their dirty laundry for years," Rachel said. "There's a lot of it in this church. I'm betting that room will be nearly full."

She was wrong. On the lovely March day when I headed to BYU for my panel presentation, I didn't find the huge room "nearly full." I found it absolutely packed, every seat taken, women standing around the periphery and perched on the stairs, women crammed in a high-pitched huddle just outside the amphitheater, jamming the doors open, determined to overhear whatever they could. After hasty consultation, conference officials decided to pipe the sound from our session into the full-sized movie theater in the student union. That room, which seated several times as many as the amphitheater, also filled up immediately.

Onstage in the amphitheater, the panel members and I whispered to each other in hushed amazement. The crowd was not only huge but strangely kinetic; everyone in the audience seemed to be moving, talking, writing in their official women's conference notebooks with an intensity I'd never seen at a Mormon meeting.

"Okay, you know the plan," I told the panel. "You each have ten minutes to speak, then we'll take questions from the audience."

"There are too many of them," whispered the apostle's daughter. "We can't just call on people—everyone will want to talk, and we'll lose control." The other panel members agreed. The unusual energy of the crowd was making us all nervous.

"It's okay," I told the panel. "People are going to write down their questions. We've got runners to bring the notes up here. I'll read the notes while you're talking, see if there are any themes. Then I'll pitch the questions over to you guys."

Precisely on the hour, I leaned into my mike, called the meeting to order, and introduced the panel members. As planned, each of the speakers gave prepared remarks about domestic violence and family dysfunction. They had written carefully worded statements that tactfully acknowledged the possibility of abuse within Mormon homes, without explicitly stating that it really did exist. The midlevel Church leader reminded the audience that righteous people would have God's protection from evils that plagued the non-Mormon world. The apostle's daughter concurred, emphasizing that women could always consult their priesthood leaders if they felt wronged within their homes. Forgiveness, said the doctor, was the highest virtue and a requirement for all good Latter-day Saints.

As each member of the panel spoke, I watched the audience with growing concern. Most crowds of Latter-day Saint women could be trusted to sit with what Primary teachers call reverence, a word that in Mormonese means staying stock-still, placid, and mentally absorptive, like moist sponges. But this audience was breaking the rules. Many of the women were jittering in their seats, raising their hands, muttering to each other. At least a dozen had begun to cry.

Before the panel members had finished their initial comments, runners were hustling up and down the aisles collecting scraps of paper on which the audience had written questions. I leafed through the first batch. The first question was about childhood sexual abuse. The second, same topic. Then another. And another. And another. All the same subject.

"I think," I told the panel through the microphone, "that there are quite a number of people here who'd like to hear you address the issue of sexual abuse, particularly as it affects children." My heart was hammering. Could the audience *feel* what had happened to me? Would someone confront me about the rumors, right there in front of this unexpectedly turbulent crowd?

"Yes," said the Church leader member of the panel, "that's a good question, and we need to discuss it directly."

The audience went abruptly silent, as though someone had flipped a switch.

"For one thing," the priesthood leader went on, "we must consider the issue of blame. Most scenarios we call sexual abuse have at least two participants, and we must be very careful to make sure that everyone involved takes full responsibility for his—or her—participation."

No more silence. A rumble of muted voices went up from the audience, steadily growing louder. As the speaker went on, the runners began to sprint, grabbing dozens of notes from agitated women, rushing to the stage, stuffing paper into my hands. "No one understands what I've been through," one note read. "I'm sick of being blamed for what was done to me," said another. "You're all protecting the system." "Why didn't God protect me when I was a child? Why won't the Church stand up for me now?" I could tell the notes were angry even before I read them; they were scrawled, scribbled, sloppy, without the daintiness of the typical Sister-Saint's handwriting. With mounting alarm, I realized that none of the *i*'s were dotted with little hearts.

Back at the panel, the doctor grabbed his microphone and rushed to the rescue. "What we have to focus on, again," he said, "is forgiveness. Yes, terrible things do happen to children—I've seen evidence of that in my practice. And those children, even when they're grown, have to pay special attention to Christ's teachings. Seventy times seven, we must forgive those who harm us. We must turn the other cheek, go the extra mile."

He was trying to impose calm and order. He might as well have tried to douse a fire with kerosene. Now the women weren't even whispering; they were talking right out loud. Some of them were shouting questions, to each other, to the panel members, to me. And the notes kept coming.

"Elder Clement said that being sexually abused as a child was like having a bad day in the first half of the second grade. Are you all agreeing with him?"

"My husband abused our daughters, and one of them killed herself. And you're telling me to turn the other cheek?"

"None of you know what it's like. Why don't you have any survivors of abuse on the panel?"

The apostle's daughter was speaking, but she'd lost the audience almost before she began. Like most Latter-day Saints, I'd been talking in front of congregations most of my life. I'd taught college for years, at BYU and Harvard. I'd never been in front of a room that crackled with as much discontent as this one. What's more, I understood exactly why the women were so upset. Everything that had been said in the meeting reinforced my own suspicion that if the whole Mormon establishment had witnessed what was done to me as a child, they would respond by saying, "Oh, my goodness, this is terrible. What do we have to do to make that kid shut up and take it?"

As the crowd continued to rumble, I realized that I had become part of the problem. There I sat, playing the patronizingly self-possessed, blue-blooded Latter-day Saint authority figure. But the truth was that as I looked out over the rows and rows of angry, weeping, hopeless faces, I saw myself. Hundreds of me. Hundreds of children with nowhere to turn, hundreds of women trapped in solitary confinement by the silence necessary to preserve the system. There were really only a couple of differences between me and the anguished abuse survivors in the audience: First, I had a microphone. Second, I knew, right to my bones, that every moment is a chance to choose either freedom or captivity. Every moment.

Feeling so nervous that I thought I might throw up, I scribbled a note to the panel members, asking them to wrap up their remarks. Then, before the lion in me lost its nerve, I took my microphone off its stand, stood up, and walked to the front of the stage. The audience quieted a bit, but not much.

"You're angry," I said into the microphone. Then, for a while, I just stood there. The hush spread; this was unusual behavior for a Mormon speaker, especially a woman. It was . . . blunt.

"I know you're angry," I told the crowd, "because I'm angry, too. Some of you have asked why we don't have a survivor of abuse on this panel. Well, we do. That would be me."

Sudden, stunned silence. The crowd looked at me as though I'd pulled a wolverine out of my girdle.

"And frankly, nothing that's been said here so far makes me feel any better," I went on. "You don't trust the people on this stage? Good. You shouldn't. Because we haven't said anything to earn your trust. We haven't done anything to earn it. In fact, the one thing in this room you can trust is the part of you that knows most of what you've just heard is garbage. Do you feel it? I do."

The energy in the room, the intense kinetic buzz, was homing in on me like a laser. It made me dizzy and held me up at the same time.

"So please, don't trust us. Don't trust anything that says God wants you to be silent or blames you for being hurt or sides with the secrets and lies that kept you from healing. You know that's poison, because believing it makes you sick. It isn't God; God is the part of you that is rejecting it, right now. Listen to yourself. There's more of God in one hurt child than in all the religions humans have ever created."

I stopped for a moment to breathe. Now that I was up on my soapbox, I found the air up there crisp and invigorating. The women in the audience were looking at me as though they expected me to be struck by lightning momentarily. One thing was for sure: I had their attention.

"That's all I have to say," I told them. "Except that I may be wrong. Don't trust me. Trust yourself. If something I said feels right to you, believe it. If it feels wrong, disbelieve it. The choice to believe or disbelieve, that's what makes you free. That's what makes us all free."

When I looked at the audience now, I no longer saw a swarm of women wearing enough hair spray to paralyze a herd of yaks. Instead, I saw the stories I had heard in my office, and more stories like them: the nine-year-old lured into her uncle's basement, the twelve-year-old pinned to the neighbor's mattress, the sixteen-year-old from a polygamous offshoot clan given to a fifty-year-old as his fourth wife, the twenty-year-old Sister-Saint obediently reading the Mormon scripture, "If a man have ten virgins given to him, he cannot sin, for they are his."

A huge calm settled over me. The buzz in the room had grown so overwhelming I thought it might begin to levitate physical objects, but the texture of it seemed to have changed. It was warm and rich and soft, a silent hurricane blowing torrents of love at all those women, all those children. It was as though the answers to all the prayers they had prayed in those terrible hours had been waiting, waiting for permission, for the choice to believe, and the choice to disbelieve.

I dimly recall being mobbed after the session ended, hugged and kissed and patted by more people than I could count. It was the first time I had stood in public without the windowpane that kept my secrets in and strangers out. For the rest of the day, when I was by myself again, I couldn't stop raising my arms in celebration, couldn't stop laughing out loud.

Picasso said, "I have worked all my life to learn how to paint like a child." That day—in the BYU women's conference, of all places—I realized that I had worked all my life to learn how to *be* like a child. To use my

Buddhist friend's terminology, I had moved through the camel phase of my spiritual journey, on past the lion, to become the child of the spirit. I looked up the quotation, which went like this:

> In the last stage the lion gives way to the child, to an original innocence. This is the Child of the Spirit for whom all things are new. For this divine child there is wonder, ease, and a playful heart. The child is at home in the reality of the present, able to enjoy, to respond, to forgive, and to share the blessings of being alive.

That evening, I sat down to write the letter that would take me out of Mormonism and on to outer darkness. My membership in the Church, my go-round with religion, had done its work. And I had finally lost my last bit of Mormon royal arrogance. I'd thought the Stream had left me in the Church so that I could heal some of my people. The real reason, which should have been as plain as dirt all along, was that I had come back to my people, all those beautiful, generous, wounded people, so they could heal me.

Death

A ll right, sweetie," says Diane, standing up and crossing the hotel room to stand by my father. "We'll get you home." She looks at me to be sure this is all right.

"Marty," she says to me, "is there anything you still want to say?"

I think about it for a moment. I do still have a few questions, mainly about what happened right after the women's conference, right after I proclaimed my trauma-survivor status and rescinded my Mormonism. Just two days after my epiphany at the panel discussion, something occurred that had never happened before and would probably never happen again. My father sent me something in the mail.

"Yeah," I say now. "Dad, why did you send me that card?"

He frowns in confusion, which is not surprising. After all, it's been ten years.

"What card?" my father says.

"The only one you ever sent me," I say. "The one with the sprig of rosemary on the front."

He says nothing, but I see in his eyes that he remembers. My father is no spring chicken, but his memory is razor sharp.

That's what the card had been about, really. Memory. Inside, he'd written a message in his scratchy hand. "Rosemary, that's for remembrance," it said. "Come pay us a visit."

I recall thinking that my father must have assumed my Allusion Manager had lost some of its perspicacity. The quotation wasn't even necessary, because the picture of rosemary, all by itself, was more than enough to remind me of Ophelia, the tragic heroine of *Hamlet,* who starts handing out flowers between going bonkers and killing herself. "Rosemary, that's for remembrance," she says, then bounces off to drown herself in the river. Maybe that's where Virginia Woolf got the idea.

"Why did you send it to me?" I ask, ten years later. "What did it mean, exactly?"

Because, like all our communication, my father's allusion-rich card had numerous possible interpretations. On the face of it, he was hinting that I'd been neglecting my parents. However, by referencing Ophelia, he might also be implying that I was insane. At an even deeper level, "that's for remembrance" could refer to the whole issue of forgetting and re-membering, such a spectacularly inconsistent issue in our family. Maybe the *Hamlet* quotation was my father's way of saying he knew I had re-membered the events I'd once repressed. Perhaps he'd overheard my mother's phone calls on the subject and had finally decided to take defen-sive action (as I child I used to notice that because he always acted so dis-sociated, she frequently spoke about him on the phone as though he couldn't hear, when he was actually picking up every word). Maybe he'd repressed memories of the incidents himself, and his subconscious mind picked out the rosemary card because it was trying to make his own memories conscious.

"Well, for heaven's sake," says my father, casting his mind back to the first and last note he ever wrote to me. "It didn't mean anything, really. Just getting in touch."

Diane, who has sat down on the arm of my father's easy chair, gives me a quick smile and a shake of the head to tell me that she, too, has the feeling my father is fibbing.

"So," I say. "You'd never written me in my life, you hadn't spoken to me for two years. Then I give a speech saying I was abused as a child, and the next day you just happen to invite me to get together?"

"Well . . . yes," says my father. "Quite a coincidence, eh?"

This time I'm the one shaking my head. "I think you were doing dam-age control. You heard about my speech, and you knew I couldn't be trusted to stay quiet anymore."

"Well!" says my father. "Well, that's just nonsense. What speech? I don't know what you're talking about."

Diane begins to laugh. "Oh, sweetie," she says to my father, "You know 'what speech.' It was big-time gossip all over Utah."

"Nonsense," my father repeats, but he's running out of steam.

"And then," I said, "you actually called me. On the phone. That never happened before, either. It seemed like you must be pretty anxious to talk to me."

·   ·   ·

I remember that phone call, vividly. In all my thirty years, my father had never initiated phone contact with me. His voice had hit me like a blow to the head, took me utterly by surprise. In a flash, I'd gone numb all over.

"Well, hello, hello," he'd said, much too heartily. "We haven't seen much of you around these parts. You must be very busy."

"Uh . . . yes," I'd said. I'd gone from making almost daily visits to no contact for years, and he was pretending it was a casual oversight? "I have been busy," I told him. "But that's not why you haven't seen me."

I don't remember exactly what we said for the next few minutes. Incongruous pleasantries, mainly. He seemed to be poking around to see what I was thinking, whether I was harboring any hostility. I just parroted his words, a few at a time, as they bounced off my blank brain. Finally, I said, "I'll meet with you, if you want. But I need to think about it for a while. I'll get back to you." We both hung up.

It took me several days to call him. On one hand, I felt emotionally, physically, and spiritually stronger than ever before in my life; perhaps it was time for a reconciliation. On the other, getting together with my father still filled me with a sick dread. And in the meantime, while I was trying to decide how to deal with my family of origin, there was so much to do.

Quitting my job, for example. And hiring a real estate agent to sell our house and making plans to move out of Utah. Even my therapy group, who loved me dearly, had advised me to run for the border after I left the Church. As apostates, it would be very difficult for John or me to find gainful employment in Mormon country. Worse yet, our children really would fall victim to the dire consequences foretold by President Dick. In fact, it was already happening.

Katie had just turned eight—the age when Mormon children are baptized—and she was gradually being ostracized by her former friends at school. To my worried eyes she seemed anxious, though she didn't talk about the reason. She didn't have to; I knew. My best friend in grade school had been the one Catholic my age in the district. Almost every year, my teachers would privately instruct me not to play or speak to the non-Mormon. I flouted their instructions because my father's status put me above the informal law; I could get away with it. But a girl with *apostate* parents? In Provo, Utah? I shivered to think what Katie experienced every day at school. I asked her about it, in a roundabout way, not wanting to instill paranoia if it wasn't called for, but she tended to go mute when I asked her whether any of her classmates ever mentioned religion.

One evening the doorbell rang, and a middle-aged woman with a plate of cookies asked if she could speak to Katie. A few shy eight-year-olds stood behind the woman on the porch. Wondering what was up, I called Katie to the door.

"Hello, Katie," said the woman in a honeyed voice, proffering the cookies. "We're having a party at that big church building down the street. You know?"

Katie nodded, her eyes huge.

"It's called a baptism party," said the woman. "You could come to it, too. There would be cake, and games, and friends. Lots of friends. And then you'd get baptized!"

I felt a most unseemly surge of rage as I watched Katie look longingly at the other girls on the porch.

"Excuse me," I said to the woman. I put my hand on Katie's shoulder and guided her into the kitchen. "Sweetie," I whispered, "listen to me. If you want to go with them, it's fine. I'll go with you. You can be Mormon if you want—it may help you fit in."

"But Mom," Katie whispered, her eyes filled with tears, "I don't believe what they believe. They told me I'm going to hell for believing in evolution, and they don't even know anything about it. I mean, if there's no evolution, how come whales have leg bones?"

The look on her small face broke my heart. I hated the woman on the porch for rubbing in the isolation of the apostates' children, for baiting my daughter into religion with friends and toys. At the same time, I was bowled over by Katie's precocious clarity, her refusal to deny what made sense to her. I'd caved in to much less pressure a million times. But I knew my daughter was aware of her choices and the consequences. One evening when she was six, I'd pointed out Jupiter in the western sky, telling her it was the biggest planet in the solar system, wondering if she could grasp what I was saying. Her reply was to squint at Jupiter and ask, "Do you think it's possible to see the Great Red Spot with the naked eye?" Yeah. Katie knew what she was doing.

Of course, during the years that followed, I would ask myself every day how the body blow of religious ostracism had affected Katie's well-being. We've talked about it a lot, whether she would have been better off if John and I had confined our religious questions to our own minds, like so many of our Mormon friends. We agree that it affected her deeply, that it gave her a passion for justice and for championing the underdog, as well as a streak of self-doubt she is now outgrowing. She seems to have been old when she was young, becoming younger and more carefree as she nears adulthood. That day with the baptism delegation was the first time I saw how clearly my daughter had chosen between authenticity and belonging, but it would not be the last. Ten years later, I am in still in awe of her courage to be herself.

At the time, we sent the delegation packing—and then started packing up ourselves. John got a job interview at a business school in Phoenix. We drove ten hours to Arizona with all the children. John's interview went well; that evening we cruised around the residential areas near the business school, pricing houses, asking the kids if they thought this might be a nice place to live.

"But," said four-year-old Lizzy, "I like the place we live now. Why can't we just stay there?"

"Because," Katie explained, "you would grow up surrounded by religious fanatics."

"Fanastics?" said Lizzy. "What are fanastics?"

"You don't want to know," said Katie. "They bring cookies, but it's really just a bribe."

Lizzy thought about this for a while, gazing from her car seat at the sky beyond the minivan windows. "Oh, well," she said at last, "I like the moon they have here."

That evening we got a phone call at our hotel. John's mother, after years of heroically fighting heart disease, had passed away during the night.

• • •

The ten-hour trip back to Provo was surreal. We were driving home to the end of life, in more ways than one. Death had come, not only for my mother-in-law, but for almost everything familiar: our childhood haunts, our friendships, our jobs, our house, our families. It was strange and sad to let go of so much at once. But it was not altogether new. I'd felt this way once before, when I decided to keep Adam, against the advice of every doctor and academic adviser. One obstetrician told me I was "throwing my life away," and he was right. By rejecting the rules and flouting the values of the community around me, I really did throw away the life I'd lived to that point. It wasn't as shallow as simply being re-jected; I'd literally killed off my *self*, my ego, the way I saw the world. My life as a Harvard academic died with my son's birth. Now my life as a Mormon was over, too. In many ways, my choices were as suicidal as jumping into the river with Ophelia and Virginia.

Still, that funereal drive home was not terrible. Not at all. It didn't feel catastrophic; it felt sacred. John and I were grieving and scared, but we no longer feared death, in any manifestation, as much as we once had. We'd already learned that throwing away one life means making room for another. *The way we are now,* the Light had told me, *this being together, is not the way you are supposed to feel after you die. It is the way you are meant to expe-rience life.* I'd begun to understand that moving toward God would entail dying many times, giving up cherished preconceptions and beliefs, re-leasing everything that contradicts the reality of experience, the reso-nance of love and truth. As long as I keep working to transcend my vast ignorance, I expect to experience this kind of death not once, not twice, but over and over, day by day, hour by hour. To follow my sense of truth means (in Eckhart Tolle's words) "to die before you die, and so to learn that there is no death."

After we left Utah, when I became a life coach, I would see hundreds of clients through hundreds of "deaths." I'd go through a few more itera-tions myself, and I'm sure there are more coming before the Big One. It's always terrifying. It always hurts. It always brings up that familiar passel of awful sensations: the burn of anger, the horrible ache of loss, the sense of the ground falling away under my feet. But once you know what to expect, there's a kind of calm that comes with the territory. Here we go again, I think, and surrender to the Void, clinging to the bumper-sticker wisdom that "what the caterpillar calls the end of the world, the master calls a butterfly." I'm still mostly caterpillar, but each metamorphosis is informed by the last. Life changes, relationships change, bodies change, beliefs change. Buddha's "noble truth" of impermanence is the only permanent thing in human existence. Once you're okay with that, dying—even with all the pain—doesn't seem as bad as you thought it was.

My mother-in-law's funeral drew a huge crowd, everyone who had been touched by her gracious, upstanding character. John was asked to give a prayer at the service but not to speak. Then, following Mormon custom, we joined the other members of the family in a receiving line next to Faye's open coffin. While teenaged cousins took care of our children, John and I embraced and shook hands with hundreds of mourners. Many were members of our home ward, who had once welcomed us so warmly and had recently taken to turning their backs when we approached. Their usual reserve punctured by the nearness of death, they threw their arms around John and sobbed.

"Come back!" said one ward member, her mascara running along the path of her tears, staining John's shirt collar when she hugged him. "Please, please, come back! We miss you." Other ward members, standing nearby, added similar pleas.

"But, Sister Sorensen," said John gently, "we still live next door to you."

The ward members only wept harder. They knew, and he knew, what they really meant. To these good Saints, our defection from the Church was a far more horrible death than the loss of John's mother. Mormons believe that love and belonging reach easily beyond the boundaries of the grave. It just can't make it over the high-voltage electric fence of apostasy. This brief contact at the funeral was intensely bittersweet; we could see how much we were still loved but also how irrevocably we were lost to our friends unless we were willing to be Mormon.

• • •

My mother-in-law's passing gave me the motivation I needed to return my father's phone call. I told him I would be glad to reconnect, but I'd like to have our first meeting in my therapist's office. I had already asked her to be there, along with John. I made it clear, however, that I planned to speak for myself, and simply wanted John and Rachel to witness the conversation. My father and I agreed on a time; then I gave him directions to the office. We hung up.

Immediately, I was seized by a huge, nameless fear of indeterminate negative consequences that would follow the instant I spoke to my father honestly. "What would happen if one woman told the truth about her life?" wrote the poet Muriel Rukeyser. "The world would split open." Though I knew it was irrational, all the training I'd received from infancy to young adulthood had taught me to fear that confronting my father would bring on the Apocalypse. It was the most frightening thing I'd ever done, but again, it had that familiar ring to it. Having a chat with Dad might not seem frightening to you. But to me, that appointment in Rachel's office was just one more date with death.

CHAPTER 3 8

The Tempest

The day of my meeting with my father shocked me by dawning just like any other. I saw the sun rise, as I had every day for a week, because I'd apparently forgotten how to sleep. I'd been staggering through the days on automatic pilot, reserving the nights for catastrophic fantasies and formless terrors. It was a good opportunity to test my "spiritual technologies." To my gratified surprise, I found that they still worked. When I sat quietly, when I listened for the Silence, I could still connect with the calm and happy child at the center of my being.

Sometimes.

The more tired and scared I became, the more my thoughts became child*ish,* instead of child*like.* The thought of seeing my father threw me into the kind of age regression many adults experience when they deal with their parents, say, at Thanksgiving dinner. I spent hours mentally rehearsing things I could say to put my father in his place: cutting accusations, clever put-downs, sarcastic insults. Unfortunately, they didn't feel like the Light. In fact, they seemed to break my connection with it. So I let myself have my vengeful thoughts, the way I had let myself chop up our cherry tree, but the part of me that had already healed knew that using spite on my father would be the verbal equivalent of taking an ax to his body. If my position was to side with love rather than violence, any form of cruelty was out.

Always open to wisdom from higher sources, I recalled a deliberately juvenile "Deep Thought by Jack Handy" I'd recently seen on TV's *Saturday Night Live.* "Today I saw a snail," said Jack, "and thought, 'I, like that snail, hide behind a shell that protects me from the world. But while the snail's shell grows from its back, mine is made of tin cans and aluminum foil.' "

I pictured my father coming into Rachel's office in a foil-and-tin-can shell, the visible manifestation of his fear. It was pleasingly ridiculous. Then I imagined that below the armor lay his true self, the soul that is part of God and therefore can never be destroyed. I determined that my strategy would be to ignore both my own fear and my father's. I would talk from my soul to his, as though neither of us were afraid. If I could stand it.

·   ·   ·

At the appointed hour, my father showed up at Rachel's office wearing a stained polyester suit rather than a shell of salvaged metal. John and Rachel rose from their chairs to greet him. He was accompanied by my mother and by a therapist my siblings had recruited to give him courage. The psychologist had never worked with my father, but she had named her only child after him. The two of us were equally represented, each with a spouse and a shrink backing us up. A fair fight, I thought.

Since it was Rachel's office, she began by allowing my parents' therapist to introduce herself, then turned the time over to me. I was glad I'd spent so many hours strategizing, because I was even more numb than I'd been while talking to my father on the phone. Reflexively, I recalled a bit of advice I'd heard him give in one of his speeches, years ago: "In a dangerous situation, presence of mind is a good thing. But absence of body is better." I knew he didn't want to be in that room any more than I did.

I started by telling the condensed version of the story I've written in this book, forcing myself to give a brief account of my memories, then describing the circumstantial evidence that suggested they were factual. I explained to my parents that I had no desire to hurt them but that in order to relate to them without feeling insane I had to be able to talk about my real memories, thoughts, and feelings. I couldn't pretend that my father was a giant of righteousness, an honest servant of God, but if they would talk to me about the abuse I would be very, very glad to have a relationship with them.

My eyes were riveted on my father, but in my peripheral vision I could see his therapist sitting up very straight, horrified, holding her breath. John and Rachel were watching my father with a kind of intense detachment, like scientists staring through a microscope at a virus, wondering what it would do. My mother stared at the floor, anger and misery rising from her in waves that were almost visible, like the zigzags of pain around the head of a cartoon character. My father pulled a set of note cards from his breast pocket, adjusted his bifocals, and began to read aloud.

"Everything Martha has said," he read from the first card, "is absolutely false. To think she would even claim such a thing is shocking. I would never defile my own child."

I remember focusing on the word *defile*. It doesn't mean to hurt or traumatize; it means to make filthy, to taint, to corrupt. Even in the process of denying my allegations, my father framed his thoughts in terms of *my* being dirty and spoiled. I'd been well versed in this perspective, having attended dozens of Mormon meetings where teachers pounded a nail into a board, then pulled it out, explaining that the wood was useless now, ruined, just like a woman who'd lost her virginity. Other illustrations included chewing a piece of gum and offering it to students or licking a peanut butter sandwich before inviting the class to have a bite. Better to die, the teachers emphasized, than to live as a defiled female.

My father was now explaining that there was no evidence of posttraumatic stress in my past behavior. "Martha was always a perfectly happy, well-adjusted child," he read, shifting to a new note card. "She drew all the time—very happy pictures. Obviously, nothing upsetting had ever happened to her."

I stared at him. I stared at my mother, who sat miserably gazing into space. I couldn't help interrupting.

"Are you kidding?" I said. "I had horrible insomnia my entire childhood and adolescence. I had such bad nightmares you told me the devil was after me. Do you remember me wearing that parka for about six years—inside, outside, winter, summer, all the time? Do you remember that I talked about suicide almost every day? I spent four years trying to starve myself to death. And you think I had no symptoms of trauma?"

"You see?" said my father triumphantly, looking up from his prepared notes for the first time. He pointed at me, but looked at his backup therapist. "Do you hear? She admits it—she's always been unstable! Just the kind of crazy person who would make up this kind of thing." Dad's favorite weapon, the double bind.

"I did not invent this," I said, trying to relax my churning stomach and keep my voice calm. "For God's sake, I have so many scars my doctors think I tore in childbirth. Where did those come from?"

My father said nothing, just began shuffling through his notes. But my mother had begun to cry.

"Mom," I said desperately, turning to her, "you asked me if he did this. You called me on the phone and you *asked* me. You said, 'Of course I believe you. I know him better than you do.' Why would you say such a thing?"

Because she was shedding tears, I'd thought my mother might be having a compassionate moment. Her voice disabused me of that notion. It sounded like a snake hiss in an ice cave.

"I assumed," my mother said, quivering with fury, "that you were joking."

I couldn't answer. She has to live with him, I thought. She has to go home after this and live with him.

"What's more," said my father, locating the card he'd been looking for and squinting a little to read it, "everyone is having this false-memory syndrome these days. Satan is running the show here, I can tell you that. There's no evidence at all that it's possible to repress a memory and then regain it."

"But you've done that yourself," I said. "You had that amnesia attack when you were working on the Egyptian book."

"That was a stroke," said my mother sharply. "That's different."

I shook my head. "No. I met the neurosurgeon who treated him. He told me there was no physical evidence of a stroke, that the amnesia was psychological."

"There was no evidence of a stroke," my mother said, "because the Lord healed your father."

I was getting dizzy. I had scars, but they weren't considered evidence; my father had no scars, but that, too, proved nothing. Every piece of evidence could be explained as an effect of God, or the devil, or the two of them together, line dancing around the lives of us wretched mortals, making bets on how we'd react to their next practical joke.

"Your religion," I said in amazement, still shaking my head at my parents, "is completely insane."

My father snapped back, going off-script again. "We raised you in the Gospel. You might want to think about how you're repaying us."

"Oh, believe me, I've thought about it," I said, desperately wanting to lash out. I stopped. Breathed. Calmed myself. "In a way, you're right," I said. "I am grateful you raised me to be religious, because at least you turned my attention to God. It's like you locked me in the deepest dungeon ever made and then threw in the key. Thank you."

I believed then, and still do, that I'd just described the function of religion in general. All faiths form around the same priceless thing: the Stream, the Silence, the Light. Then, human nature being what it is, that holy core begins accreting a shell of mindless corruption. It is, in a word, defiled. And since this power is the most precious thing in human experience, its dark side is the purest form of evil.

"Sharper than a serpent's tooth," my father said. He wasn't reading this; it was a spontaneous quotation, tossed up by his Allusion Manager. The quotation is from *King Lear,* and he knew I would finish it in my own head. "Oh, how sharper than a serpent's tooth it is to have an ungrateful child." I felt my muscles relax a little. Now that my father had begun to converse with me in the usual way, through literary references, the situation felt a dab less alien. I knew how to speak Allusion.

"Remember Cordelia?" I said, picking up the allusion to *King Lear* and moving it forward. Cordelia is the third of King Lear's daughters, who loves him too much to flatter him and is sent into exile as a result. "I'm not doing this because I don't love you. I'm doing it because the truth and love are the same thing. If we can't tell each other the truth, there can't be any real love between us. If we do tell the truth, we can get over anything. Anything."

My father dropped his eyes to his note cards, muttering, looking for a fitting response. There was rage in his face, his voice, his posture. I watched him search his notes, this angry old man in his dirty clothes, and right before my eyes, something changed. It wasn't a transformation in

the way my father looked, but in the way I saw him. It was strangely obvious that the furious figure on Rachel's office sofa wasn't my father at
all. In fact, that creature wasn't even real. It was like a strange clay mannequin, almost entirely divorced from his soul. That soul, however, still
shone—I swear, I could *see* it. And the reason I could see it was that I
loved it. With all my heart.

Children who are hurt by their parents pay a terrible price, because
they can't help loving their tormenters. But I suddenly realized that this
torment can also be a gift, because to know the shining soul hidden behind an enemy's shell is to understand that we are all safe, all lovable, all
loved. At that moment I could see—not by imagination but by simple
observation—what the Buddha meant when he sat down to meditate and
all his demons flew shrieking into his face. "You are illusion," he'd told
them. And the demons had turned into flowers, settling gently around his
still, breathing form.

"You think you're so very smart," said my father, acid in his voice.
"You ought to think where you got that brain, young lady."

I decided to ignore this feeble dig. "You know," I said, rather than jab-
bing back at him, "I've always thought that *King Lear* and *The Tempest* are
the same play, with one difference."

My father couldn't help it; he loved Dueling Allusions as much as I
did. He looked up from his note cards with a quizzical eye.

"Think about it," I said. "Both those plays are about kings in exile.
Prospero and Lear. They both end up in the wilderness, both out in these
huge storms. They both have daughters they want to protect. Only Lear
can't do it. Everything he loves, he destroys."

The witnesses in the room—everyone but me and my father—
looked puzzled. It probably seemed odd to them that I'd gone into a literary analysis in the middle of a family confrontation. They didn't have
trick frontal lobes that replayed Shakespeare's plays to them on a continuous basis, whether they liked it or not. But my father was right; my
brain and his were built from the same DNA.

"I think there's just one reason *The Tempest* has a happy ending," I tell
my father. "There's one thing Prospero does that Lear doesn't."

"Well," said my father, "of course, Prospero has his magic. He's a
sorcerer."

"No," I said. "That's not it."

My father thought for a moment, and then his face went suddenly calm, and I knew he understood.

"Prospero forgives," said my father.

I nodded.

"Have you ever heard that forgiveness is giving up all hope of having had a different past?" I asked him.

He didn't answer.

"I'll never condone what you did," I said, "but for what it's worth, it just occurred to me that I've forgiven you. I've given up all hope that you didn't do what you did, and I can live with it. On the other hand"—I shook my head—"I think you're still trying to have had a different past. It won't work."

My father gave a snort of disgust, but it didn't matter. Whatever he did, I could feel something magical flowing through that room. Not the magic of fundamentalist religion, of devils named Stan that inflict scars on the unrighteous and miracles that automatically erase them from the tissues of the servants of God. Not the magic of the "seer stone" Joseph Smith said he used to translate the papyri that ignited a chain of events that would later devastate my five-year-old life. The magic I felt was both quieter and more powerful. I did believe that it could heal us, body and soul. I did believe it could work miracles. But that wasn't the point.

"Remember what Prospero says to Ariel?" I asked my father. "When he forgives the people who betrayed him?"

It's a rhetorical question; of course he remembers. " 'They being penitent,' " my father murmured, quoting Prospero's speech, " 'the sole drift of my purpose doth extend / Not a frown further.' " He stared at the carpet as he spoke, but his face wore an expression of terrible sorrow. I could almost hear the beat of his heart, drumming out the same prayer that had haunted me for so many months, so many years: *Please please please please* . . .

"And after that," I said, "Prospero doesn't need the parlor tricks. Not anymore. Remember? 'But this rough magic I here abjure . . .' "

My father nods, and we quote the end of the speech in unison: " 'I'll break my staff, / Bury it certain fathoms in the earth, / And deeper than did ever plummet sound / I'll drown my book.' "

• • •

Rachel told me later that as she watched this conversation, she felt as if she'd shown up at a courtroom expecting a normal trial and instead watched as opposing counsel began performing selections from Cirque du Soleil. "I've never seen anything like it," she said. "I didn't know what the hell you two were talking about, but you and your father are so . . . connected. There was almost a sweetness to it. And sadness. Mainly sadness."

I had to agree with that, because despite our moment of literary bonding, no concord arose from that meeting in Rachel's office. I kept claiming that what I remembered really happened, and my parents kept claiming that it didn't. The people in my father's camp—my mother, my siblings—stayed in it. My allies continued to believe me. That was where we began, and it was where we ended. I do think (though I could be wrong) that by the end of the session, my parents' psychological counselor was feeling a bit nervous about the name she'd given her baby.

Part of me, the unquenchable, irrationally hopeful part of me, was crushed that our meeting changed nothing. For a few weeks, I would feel as if my heart were being ripped from its cage of ribs over and over, like Prometheus's liver. But I hadn't really expected anything else. If my parents had made any concessions that looked remotely like agreement with me, they stood to lose everything—their lives, their worldview, their social status. They would have to die before they died, and it was a little late in the game for them to start that sort of thing.

After a couple of hours, we all agreed that we had an official stalemate. I told my parents that if they could tolerate the way I had come to think and speak, they should give me a call. I tried as hard as I could to stay in that moment when I had felt my father's spirit shining, when I could see both my parents for the scared, confused, incorruptible souls they truly were. But by the time we said good-bye and my parents left, I could barely see them through the clanking and shuffling of their fear-shells, all the tin cans and aluminum foil.

CHAPTER 39

Designing a Life

Y ou poor thing!" says Diane, patting my father's shoulder. "All
these questions, all these memories."

"It's like a military tribunal," my father mutters, still angry,
but responding to her kindness despite himself.

"Or a battle," says Diane. "You used to talk about the battles you were
in, during the war." Even as a child, Diane could get my father into the
war-story mood. His face changes as she speaks. He looks brighter, more
intense.

"Remember?" my cousin continues. "How everything slowed down
and you felt as though you were somewhere else?"

"Yes," says my father. "Oh, yes, that's true."

"And the bombs . . ." Diane prompts.

"Oh, the bombs," my father says, going right into the routine. "You'd
see them come arcing over the field." He moves one hand through the air.
"It always seemed they were moving so slowly, but at the same time, you
couldn't run fast enough to get out of the way. And it all felt choreo-
graphed. Like a ballet. As though everything had been worked out ahead
of time; who would die, who would live, all of it."

"And," Diane says, "you used to say, you felt as though you weren't
even in your body at all."

"Yes," says my father. "I might as well have been a million miles away."

Diane leans over to put one long arm around my father's frail shoulders, giving him a sideways hug. "Oh, sweetheart," she says. "You have
such a big, fat, whopping case of posttraumatic stress syndrome."

My father looks confused, both pleased and displeased by his niece's
embrace.

"And you passed it on to Marty." She corrects herself. "To Martha."

My parents always disapproved of nicknames, as they did of casual titles like Mom and Dad. Too intimate.

"All we're trying to do here," Diane tells my father, "is heal our family. Do you see that? Your generation didn't have much chance. What year were you born?"

"Nineteen ten," says my father. He seems calmer. Thoughtful.

"Well, there you go," Diane says, holding up an open palm. "Nobody had therapists when you were growing up. Hardly anybody had *cars*."

My father nods, relaxing even more. Diane looks at him with a mixture of tenderness and intense purpose. When her own father died, she unofficially adopted mine. She loves him as much as I do, but being a self-proclaimed bossy oldest child and having had too little contact with him to give up, she's more determined to fix him than I am.

"The truth heals," Diane says. "It really does. And talking about what happened in our homes isn't much different from telling war stories. They're terrible memories, but just communicating about them lets the poison out."

"I don't know what you're talking about," says my father. "I've never told a war story in my life. I never talk about the war. Ever."

Diane and I look at each other, speechless. Then my cousin bursts out laughing. "Our family is so *zany*!" she says. "This is just like *Alice in Wonderland*. Like the Mad Hatter's tea party!"

Now I'm laughing, too. "It's not just our family," I say. "It's this whole damn state." I'm pleased to note that the taste of these words is not bitter at all. I can say them happily because I have distance on my side; I'm no longer a Utahan, any more than I am a Mormon.

"Are you finished, Marty?" Diane asks me.

"Yes," I say. "I am. I'm finished." I find myself smiling at my father, swept by sorrow, and also, to my astonishment, with affection. "Thank you for sitting here with me," I tell him. "And thank you for everything you did. Really. Everything."

My father doesn't answer, just stands and reaches for his sunglasses, the ones he wears inside and out, no matter how cloudy or dim the light may be. Now, watching him don his battered hat and wipe the sunglasses with a handkerchief, I feel something that once would have seemed unthinkable: love and gratitude, not in spite of the worst things he ever did to me, but also because of them. Don't get me wrong; I still disapprove of his actions enough to want to clock him with something really heavy. I still think he lives in a web of lies, a craziness so pervasive it pulls other people into it like a spiritual black hole, so dense no light can escape. I still won't believe those lies, or hang out with people who require it of me. But I remember what Elizabeth Cady Stanton once said: "In education, in marriage, in religion, in everything, disappointment is the lot of women. It shall be the business of my life to deepen this disappointment in every woman's heart until she bows down to it no longer." My father had deepened my disappointment in life, in religion, in God, until I could bow down to it no longer. And that, paradoxically, was why I learned that I was free.

I stand up, too, and notice that sometime in the last ten years, my father has become shorter than I am. Diane puts her arm around him again, and gives him a kiss on the cheek. I hug him, and though it's like embracing a block of wood, there is no resistance from within me. I bid my father good-bye and watch as Diane leads him through the door. It closes behind them. The closet door opens, and Miranda emerges to envelop me in her long, motherly, cousinly arms, and I faint dead away.

· · ·

About a week after I met with my father in the hotel my cousins and I now called the Incest Inn, Diane received a letter that made even me, a death-threat veteran, somewhat nervous. The author informed Diane that he knew "the kind of person she was" and went on to list a catalog of complaints. The penalty if she continued to mess with her family, the letter said, would be worse than death. "I learned how to do things in prison that will make you wish you were dead," it said. "And don't bother looking for DNA on this letter. I know better than to lick a stamp."

Diane called Phoenix to read me this letter, because it mentioned me or, more precisely, the fact that Diane had set up the meeting between me and my old man. "Tell your cousin she's full of shit, and she'd better stay away from her father." I told Diane to go bunk with her boyfriend. Also to get a very large dog. But nothing ever materialized from the threat letter. In fact, it had a positive effect. It gave me a sense of closure. Once someone you love has been threatened with injury and mayhem should you ever contact your parents, it really does feel as though you've given the filial relationship the old college try.

•   •   •

One day after we'd moved to Arizona, I passed an open patio door to see a rattlesnake coming across the threshold. I let out a yip of shock and fear, called to the children to stay in the family room, and considered the situation. John was out of town, making it improbable that he would intervene before the situation was resolved. There I was, holding a broom, several feet from the snake. There it was, halfway in, pausing to look at me, tasting for me with its tongue. After a moment, my heartbeat began to slow down. I remembered that snakes can only strike in a small radius around their bodies, that the human hand can move four times faster than a striking snake, and that I was holding a broom, which I could use to fend off attack. Thank you, Discovery Channel.

At the moment I realized the snake was too far away to hurt me, I noticed that it was really rather beautiful. I began to admire the subtle mottling of brown and black diamonds, the elegant curve of the snaky body. And as I did so, an unexpected surge of empathy rose in me. I could imagine what it must feel like to be the snake, to find oneself in this odd place, where the air and floor were so much cooler than they ought to be.

"Dude," I said to the snake, "you and I are both going to be so much happier if you turn around and go the other way."

A few seconds later, the beast took my advice. It cautiously twined itself around, afraid to turn its back on a creature as large and terrifying as a human. When its belly touched the sun-baked warmth of the patio tiles, it shot off as fast as it could go. I found this endearing. I stood there with my broom and genuinely loved the snake, who, after all, was just being a snake.

This is how I feel about my father, my family, and the Latter-day Saints. They are themselves. They do whatever is their nature to do, make choices I have no right to judge or condemn. They are beautiful. I love them.

As long as they're a certain distance away.

CHAPTER 40

Paradise Lost and Found

A few weeks after the meeting with my parents, six years after moving back to our home town, John and I got out of Dodge yet again, heading south through the high Utah plateaus to the low Arizona deserts. John had taken the job teaching business school in Phoenix, which would give us a chance to plant our feet solidly on new ground, far from turf dominated completely by the Latter-day Saints. As refugees go, we were in very good shape: all our limbs intact, minimal parasites, a place to live. But even before we left, I felt homesick for the sweet dry air of the mountains, for the reliable niceness of the good Saints in every shop and office, for the network of love and duty that binds the Mormon community so tightly together.

Ironically, the quotation that kept echoing in my head as we left Utah Valley came from the Book of Mormon. At the end of Joseph Smith's magnum opus, the last surviving Nephite, a man named Moroni (who would later, in angelic form, lead Smith to the golden plates) writes about the eradication of his people and his own isolation. Like a good Latter-day Saint, I knew chapter and verse.

> Behold, the Nephites who had escaped into the country south-ward were hunted by the Lamanites, until they were all de-stroyed. And my father also was killed by them, and even I alone remain to write the sad tale of the destruction of my people. But behold, they are gone, and I fulfill the commandment of my fa-ther. And whether they will slay me, I know not. Therefore I will write and hide the records in the earth, and whither I go it mat-tereth not.

I always found this passage haunting. I think I identified with Moroni's plight from the time I was five years old, when my whole world died, "and my father also was killed," at least in my little-girl heart. I officially left Mormonism on premises befitting an adult: because I had come to think of Moroni's story as memorable fiction, rather than history; because I believed Joseph Smith was a brilliant man, but not God's only mouthpiece. But really, my soul had fled Mormon country long before I knew anything of scriptural scholarship, way back when a blend of religion and insanity separated my soul from life and love. Surrounded on every hand by friends and family, I had grown up feeling desperately alone. The harder I tried to make Mormonism my home, the more I realized it never had been.

.   .   .

I remember looking in the rearview mirror at my children as we drove away, remembering what it was like for me when Adam was diagnosed with Down syndrome. I'd been told there was a high risk he would die at birth, and I confess that before he was born there were moments I thought this might be a relief. If my baby died, I could grieve him and move on. To include him in my life meant coping with his disability every day. I didn't know if I could handle that.

In the end, of course, it was Adam's "handicap" that began teaching me how to be happy—or perhaps I should say to stop doing things that made me unhappy. My fear and sadness were so unbearable that eventually I gave up the way of thinking that created them. Over and over, I groped past the shallow scrims of intellectualism and perfectionism to find something deeper and truer beyond them. Love, I discovered, is the only thing human beings do that really matters a damn. Happiness, like beauty, is its own excuse for being.

"Adam fell that men might be," says another passage in the Book of Mormon, "and men are, that they might have joy." Naming my son Adam had helped emblazon this beautiful statement on the fibers of my heart, and I am deeply grateful to Joseph Smith, that dynamic, charming, libidinous narcissist, for writing it down—even though I happen to believe he made it up.

My defection from Mormonism changed me in the same way Adam's disability did: it became an open-ended tragedy that I wouldn't give up for anything in the universe (not even my own planet) because it helps me let go of beliefs that had damaged my soul. An erstwhile friend of mine in the Oak Hills Fourth Ward once said he thought the only prayer we offer spontaneously is "Why am I in pain?" Knowing that I am considered wicked and perhaps insane by people I love is so painful that it continually drives me to this prayer, drives me to seek sustenance even more stable and powerful than human acceptance and company. *Please, please, please, please* . . .

When I persist in this prayer, sooner or later (the more I practice, the more it becomes "sooner") something wonderful happens. My status as an untouchable feels so terrible that something deep inside me finally lets go of it, of all identity, of all attempts to prove or please or control anyone at all. At that moment, I rediscover the stillness in my own heart of hearts. Then I feel its connection to the Stillness all around me, the gorgeous, blissful Stillness that holds every heart, every mind, every tree and rock in its infinitely loving embrace.

I am here. Always. I am always right here.

And it is, it is, *right here,* nearer than near: connection, comfort, safety, belonging. Home. Lao-tzu said, "The master can travel all day without ever leaving home," and while I'm no master, I have returned home frequently enough to know he was right. I'm starting to believe that my homing instinct will guide me back anytime I consult it, from anywhere in creation. I think that may be the reason for this whole terrifying, excruciating mortal existence; to wander away from home, then find the way back, so many times we learn from our toes up that no matter how far afield we may stray, we can always, always, always get there from here.

.   .   .

Our little family reached Arizona in the summer of 1994 and set up a physical home all over again. It took us a while to become desert rats, to acclimate to the industrial-strength sunshine and the prickly plants. During our first sixty-degree December, Katie taught Adam and Lizzy to sing

"I'm Dreaming of a Beige Christmas" and "It's Beginning to Look a Lot Like Labor Day." We avoided the towns around Phoenix where Mormons live in great abundance, and we were happy.

One day I left my children in the family room for a few minutes, turning the TV to *Sesame Street* to keep them quiet. When I returned, the program had changed. I'd accidentally tuned in to a broadcast from KBYU, Brigham Young University's public station. There on the screen was my father, his eyes locked on to the speech he was reading, his hands fidgeting nervously with the pages. My first reaction was a shock of horror, the kind that once filled my nightmares. Next came anger, a fierce unbidden spasm of it, telling me to get my kids away from him, *now*! Almost as soon as I felt this, it was over; I could see that Katie, Adam, and Elizabeth had no interest in the man on the screen, and he had no power over them. I stood there for a long moment, watching my children with their grandfather, and then another feeling arrived. It was a sweet and terrible sadness, like cold spring rainwater, that slowly saturated my whole body. I can't say it felt good, but something told me that this rain was the water of life, that grief is as healing as it is painful.

For a few minutes, I listened very carefully to my father's speech. I understood each word he used. The words were organized into complete sentences. The sentences seemed to be related to each other. And yet, I had no idea what he was talking about. Nothing made sense. Nothing hung together. The world began to spin in my head, and for a minute I remembered what it had been like to mold my life around the weird, circuitous logic of my father's religion. I turned off the TV feeling a blend of sorrow and validation. I didn't mention to the kids that the man they'd just seen was their grandfather, because I'm not sure it was. That figure was the marionette, the puppet owned and operated by a complex religious culture. Even if my children watched every speech my dad ever gave, even if they visited him every day of their lives, they wouldn't have known their grandfather. I didn't know him. I don't think he ever did himself.

·   ·   ·

The strange thing is that in a way that felt strangely inevitable I ended up following my father's footsteps into my own version of the family business: giving philosophical counsel. I finished my PhD program the first year we lived in Phoenix, and shortly after that the business school where John was working hired me to teach a couple of courses as well. This was where I came to realize that the experience of leaving the Saints had built most of the foundation for my life's work.

I was teaching career development, helping students create successful lives. But to me, that didn't necessarily mean huge salaries and a Donald Trump social profile. It meant learning to go home and stay there, in that place where joy is not dependent on wealth or image, and even the deepest sorrow is a guide toward healing and happiness. During my years in Utah, through all those days of spiritual trial and effort, all those nights of psychological struggle, I'd developed a repertoire of techniques that helped me do this. In Phoenix, I began teaching these techniques to my students.

"You'll know when you're in the wrong job interview," I'd say during a lecture, "because the pit of your stomach will tell you to get out. Your first daily priority should be stillness, attention to what you really know and what you really feel. Don't 'network' into meaningless relationships with colleagues who bore you; find the people who can make you laugh all night, who turn on the lights in your heart and mind. Do whatever work feeds your true self, even if it's not a safe bet, even if it looks like a crazy risk, even if everyone in your life tells you you're wrong or bad or crazy."

What I was really telling them was how to be a Leaf in the Stream, though of course I never called it that. Nor did I quote Jesus' question, "What profiteth it a man if he should gain the whole world, and lose his own soul?" I rarely used Buddhist terms like *awakening* or *right action*. But all these concepts, all the things I'd learned in my search for God, drove every piece of advice I gave my students.

After a while, a few people asked me if I'd be willing to speak to them about such things outside of class. They said they'd be happy to pay me. I resisted for some time, but that's the thing about business-school students: they tend to be pit bulls. I finally gave in, thinking that I'd spend a few hours with a few students, simply pointing out to them that they already knew, deep down, what they should do with their lives. A year later, I'd quit teaching and was working with clients full time. Reporters still called me for quotes in newspaper articles, and in one of them I read that I'd become a "life coach." I was pleased to have a name for what I did, even a cheesy one. My Harvard professors may roll their eyes, but I loved my job with all my heart. I'd also started writing books and articles, on many topics but with only one theme, Dante's theme: the journey through the inferno as the road to heaven. Paradise lost and found.

In my case, the inferno-road led through Provo, Utah, the well-meaning bureaucracy of Mormonism, the community of Saints. Yours probably passes through some other territory, but we all make the same trip. We believe without question almost everything we learn as children, stumble into the many potholes and pitfalls that mar any human endeavor, stagger around blindly in pain and outrage, then slowly remember to pay attention, to listen for the Silence, look for the Light, feel the tenderness that brings both vulnerability to wounds and communion with the force that heals them. Don't worry about losing your way, I tell my clients. If you do, pain will remind you to find your path again. Joy will let you know when you are back on it.

I still make the journey every day, which is why I wrote this book. Many people, especially I myself, have asked me repeatedly why I'd do such a thing. I hate conflict, have an enormous fear of being disbelieved, and remember just enough of the old-fashioned Mormon temple ceremony to be paranoid about lethal reprisal from the lunatic fringe of my father's fan base ("and whether they will slay me, I know not . . ."). But as much as I dread the consequences of openness, I know the consequences of secrecy are worse. I've read research that indicates that people who hide a history of traumatic experience live shorter, less healthy, less happy lives than those who tell their stories. I know, at a much deeper level, what keeping secrets did to me, and even more, to my father. He did more than die for his religion; he gave it his life. He almost gave it mine. The memory of that is so awful it leads me down Dante's road many times every day—and each time, the awfulness makes me keep going, all the way through hell and back to paradise.

Once I am home again, I know that my father's true self is not the man who lied and covered up and sacrificed his children's happiness for his religion, any more than it is the amalgamation of photons coming from a television screen in Phoenix. His true self is the being at the core of his personality, the part I have never reached, a being of incorruptible love who is simply trying to find the way home. I have no way to judge whether he could have found another path. Maybe he thought that if he just kept being *more* Mormon, more devoted to religion, he'd break through and find peace. Maybe he pushed this logic so far he thought himself a second Abraham, offering his own child in the hope of receiving divine favor, understanding, union with God. Maybe there was some genuine logic behind his behavior, albeit logic forced on him by conditioning and socialization.

Or maybe he was just plain nuts.

Even if I never know the explanation behind what happened to me as a child, I do know this for sure: Whether or not my father had the freedom to choose his thoughts and actions, I do. I am free, and always have been; free to accept my own reality, free to trust my perceptions, free to believe what makes me feel sane even if others call me crazy, free to disagree even if it means great loss, free to seek the way home until I find it.

All the great religions I have studied, including Mormonism, hold that this irrevocable soul-deep liberty is the key to the end of suffering and the beginning of joy. The Buddha said that just as you can recognize seawater because it always tastes of salt, you can recognize enlightenment because it always tastes of freedom. About a year after I discovered I'd become a life coach, I stumbled across a Buddhist prayer that felt so true to me it almost stopped my heart. The last section goes like this:

> As long as space endures,
> And as long as sentient beings exist,
> May I also abide,
> That I may heal with my heart
> The miseries of the world.

I didn't think about these words, I felt them resonate clear through me, as though I'd gotten a blast of pure peppermint, as though every cell of my body was independently falling in love. Of course I'm not saying I can fulfill the promise of that prayer, only that I want to die trying. Maybe I already have died trying, once or twice. I think that may have been what I was doing when I left the Saints. Maybe, at some level far beyond thought, that was how I chose to use my soul's freedom.

I can imagine talking to the Light about this, before I was born, before my father and mother were born, when there was no separation between us, not even an illusory one. "That!" I would have said. "That prayer—that's the description of the job I want!" I figure the Light would have said, *Hang on there, kid. I gotta tell you, the training for that one is a bitch.* Then I'd have said, "Who cares? Sign me up! *Please please please please* . . . ?" And the Light, laughing that indescribably delicious, comforting, intoxicating laugh, would have said, *Okay, sweetie. If it's really your heart's desire, of course you can have it.*

That's how I picture it happening. And every day, the drone note of my life is the same: *Thank you thank you thank you thank you thank you* . . . As the rabbi Hillel put it, "I walk, I fall down, I get up. Meanwhile, I keep dancing."

Epilogue

L izzy was nine years old when she asked me her first serious religious question.

"Mom," she said, "why did Jesus have twelve opossums? I mean, what did he *do* with them?"

The first thing that crossed my mind was an innovative, zoologically diverse reconception of da Vinci's *Last Supper*. This was followed by a spasm of concern. My children have virtually no religious training— should I have signed them up for some sort of church?

Almost as soon as the thought occurred, I'd decided the answer was no. Like most Mormons who leave the fold, I have never signed up for another brand of formal religion, but my children, like anyone else who knows me well, can't help seeing how obsessed I am with God.

I suspect this is why Lizzy came to me with her inquiry about the twelve opossums. It was an excellent question, a child's question, which is the only kind that leads to a genuinely spiritual answer. A Zen master might see it as an illustration of "don't know mind," the honest, unpretentious openness that is necessary for enlightenment. Lizzy is approaching her own spiritual quest with a mind and heart untrammeled by the luggage attending most organized religion. So, instead of signing her up for Sunday school, I decided to take my daughter as my role model. After all, the central goal of my life is to stay in the place of the spiritual child, unfinished and curious. Lizzy and I went on line together to find out about the opossums, and discovering that they were apostles barely dampened the fun.

Speaking of Zen masters, Adam is my own handy home version, the compact, blond model. He has never stopped being my spiritual teacher. One day when we were sitting down to eat dinner (take-out—I haven't cooked at all since my bread-baking days), Adam had us all stop while he said a completely unintelligible grace. We knew he was finished praying when he emphatically said, "The end." As we began to eat, I turned to him and asked, "Adam, where does God live?"

Adam's eyes crinkled into the new-moon shape that accompanies his smile, and he thought for a long moment. Then he said, "God lives in pizza."

We all laughed, chomping into our pepperoni and cheese.

"God lives in salad," Adam continued. "God lives in water. God lives in ice cream."

The laughter at the table hushed as we all began to see the deeper meaning in this. Here we were, consuming objects that sustained the miracle of life. Everything on the table had come from something living, either animal or vegetable. In some unfathomable way, life was being passed from one aggregate of stardust to another: a cow's milk, a stalk of wheat, a leaf of lettuce, all busy being transformed into . . . us. Adam was absolutely right.

The next day, while I was writing about this dinner-table epiphany in an e-mail to a friend, Adam happened into the room. By way of fact-checking, I decided to repeat the previous night's question. So I asked again, "Adam, where does God live?"

Adam stopped, cocked an eyebrow, and sighed: *When will she ever learn?* Then he said, very firmly, "Mexico."

And that was true, too.

. . .

Of all my children, Katie was the one most affected by her parents' tu-multuous roller-coaster ride through Mormonism. She was the only one old enough to attend Latter-day Saint Sunday school, the only one who was taunted by Mormon peers. She developed a shell of her own, be-coming a tad belligerent toward fundamentalism of any stripe. We've talked philosophy endlessly, and at eighteen, she is more aware of her own beliefs than I was at thirty. She is sharp of both mind and tongue, prone to skewering simplistic fundamentalism with jokes I find hilarious.

At the same time, I know that while religion is not Katie's cup of tea, God is. Like me, she was born with a longing for spiritual communion in the marrow of her soul. I realized this one Fourth of July night when Katie was five. While John stayed at home with our two sleeping toddlers, I loaded Katie into our minivan and drove up onto the foothills of the Utah mountains. I parked at the top of a steep hill. Then Katie and I climbed up onto the van's roof, from which we had an unobstructed view of the fireworks display just beginning in the valley below.

It was awesome. For over an hour, great thundering, whistling showers of light bloomed and faded right at our eye level. We oohed and ahhed. I taught Katie the Japanese word for fireworks, *hanabi,* which literally means "flower fire." Then we subsided into silence for fifteen or twenty minutes, after which Katie said, "Fireworks make me feel like I'm home."

I was puzzled. "Well, I guess we wasted a trip, then."

"No," said Katie, "I mean I feel like I'm home, and I'm safe, and it's okay to go to sleep. It's kind of hard to explain."

"Ah," I said, getting it. I thought about leaving things at that, but it seemed right to go on. "You know, I believe that when we see something as beautiful as this, it's almost like a memory of what we really are, where we really belong."

I could feel Katie going very still in the darkness beside me.

"And I don't know what God is," I told her, "but that feeling—that beauty, that memory, whatever it is, wherever you find it—I think that must be part of it. That's one of the things I mean when I say 'God.'"

There was another long silence, and then Katie's small voice whispered, "Mommy, for the first time, I'm crying because I'm happy."

That voice, soft and high-pitched though it was, didn't sound like an untutored child contemplating a novel concept. It sounded like an ancient soul, groping along in an unfamiliar body, beginning to remember itself. And though Katie has already traveled a great distance along her own spiritual path, I still see in her this brave, inquisitive, perpetually awakening soul. I think that's what she is, at the very center. I think that's what we all are.

As a student of sociology, I know I'm not the only one who feels the yearning for spiritual completion, or who enters and then leaves religion in an effort to fulfill it. Millions of people, from all faiths, are doing it as you read these words. I've watched it happen to plenty of non-Mormon friends. One of my Harvard roommates went back to his hometown after his mother's death to become the cantor of the local synagogue. Two Islamic friends became ardent students of Arabic, in the hope that reading the Koran as it was originally written would facilitate their spiritual awakening. A Dead Head buddy, who followed Jerry Garcia around the country for years, went back to weekly Mass after he'd dried out in a twelve-step program, explaining to his stunned drinking buddies that only a spiritual life could fill the vacuum in his soul.

All these people felt what *The Cloud of Unknowing* calls the soul's "naked intent toward God." The key word here, I think, is *naked*. Any spiritual practice is ultimately just a way of stripping off the illusions we have learned from other flawed mortals, letting go of whatever holds us back, opening ourselves completely to what comes next. It feels like a terrible risk, to be so vulnerable, to disobey the rules, to end up losing the things and people we love.

When I live this way, the wounded five-year-old in me still tends to quail. I know my little fears are inconsequential next to what many others face, but they send me into frequent tailspins nonetheless. A client I was seeing decided to break up with her boyfriend; when he called in a drunken rage and told me to butt out, I was tempted to stop working with her. I quit a job with one magazine to take another that paid less, but felt more in tune with the Stream, and when the editor of the first magazine angrily promised my agent I would fail as a writer, I felt skittish for months. After a member of my family published my father's biography, describing me as an unstable victim of false-memory syndrome who had inflicted the trials of Job on my parents, I couldn't help feeling depressed. Typing these words, right now, makes me so nervous I want to hide in the crawl space under my house and eat a twenty-pak of Twinkies. I could go on and on. Believe me, I often do.

But then, right in the middle of a grand mal fuss, I sometimes have the sense to open my eyes, to become present, to see the flower fire blossoming in the sky, and to remember what I've learned. For example, I've learned that the worst pain, fear, and torment I've ever experienced has only deepened my ability to experience joy. I feel this even when I'm hurting, because while pain and pleasure are mutually exclusive, pain and joy are not.

The more I tune in to the source of my own being (and every religion I've studied has helped me find ways), the more anger, sorrow, and fear seem confined to the shallows of my personality, while my true self— and yours, and that of every being—is like a sea whose depths are always tranquil, however troubled the surface may become. Pain reminds me to return to the deep, calm, gentle sea, so that I find myself crying because I'm happy, *and* because I'm sad, but never because I'm in despair. Once you're sure that God is waiting in the acceptance of every true thing, even pain, I'm not sure despair is even possible.

This makes a paradoxical gift of the fact that I still grieve every day for the people and things I lost when I left the Saints. The sequence of faces, the list of names, drifts through my mind over and over, like a hazy Rolodex.

I haven't initiated contact with my parents, nor has either of them tried to contact me, since the conversation with my father at the Incest Inn, ten years after my memories returned, three years before I wrote this book. I know, through my father's published biography and a few third parties, that my actions have caused them great distress. I'm sure that writing my own version of the story will cause more. But I know it won't change the minds of any faithful Latter-day Saints, and after years of searching my soul, rehearsing my family's version of events over and over in my mind, reexamining the return of my memories and the surrounding circumstances, I am convinced that my memories are real. Writing my side of the story has allowed me to relax and love my parents, in that beautiful rattlesnake way, however they may regard me.

My siblings and I have had very little interaction—a funeral, a few phone calls—since our landmark session with Mona. There is still no explicit gag rule limiting our conversations, but we live in different worlds now, different universes. The last time I spoke with one of my sisters, she mentioned that she's discovered that there's no real evidence Mormons ever practiced polygamy. I just dropped my jaw and stared at her, feeling the vertiginous sensation of our last bit of common ground slipping out from under us. I can still feel and treasure my siblings' love, in a New Age, astral-plane kind of way, but we no longer live in the same reality. I am the one who broke the family code, and that seems to have created an irreparable breach in my connection to my siblings.

Mona the therapist went on to write a book on sexual abuse. I read it; it's not bad. My hope for her is that she has decided to stick to the written word.

I had little contact with my therapist friend, the one I called Laura, after the conversation in which she advised me that I must "honor the secret" of my past to protect the Mormon Church and my father's work as an apologist. A few weeks before I finished writing this book, I heard that Laura had committed suicide. I don't know if she was honoring any secrets besides mine; if so, she took them to her grave.

Rosemary Douglas, the woman who helped me through the terrible period of silence, has served in many leadership positions in the Latter-day Saint women's auxiliary organizations. She loves the Mormon Church, and she embodies all that is best about it. She has written me a few times, recounting the sincere efforts of many Latter-day Saints to address the organization's failings and make the world a better place for Mormons and non-Mormons alike. She still believes that the only path to salvation is through the Church and wishes fervently that I will repent and recommit to it—but she also clearly loves and accepts me as I am. I think most of the Latter-day Saints are very much like Rosemary.

The psychologist I called Allen, who took on a client whose father was "financially important to the Church," suffered a series of severe strokes not long after our meeting in the hall. Last I heard, his memory and his ability to speak were both severely compromised. I think Freud would have a thing or two to say about that.

The September Six continued to write about Mormonism from the outside, except for one man who applied for, and was granted, rebaptism. Newspapers reported that a woman who also asked for rebaptism was told by local Church authorities that she had "to stop thinking the General Authorities could do wrong."

John's family took a deep breath and continued to accept both him and me, though it can't have been easy for them. They have my heartfelt gratitude, forever.

Rachel Grant still practices in Utah, though the stories she hears in her office continue to make her skeptical about the mental health of the Latter-day Saint community. Three years after I concluded my treatment with her, when professional ethics permitted, we reconnected as friends.

Whenever I return to Utah or she visits Arizona, Rachel and I have ongoing conversations notable for their irreverence. She recently described
to me a lesson taught in a class for the Mormon women's organization,
a lesson that specifically mentioned the problem of child sexual violence. A major part of the presentation consisted of gluing a packet of
SweeTARTS to a piece of poster board, then inscribing it with "Let's protect our little sweet-tarts from sexual abuse."

Utah County, still known to its residents as Happy Valley, continues to
have the highest per capita consumption of Prozac in the world.

Deborah Laake, the journalist whose book about the Mormon temple
rituals was on the *New York Times* best-seller list, committed suicide in
1996. She was fighting cancer, which undoubtedly contributed to her decision to end her life, but a friend of Laake's who knew her well told me
that the ostracism from the community of Saints was the real reason she
gave up on life.

Steve Benson, the Pulitzer Prize–winning cartoonist who left the
Church after publicizing his prophet-grandfather's deteriorating health,
is no longer under police protection. Instead, he joined the police force
himself, which probably makes him feel safer, though he's never told me
this in so many words. Steve's wife, Mary Ann, was my first close friend
in Phoenix, and our families remain immensely fond of one another.

Diane, Miranda, and I stay in close touch through e-mail, phone calls,
and the occasional visit. My cousins still put the fun in dysfunctional, and
I adore them.

The Church of Jesus Christ of Latter-day Saints continues to ride the
fine line between protecting doctrines from contradictory evidence and
calling attention to their nonscientific beliefs. In 2003, a Mormon geneti-
cist in Washington State was threatened with excommunication after
studying the DNA of several American Indian populations and discovering that they were of ancient Asian ancestry, without a trace of Middle
Eastern blood. After the press and dissident Mormons kicked up a fuss to
protest the excommunication, charges were dropped. The scholar remains a Latter-day Saint in good standing, and the publicity surrounding
the incident has quieted down nicely. As a notable man once said, people
underestimate the capacity of things to disappear.

I've lost track of the rest of the Latter-day Saints, along with my roommate the cantor, my Muslim friends poring over their Arabic versions of the Koran, my Dead Head buddy whose only alcoholic indulgence now is the Blood of Christ. I wonder about them sometimes: Are they content, spiritually fed, happy in the traditions they learned as children? Or have they followed their spiritual paths all the way through religion and out the other side, as I did? Though the details of my story are unique, I am sure the pattern is not.

As for me, I have been granted a richer life than I ever thought possible. Living as Leaves in the Stream has led our family into many great adventures, as well as sustained simple pleasures, and it's impossible to say which I've loved most. My writing has introduced me (and sometimes the whole family) to amazing places and, even more, amazing people. As if that weren't enough, I get paid for indulging my great obsession: pondering how we overburdened mortals can find our true selves, our right lives, our way back into the presence of God. Some of my clients might be startled by this language, offended by the woo-woo sound of spiritual terminology, sick to death of religion. Lord knows, that's okay by me. Whatever they want to call it—homeostasis or optimal functioning or a positive serotonin balance—I'm more than happy to comply, as long as we get there together.

"The roads are different," wrote the Sufi poet Rumi, "but the goal is one. When people reach the goal, all those who yelled at each other along the road, 'You are wrong!' or 'You are a blasphemer!' forget all possible differences. There, all hearts sing in unison."

I like to believe that there is some destination awaiting us where all our hearts will sing in unison: me, my father, my family, my people, our whole troubled and troublesome species. Maybe we'll all simply die and enjoy a common, stress-free oblivion. Maybe, though, we'll arrive at a place and time (or something beyond space and time) where we'll sit around laughing and swapping stories about the messes we made during our respective treks through the blind maze of mortality. We'll toast Muhammad, wave to the Buddha, high-five Jesus, Mary, and Rabbi Hillel, scratch the twelve opossums behind their ears. Then I plan to sit back to watch the flower fire, knowing that I'm home and I'm safe and it's okay to go to sleep.

Martha Beck is a writer and life coach who lives in Arizona with her family. She is the author of *Expecting Adam, Finding Your Own North Star,* and *The Joy Diet.*